Women in Non-Traditional Occupations

Also by Barbara Bagilhole

EQUAL OPPORTUNITIES AND SOCIAL POLICY: Issues of Gender, Race and Disability

WOMEN, WORK AND EQUAL OPPORTUNITY

Women in Non-Traditional Occupations

Challenging Men

Barbara Bagilhole
Associate Dean (Research) for the
Faculty of Social Sciences and Humanities and
Reader in Equal Opportunities in Social Policy
Department of Social Sciences
Loughborough University

palgrave
macmillan

First published 2002 by
PALGRAVE MACMILLAN
Houndmills, Basingstoke, Hampshire RG21 6XS and
175 Fifth Avenue, New York, N. Y. 10010
Companies and representatives throughout the world.

PALGRAVE MACMILLAN is the global academic imprint of the Palgrave Macmillan division of St Martin's Press, LLC and of Palgrave Macmillan Ltd. Macmillan® is a registered trademark in the United States, United Kingdom and other countries. Palgrave is a registered trademark in the European Union and other countries.

ISBN 0–333–92926–8

This book is printed on paper suitable for recycling and made from fully managed and sustained forest sources.

A catalogue record for this book is available from the British Library.

Library of Congress Cataloging-in-Publication Data

Bagilhole, Barbara, 1951–
    Women in non-traditional occupations: challenging men/Barbara Bagilhole.
        p. cm.
    "Reader in equal opportunities in social policy."
    Includes bibliographical references and index.
    ISBN 0–333–92926–8 (cloth)
    1. Women – Employment. 2. Occupations. 3. Equality. 4. Sex discrimination in employment. I. Title.

HD6053 .B245 2002
331.4–dc21

2002026753

10 9 8 7 6 5 4 3 2 1
11 10 09 08 07 06 05 04 03 02

Printed and bound in Great Britain by
Antony Rowe Ltd, Chippenham and Eastbourne

Contents

List of Tables   vi

Acknowledgements   vii

Introduction   1

1 An International Perspective on Women's and Men's Work:
   Gender Segregation of Labour Markets   10

2 Explanations of Continuing Occupational Segregation and
   Identification of Potential Levers for Change   26

3 Concepts and Themes around the Difference between
   Women's and Men's Work   44

4 Four Non-Traditional Occupations for Women   58

5 No Change at Home?   76

6 Structural Barriers   96

7 Hostile Reactions: Male Culture   114

8 Equal Opportunities Structures and Policies   133

9 Men Were There First – Becoming One of Them!   149

10 Titles Don't Always Count   165

11 Challenging Gender Boundaries: Common Themes and
   Issues for Women in Non-Traditional Occupations   180

Appendix: Details of Case Studies   194

References   198

Index   219

List of Tables

1.1 Occupational segregation by sex in selected European
    countries and the USA   14
1.2 Employment by sector, employees and self-employed
    aged 16 and over   18
1.3 Employment by occupation, employees and self-employed
    aged 16 and over   19
1.4 Occupational segregation, employees and self-employed
    aged 16 and over   19
1.5 Top occupations for women and men in the USA   23

Acknowledgements

I would like to thank all the women Civil Service managers, academics, construction engineers, and priests in the Church of England who so willingly and enthusiastically gave up their time and confidences. They were all very open and frank about their experiences of working in male-dominated occupations, even on issues that were very sensitive and at times painful for them. Should any of them chance to read this book, I hope they will be happy with the representation of their views, experiences and perceptions.

I would like particularly to thank my colleague Ruth Lister for her past and continuing support in my academic career, and for coming up with the brilliant initial idea for this book. I would also like to thank another colleague, Linda Hantrais, who conscientiously and meticulously read the first draft of this book, and came up with so many helpful and constructive ideas to improve it.

When I first started my academic career in 1991, I went to a seminar given by Jo Campling on 'getting published'. Her advice in that seminar and subsequently has proved to be indispensable. This is my third book with Jo, and as always she has acted as a wise adviser, confidence booster, encourager and supporter, and deadline enforcer.

My thanks go to my sons George and Ben, and my mother Joyce for their continuing support and love, and to my cats as the best companions and patient listeners through many hours of writing this book. Finally, I would like yet again to especially thank my partner Rupert for his love and making life fun.

Introduction

'Anything you can do I can do better! I can do anything better than you!' 'No you can't!' 'Yes I can' 'No you can't!' 'Yes I can! Yes I can! Yes I can!'

'Annie Get Your Gun', Irving Berlin, 1971

Man for the field and woman for the hearth:
Man for the sword and for the needle she:
Man with the head and woman for the heart:
Man to command and woman to obey:
All else confusion.

Tennyson, *The Princess*, 1847

Women who enter non-traditional occupations can be said to have to masquerade as men, but not quite as literally as their sisters did in history. One stark example of this was James Miranda Barry, on whose true story Duncker (1999) based her novel. She was a woman who pretended to be a man for 50 years, and pursued her career over three continents as a surgeon officer in the Victorian British Army. Edinburgh University, where she studied medicine, was for men only and therefore provided the catalyst for her performing life as a man. Barry wore three-inch soles to her boots, shoulder pads and a long overcoat at all times. Only after her death in 1865 was it revealed that she was a woman. She may have been one of many women in Victorian times who were compelled to pass as a man, or otherwise be prisoners of their gender and unable to pursue their desired careers.

The following poignant piece of conversation between Barry and her father from Duncker's novel expresses aptly how some women who desire to enter non-traditional occupations are expected to conform.

> 'Listen, soldier,' said Francisco, 'would you like to study properly? At a university?'
>   'Yes,' I whispered, suddenly feeling sick and shivery.
>   'Well, that's what you're going to do. There's just one thing that you'll have to remember from now on. You never will be a girl. But you won't find that hard. You'll just go on being a tomboy' ... 'Welcome aboard, James Miranda Barry. You'd be wasted as a woman. Join the men.'
>
> (Duncker, 1999, p. 60)

This book is also about women in non-traditional, male-dominated work. Its overall aim is to examine and analyse common issues and concepts concerning these women. The overall question it explores is: if women work in non-traditional, male-dominated work, are they agents for change or changed themselves? Cockburn (1991, p. 2) stated that 'many feminists increasingly moved into ... employing organisations taking their struggle with them ... [and] by such "entrism" women have for the first time approached the places of power and begun to challenge powerful men and the way they operate'. But is this the case in non-traditional occupations? Are these occupations full of feminists challenging male dominance? Or are they full of conforming women who have changed themselves for the sake of their career success? This book seeks to find out which is the more accurate assessment.

To answer these questions it looks in detail at four case studies of non-traditional occupations where the author has conducted qualitative empirical research: Civil Service management, academia, construction engineering and the priesthood in the Church of England. The four occupations make their appearance together (in Chapter 4), but are cited in subsequent chapters as and when the themes under discussion draw them into view. Thus the case studies are of course not presented as typical (although they may be), but rather as theoretical explanations for the complex processes which accompany women in male-dominated occupations.

The perspective of research on the segregation of the labour market has changed. Analysis in the 1970s and 1980s stimulated research on the exact measurement of occupational segregation, resulting in a debate on the usefulness or otherwise of different indices. However, by the 1990s, the usefulness of a single indicator was questioned.

Therefore, instead of measuring horizontal segregation at a national level, more and more studies adopt a case-study methodology, trying to explain occupation segregation by determining the factors behind it (Platenga and Rubery, 1999). As Gonas and Lehto (1999, p. 25) argue:

> The persistence of gender segregation is bound up to a large extent with internal processes in organisations ... To reach some kind of understanding of the forces that shape and reshape segregation patterns, researchers have to go beyond quantitative statistical analysis. They have to probe deeper into organisational cultures ... and reveal the silent, hidden processes at work behind the official ideologies of eo [equal opportunities] and equality. The demand for qualitative research is very strong and it is important to develop this line of research.

The empirical research reported in the book was carried out over seven years and received funding from a number of sources (see the Appendix for information on samples and sources of funding). I would like to thank all those women who cooperated with the empirical research. Should any of them chance to read this book, I hope they will be happy with the representation of their views, experiences and perceptions. Through them, I have attempted to analyse 'gender relations ... in lived experience' (Evetts, 1996, p. 6). Fraser (1999, p. 5) argues that the 'interests, concerns and, indeed, the voices of women as workers are hidden, and their worries and needs in relation to paid labour remain unexplained'. Hopefully, this book will go some way to remedy this omission.

What do we mean by non-traditional occupations?

For the purposes of this book non-traditional employment is taken to denote any occupation which is, or has been, traditionally undertaken by a man. Of course the terms 'non-traditional' and 'traditional' with regard to gendered work remain culturally and historically specific. For example, it is still relatively unusual to find women engaged in the construction industry in the UK and Europe generally. However, this is not so in other parts of the world, especially in poorer countries, such as India, where particular social, cultural and economic conditions affect women's employment activity (Bagilhole, 2000a). Importantly, such differences in the allocation of work are proof of the fact that work roles are not necessarily assigned on the basis of biological or physical attributes.

No finite international or national agreements have yet been achieved on how to define an occupation as 'non-traditional' for one sex or another. However, governments, agencies, institutions and employers in different countries have increasingly had to reach a contextually agreed definition in relation to anti-discrimination legislation, or the funding of special training and employment schemes for the under-represented sex. The most widely used cut-off point has emerged as between 30 and 33 per cent; if one sex is represented by roughly less than a third of those involved in an occupation, it is designated as non-traditional for the under-represented sex.

Overwhelmingly, where women in paid work have been studied, the focus has unsurprisingly been on what have come to be regarded as stereotypical 'female' areas of employment such as teaching, nursing and clerical work. Nevertheless, there have always been women who have 'stepped outside the stereotype' (Whittock, 2000, p. 7). However, apart from the two world wars when there was a general, if often grudging recognition, of women's participation in non-traditional forms of work, such activity has been 'hidden from history' (Rowbotham, 1974, p. 1). Therefore, in an effort to recover what Connell (1993, p. 188) refers to as 'a marginalised form of femininity', this book introduces the reader to women in four non-traditional occupations.

Why study women in non-traditional occupations?

Women and paid work are increasingly seen as a popular and fascinating topic both worldwide and across disciplines. This reflects the continuing marked rise in women's involvement in labour markets in all countries, and governments' continual desire for their increased participation in order to utilise their talents and skills to the full. Therefore, as women make inroads into non-traditional or previously male-dominated occupations, this becomes an important topic. More women have been gaining the qualifications to embark on careers formerly dominated by men, and more women have been stepping onto the lower rungs of such careers formerly dominated by men. Therefore, the topic is widely recognised as a significant and essential element of equal opportunities.

It would be disingenuous to claim to have initially chosen to focus on these particular groups of women for the purpose of comparing and contrasting their experiences. There was no prior planning about which groups to investigate. Rather they were decided upon for different but, in the end, a fortuitous convergence of reasons. They are women in men's jobs; the Civil Service was feminised but men retained the management of it; academia has been identified as one of the last bastions of male power; construction is the most male occupation after coal mining; and the Church of England refused to ordain women as priests until the 1990s.

Interest in the careers of such women developed through my research on women in the Civil Service, which is vertically segregated with women concentrated at the bottom of the hierarchy and in a minority at the top. My subsequent research on women academics, construction engineers, and priests in the Church of England, demonstrated similar dynamics of exclusion and marginalisation found in my earlier study of Civil Service managers. At the organisational level these occupations consist of discriminatory environments, where women's careers are shaped in a detrimental way as a result of their gender. This, therefore, raises the question central to this book. Are women changed by this environment, becoming more like the men around them, or do they change the environment?

The book does not purport to cover all the issues raised by this topic, nor can the above question be claimed as the original *raison d'être* for this strand of my research. Rather the work has evolved and developed from the perception of the overlap of women's experiences in different male-dominated occupations. By listening to the women and giving them a voice through my qualitative research using in-depth interviews, I have gained a useful insight into their experiences that can contribute to knowledge in this area. The discipline of listening to those who 'live the experience' of working in non-traditional occupations has proved immensely interesting and rewarding. It has also rung bells with my own experiences in paid work, particularly working as a bank clerk, straight from school, and teaching a man my job – a man who was being paid more than me before the Equal Pay Act was introduced. Also I was told that even though I had A-levels, the normal requirement to take banking exams, women did not take them and even if they insisted on doing so they could only aspire to being a personal assistant to the branch manager, never the manager herself. Finally, my latest career as an academic has resulted in me yet again experiencing an occupation geared to and kept almost exclusively for men, but it has also allowed me the privilege of investigating and pursuing the issues involved through my research.

Common themes appear to emerge when women enter non-traditional occupations where they seem to have a fairly consistent experience. Often the women who enter fields predominantly occupied by men are highly qualified and less likely to have partners or be married and, if married, less likely to have children than their male colleagues. If they do have partners and families, they continue to bear the major workload and responsibility for housework and carework. They do less well than male colleagues in the recruitment, selection and promotion processes of their occupation, and they report the existence of a 'glass ceiling' affecting professional advancement. They are paid less than the men and cluster in lower-status specialities within their professions. Finally, they suffer from reported incidences of sexual harassment and discrimination. Women in male-dominated occupations demonstrate the dynamics of exclusion and marginalisation. As Spencer and Podmore (1987a, p. 1) point out: 'The severity of the damaging effects of this for women varies between the different professions discussed, but in each case it is clear that women encounter considerable difficulties in their careers as a result of their "deviant" gender.'

Thus, I have become fascinated by women in male-dominated occupations and by their apparently shared experiences across different occupations. I have also reflected on my own shared experiences with them in the academic workforce. I was an 'outsider' who joined without knowing I was an 'outsider'. An innocent who was genuinely shocked and dismayed by the entrenched numerical dominance of men and the traditional male culture which prevailed in universities in the early 1990s. Coming from working as an Equal Opportunities Officer in a local authority that was considered progressive in this field at that time, it was an amazing experience to be the only woman in academic meetings, and to be greeted by the 'chairman' [sic] as 'gentlemen, and oh the lady from social sciences'.

It is too simplistic to argue that women pose a threat just by their presence in most organisations. Rather, it is by their claims to equality. Women entering non-traditional occupations equivalently (or better) qualified for professional roles than their male colleagues are seen as a threat, whereas women cooks, cleaners and secretaries are not. 'Somehow when integration supports men's super-ordinate status there is no objection. Men cheerfully permit women into their workplaces when they are secretaries to their manager roles, and nurses to their doctor roles' (Epstein, 1997, p. 206). On the other hand: 'Women who in their career choices, ambitions and behaviour, seem to challenge gender stereotypes will be perceived as odd, as different (or even deficient) in essential aspects of femininity, caring and relatedness. They will be admired by a few but they will mostly be criticised, by other women as well as men, in their attempts to break new ground' (Evetts, 2000, p. 60).

Summary of the contents of the book

In the first three chapters, the book presents a broad international overview of women in employment and of the literature on segregation and equal opportunities. Then, in the remaining eight chapters, it moves on to an analysis of the author's empirical work on women in four 'non-traditional occupations'. The empirical chapters present detailed evidence confirming the trends identified at the macro-level and in the literature.

Chapter 1 presents an international perspective on women and men's work. It analyses statistically where women and men work and in what numbers. It offers an international view by comparatively exploring both horizontal and vertical occupational segregation data from the UK, the rest of Europe, and the USA. It investigates trends and changes, but also, importantly, the static and intransigent nature of this occupational segregation, which has been identified as extensive and pervasive and one of the most important and enduring aspects of labour markets around the world.

Chapter 2 provides explanations of the continuing segregation exposed in the previous chapter. It examines various key theoretical and ideological explanations for the continuing horizontal segregation of labour markets into male-dominated and female-dominated occupations; the vertical segregation of occupations with women concentrated at the bottom of occupational hierarchies; and potential levers for change. These potential levers for change include negative economic impacts on occupations, 'critical mass' theory, role models and mentorship, and women's agency.

Chapter 3 analyses the concepts and themes around the difference between what is identified as 'women's work' and 'men's work'. It investigates the various gendered concepts, discourses, language and symbolism which are important in the process of differentiation between the types of jobs and occupations that are seen as suitable for either women or men. These include important issues of leadership, and management, technical ability, and pastoral and caring skills.

The subsequent chapters are organised around the common themes on women in non-traditional, male-dominated occupations identified above. They draw on qualitative empirical research by the author on women in four occupations: Civil Service management, academia, construction engineering, and priesthood in the Church of England.

Chapter 4 highlights each of the four male-dominated occupations in turn, examining the history of women's involvement in them, including dates when they were first allowed entry and under what conditions, the numbers of women in them, and where they are in the hierarchy of the organisations.

Chapter 5 investigates the fundamental relationship between paid work and unpaid work for women in male-dominated occupations. It examines the way in which women combine wider and heavier responsibilities to their families and home with their paid work demands. It looks at the impact of personal responsibilities on paid work. Do these women succeed less well in their career because of either real or assumed, present and future outside responsibilities?

The chapter also examines the consequences of paid work on personal responsibilities for women. It investigates the effects of doing non-traditional jobs on women's home role, and roles of wife/partner and mother. Do they accommodate taking a masculine role at work and a feminine one at home? Who does the housework? Who takes responsibility?

Chapter 6 examines the effects on these women of structural difficulties and barriers they face in these male-dominated occupations. It demonstrates the consequences of both their assumed domestic responsibilities and the reality of these responsibilities. These structural disadvantages begin with entry into the occupation through recruitment and selection processes. Then, on a day-to-day basis, structures and procedures adversely affect their pay, career development and opportunities, and chances of promotion.

Chapter 7 investigates the cultural environment of these non-traditional occupations that impact on women and prevent them from achieving 'like men'. When women enter these occupations they encounter hostility, both overt and covert opposition, and resistance to their success. The chapter examines women's experiences of relationships with colleagues, managers, clients, customers, lay people and the community, which can and do negatively impact on their achievement and feelings of competence and confidence. This chapter also importantly raises and analyses the issue of sexual harassment.

Chapter 8 investigates the effects of specific equal opportunities policies and procedures within occupations and particular organisations. It explores issues which include hours of work, demand for continuous careers, childcare, maternity leave, flexible working, and the availability of training.

Chapter 9 examines the proposition that women are being changed by the roles they take on in non-traditional occupations. It explores the impacts on women of the hierarchy and establishment, and traditional way of doing these occupations. The well-established ways of being a manager, academic, engineer or priest make their mark on women. This is because men were there first, and they have set down a male model for the occupation. Therefore, to achieve success on male terms some women are conforming and changing, and becoming 'honorary men', or 'queen bees'.

Chapter 10 investigates the alternative proposition, that women are changing the occupations, that they are chipping away and changing these gender regimes rather than themselves.

Certainly it can be shown that women hold different posts to men in these occupations. Also they do different types of work in different proportions to men, and take on different roles even within the same occupation. An example is performing more pastoral and caring work, which is either self-imposed or enforced by the expectations of colleagues, managers and clients. Also, evidence is examined on how women change the job, change the accepted way of doing things, and challenge the ways things are done.

Chapter 11 draws together the common themes and issues which emerge from the analysis of these women in four non-traditional and male-dominated occupations, with the objective of coming to a clearer understanding of the consequences for the women themselves and for the occupations. The final question addressed is: are women changing these occupations or are they in the process of their engagement in this work being changed themselves?

The inspiration for this book comes from my reflections on my research and my own experience over many years of being a woman in non-traditional paid work. This has involved listening to and attempting to understand experiences through women's own voices, and my own. It attempts to take the work further and begins to chart out future directions for research in this area.

1

An International Perspective on Women's and Men's Work: Gender Segregation of Labour Markets

> Sex segregation has a history as old as the labour force itself
> Reskin and Roos, 1990, p. ix

The pervasive nature of labour market segregation by gender

This chapter presents a statistical analysis of where women and men work and in what numbers. It offers an international view by comparatively exploring both horizontal and vertical occupational segregation data from Europe, in particular the UK, and the USA. It investigates trends and changes, but also importantly the static and intransigent nature of this occupational segregation, which has been identified as extensive and pervasive and one of the most important and enduring aspects of labour markets around the world.

Although modern industrialised workplaces have different segregation patterns, one type of segregation is endemic: 'Almost every workplace in modern industrial societies is either gender-segregated or all one gender' (Lorber, 1994, p. 194). However, it is important to acknowledge at the beginning that gender segregation is mediated by other patterns of disadvantage. Women should not be considered as a unitary category but as having identities formed in gendered processes that vary according to various factors including class, age, marital and parental status, whether they are white or black (including differences between ethnic minority groups), lesbian or heterosexual, and whether or not they experience disabilities. Women are not a homogeneous group.

Gender is one basis of oppression which intersects with other areas of oppression (Wieringa, 1994). Putnam Tong (1998, p. 8) argues that a true understanding of the sources of women's oppression requires a deep analysis of 'how sexism is and is not related to all the other isms that plague human beings (racism, classism, ageism, ethnocentrism, ableism, heterosexism, and naturism)'. Different women 'emphasise those political issues that are most salient to their own social location' (Hartsock, 1998, p. 251). Feminist theorists therefore often find themselves struggling simultaneously against the questionable belief in universal sisterhood and the risk posed by a relativist stress on difference. While the experiences of women originating from different locations within a society, a culture, or different parts of the world cannot be the same, it is possible to identify common interests and common disadvantage for women. Hence the identification of a gender segregated labour market (Hartsock, 1998).

While arguments against essentialism of either a biological or social constructionist nature are well established by feminists, it must be acknowledged that gender is a key constitutive part of the field of social, cultural and economic divisions in society. Although divisions can be seen as 'complex, fractured and sometimes contradictory' (Halford et al., 1997, p. 12), as J. Acker (1992, p. 251) states there are no '"pure", gender-free, economic, social or cultural processes, and gender is always implicated'.

While women's experiences of disadvantage are tempered and altered by other social divisions, nevertheless, they do have considerable shared experience within their group (Bagilhole, 1997). Deem (1996, p. 100) raises a note of caution that overemphasis on the exploration of 'the different positions and identities taken by women, omits the possibility that there are still systematic modes of discrimination ... and distinct patternings which relate to gender'. Thus Deem (1996, p. 85) argues that 'it is important that we do not let the current fashion for focusing on difference and identity distract our attention from the possibility that the economic, the political and the cultural have more of a systematic influence on inequalities than might be supposed from an analysis which concentrates only on the politics of the differential identities of women'.

Material differences still exist beyond and outside identities. Age, ethnicity, class and disability all mediate the impact of employment on gender relations. These are not simple issues. Nonetheless a few general patterns emerge. Studies of ethnicity in the UK and the USA (Bhavani, 1994) have revealed patterns of segregation by race and occupation. Many studies in both the UK and USA identify a tendency for ethnic minority women to be concentrated among low-status occupational groups (Bhavani, 1994; Sokoloff, 1992). There has been a small rise in the share of black women in higher-grade employment in the UK (Bruegel, 1994), but black women continue to be under-represented in this group relative to white women. There is also a wide variation between the employment rate for ethnic groups in the UK, especially for women; with 69 per cent and 64 per cent of white women and black Caribbean women working respectively, compared with only 21 per cent of women of Pakistani and Bangladeshi origins (Bagilhole and Dugmore, 2001). In terms of age, economic activity rates for men and women in the UK are the closest for those aged under 25 – 59 per cent of young women and 63 per cent of young men. Whereas 60 per cent of women aged 45–64 are economically active compared to 77 per cent of men of the same age (Bagilhole and Dugmore, 2001). Also, disability has an important impact on rates of employment in the UK, with only 37 per cent of women with disabilities and 39 per cent of men with disabilities in employment (Bagilhole and Dugmore, 2001).

Nevertheless, despite the dramatic increase in women's participation in the labour force worldwide during the twentieth century, women are concentrated in a narrow range of occupations, often seen as 'women's work'. Occupational segregation by sex differs across countries, but it is 'extensive and pervasive and is one of the most important and enduring aspects of labour markets around the world' (Anker, 1998, p. 3). Not only is it extensive in all countries, this is true no matter how they are economically or politically organised, from industrialised capitalist countries to former communist countries and developing countries.

The persistence of sex segregation across different types of occupations and between high and low status occupations has been extensively documented, and remains despite technological advances in work organisation. As Rubery et al. (1996, p. 3) argue, occupational segregation is 'central to the persistence of gender inequality in the labour market, where female and male-dominated jobs are organised according to different principles, including pay, working time and integration into career ladders and organisational structures'. The sex segregation of occupations has two dimensions, horizontal and vertical. On the whole, women and men have different types of occupation (horizontal segregation), but where women and men are found in the same occupation, even if women predominate, they are most commonly found in the lower grades (vertical segregation) (Hakim, 1979). Both forms of occupational segregation have different consequences for women than for men. 'Women's class situations are characterised by ... low wages, intermittent employment, and subordination to men in the workplace and often at home. Men's class situations are characterised by ... higher wages, lifelong employment, and either dominance over women or little contact with them in the workplace and dominance in the home' (Acker, 1989, pp. 18–19).

The following call for action from Anker (1998, p. 5) demonstrates this: 'Given the extensive nature of occupational segregation by sex and its undesirable effects on the economy, women and society, reducing sex segregation of occupations should receive urgent and priority attention by policy-makers, laypersons and researchers.' This is reflected in the European Union's desire for the entry of more women into the labour force and into better positions in economic terms (European Commission, 1998).

While occupational sex segregation has declined in recent years for certain groups, for the majority of workers it remains a fact of everyday working life. Moreover the selective decline has to be contextualised by counterbalancing phenomena: an increase in women entering female-dominated occupations; feminisation of some occupations; resegregation; and accompanying adoption of either industry-wide or establishment vertical segregation. Despite several decades of women's expanded labour force participation, women and men still tend to work in different industries, in different occupations, and, even if they share a profession, in different roles and positions, with men generally at the top and women generally at the bottom of the hierarchy.

There remains the question of how to measure this segregation. In the 1970s and 1980s, research on the exact measurement of occupational segregation resulted in a debate on the advantages and disadvantages of different indices. However, by the 1990s this debate had reached an impasse, despite the plethora of new proposed indices. The usefulness of a single indicator was questioned as indices were found to disguise trends in segregation and failed to distinguish vertical segregation from horizontal segregation (Platenga and Rubery, 1999).

However, an interesting and illuminating measure of horizontal occupational segregation proposed here is the 'segregation index'. This uses a figure that indicates the percentage of workers of one sex that would have to change jobs in order for the occupational distribution between the sexes to be balanced (Reskin and Hartmann, 1986).

Using the 'segregation index', Table 1.1 shows the extent of occupational sex segregation in some European countries and the USA. It shows that segregation remains high, even in some countries that have extensive equal opportunities policies. Denmark, Luxembourg,

Table 1.1   Occupational segregation by sex in selected European countries and the USA

Country	Segregation index
Denmark	49.7
Luxembourg	48.9
Norway	47.9
Ireland	47.6
United Kingdom	44.4
Sweden	43.2
The Netherlands	39.9
Austria	39.2
Switzerland	39.2
United States	38.4
France	38.3
Germany	36.4
Italy	24.6

Source: Adapted from Jacobs and Lim (1995, p. 276).

Norway, Ireland, the United Kingdom and Sweden would all require over 40 per cent of the female workforce to move into 'men's jobs' or vice versa for a balanced workforce.

However, caution must be exercised when this index is used comparatively because a major weakness is its sensitivity to different types of occupational classifications. The broader the occupational categories and classifications are in a country, the lower the index tends to be, and this may explain the lower figure for Italy.

This chapter will now continue by examining occupational segregation statistics for the European Union, the UK on its own, and finally the USA.

The European Union

Female economic activity rates vary among European Union (EU) countries. However there has been both an absolute and relative progressive increase in women's employment, coupled with a decrease in single-earner households throughout the EU. Women are continuing to enter the labour market in their millions, despite recurring recession and employment crises. The percentage of women in paid work in the EU rose from 35 per cent in 1975, to 41 per cent in 1991, to 51.1 per cent of women between the ages of 15–64 by 2000 (Jacobs et al., 2000). Between 1989 and 1999, the EU employment rate for men fell by almost 3 per cent, while for women it rose by 6 per cent (Eurostat, 2001).

This basic trend has redrawn the contours of the labour market. However, this does not mean that women have won occupational equality. This feminisation of the working world has not produced an equal distribution of jobs between the sexes and occupational segregation remains a central characteristic of all EU labour markets (Eurostat, 2001). Women and men remain horizontally and vertically segregated in the labour market, with women in less secure, low-paid jobs, essentially in the service sector, which accounts for 80 per cent of female employment. Gender pay gaps persist, and there is a strong relationship between sex segregation and low pay in every member state (Eurostat, 2001).

There have been two contrasting trends; a further concentration of women in lower-level female-dominated clerical and service work, and the increasing employment of women in higher-level professional jobs. The feminisation of clerical work in many countries of the EU has reached ever new heights with this category now containing the largest concentration of women workers. Also, in all member states, some women have gained access to highly-skilled professional jobs (Platenga and Rubery, 1999). However, importantly, there is still strong evidence of persistent sex segregation within this category, and where women are entering the better paid, high-level jobs there are falling levels of pay and men are departing for better paid jobs elsewhere in the economy. Also, these women remain crowded into the caring professions and the public sector (Eurostat, 2001). Several factors account for this, including the issue that women may be attracted to the shorter working hours or flexible leave arrangements in the public sector, which appears to be less discriminatory in its employment practices.

While the dominant view may be one of strong similarities in patterns of segregation between countries within the EU, closer inspection reveals important national differences, of which the following are some examples.

According to Meadows (1996) many southern EU countries show a different pattern of employment segregation to other countries. The difference is that in places such as Italy or Spain men appear more willing to take jobs traditionally held by women in northern EU countries (for example, catering, and waiting at tables). However, in Italy, policies have made very few inroads into equalising pay for women and men. Even when women have the same skills and qualifications as men, they tend to be employed in less well-paid jobs. Women are also frequently excluded from schemes involving bonus payments or allowances, and they tend to work shorter hours than men and to avoid overtime because of their family responsibilities and the absence of publicly provided childcare and eldercare services. More than two-thirds of the women employed in the service sector, for example, work reduced hours, even though part-time work is poorly developed in Italy (Del Re, 2000).

In contrast to Italy, Sweden, like other Nordic states, has a strong public sector which has funded and run most childcare and eldercare. Also, under the parental insurance scheme, either parent can take paid leave to look after young children. Despite this, gender segregation in the labour market remains. Patterns of segregation in the labour market are clearly reflected in the divisions between typically male and female occupations, and mixed occupations seldom mean that women and men do the same jobs. Men still earn more and are in the majority in higher status positions (Bergqvist and Jungar, 2000).

As Bergqvist and Jungar (2000) show, about three-quarters of all women entering the Swedish labour market during the 1960s joined already female-dominated occupations, while a quarter joined male-dominated occupations. Also, there was little change in the gender composition of different occupations between 1970 and 1990, despite an underlying political intention to break up segregation patterns.

In the Netherlands, labour market statistics show a traditionally low participation rate of women in paid labour. The Netherlands has the lowest female participation rate of all Western countries, if the volume of hours of female labour is taken into account. There is no other country in the EU where proportionately more women work in part-time jobs (over 60 per cent). This is partly due to the lack of sufficient childcare facilities. The traditional gender arrangements are institutionalised in a breadwinner–caretaker model. Part-time work enables women to combine paid work and raising children, while men work full time, providing for the greater part of the family income (Benschop et al., 2001).

In France, occupational segregation has changed slightly in the 1990s in two ways: women gained a greater presence in the more technical and skilled occupations; and the proportion of women in some of the most highly female-dominated occupations stabilised or even decreased, while women gained increasing access to traditionally male occupations (Gonas and Lehto, 1999).

However, despite this slight attenuation of segregation, the general pattern has not been dramatically transformed. In fact, there is evidence of increased occupational segregation in France in the late 1990s. Policies in the form of benefits and tax deductions, intended to enable parents to share more equitably their family obligations towards dependants through using the services of childminders, have created and developed more domestic service jobs. Thus, one of the unintended consequences of these policies has been to increase labour market segregation, since these childminders are almost exclusively women. 'The domestic services sector is increasingly feminized, thereby reinforcing some forms of inequality in the labour market' (Lanquetin et al., 2000, p. 87).

When looking at vertical segregation, it is difficult to ascertain the true number of women managers in the EU because different countries use different classifications, plus some countries do not collect this data at all. Depending where one draws the line and starts counting managers, the proportions vary, although it is clear that men have close to a monopoly on the most senior positions and greatly outnumber women in middle-level managerial jobs in virtually every country. Throughout the EU, women's advance into senior management positions has been very slow. Fewer than 5 per cent of women are in senior management roles and this percentage has barely changed since the early 1990s (Davidson and Burke, 2000). 'Years after the EU adopted equal opportunity laws, European management is still a man's enclave' (Vinnicombe, 2000, p. 9). Also there are considerable differences by employment sector with banking, finance and insurance having more women managers.

It might be assumed that female managers would have the greatest chance of success in Scandinavian countries where some of the highest numbers of women are in the workforce, and family and equal opportunities policies are strongly enforced by legislation. Yet the number of women managers is not significantly higher in Scandinavian countries than in the rest of Europe (Davidson and Burke, 2000). Also, in West Germany, the expectation that changes in organisational arrangements and new management strategies would open opportunities for women via new (soft) skill requirements has not been realised, and vertical segregation has changed only very slowly, with few women making some inroads into managerial jobs (Gonas and Lehto, 1999).

The UK

United Kingdom statistics suggest an upward trend in women's employment generally. However, an analysis of women's working patterns suggests that occupational segregation between women's and men's work barely changed in the twentieth century. Despite sex equality legislation, female workers remain ghettoised in traditional female occupations, men are not noticeably entering women's work, and there have only been very slight increases in the number of women entering some non-traditional occupations. Therefore, there has been very little challenge to established notions of women's and men's work. The majority of UK workers work in same sex groups. Also, women's employment is even more concentrated than men's, and their range of occupations and industries more restricted.

Whittock (2000) demonstrates that despite the steady increase in the number of women in paid employment, certain occupational groups have remained either stereotypical women's or men's occupations. For women these include: professional and related in education, welfare and health; clerical and related; and catering, cleaning, hairdressing and other personal services. For men they include: processing, making, repairing and related (metal and electrical); construction, mining and related; and transport operating, materials moving and storing and related. Even within these occupational groups there is further evidence of stereotypically segregated jobs. For example, the largest number of women in the professional and related occupational group is categorised as nurse administrators or nurses.

Women are over-represented in part-time employment, accounting for the majority of part-time employees in all occupational groups (EOC, 2001). The wage gap between women and men in paid work also prevails, with full-time working women earning 80 per cent of the male full-time hourly rate (EOC, 2001). Women working part time have seen only a 7 per cent rise in pay parity with full-time working men since 1971 (Rake, 2000), confirming UK women as among the worst paid in Europe.

As Table 1.2 demonstrates, in many major sectors of employment, horizontal segregation continues to be endemic, with women remaining concentrated in fewer sectors than men.

Table 1.3 shows that women and men are also segregated across occupational groups, and that only in the group 'associate professional

Table 1.2   Employment by sector, employees and self-employed aged 16 and over

Major sectors	Women (%)	Men (%)
Construction	9	91
Agriculture and fishing	22	78
Energy and water	23	77
Transport, storage and communication	25	75
Manufacturing	26	74
Education	71	29
Health and social work	81	19

Source: EOC (2001) analysis of Labour Force Survey Spring 2000, Office for National Statistics.

and technical' do the two sexes approach parity. Also, men remain concentrated in the higher paid groups in both the non-manual and manual occupations.

When employment sectors and occupational groups are broken down further by selected occupations, an even greater degree of segregation is exposed (Table 1.4).

Table 1.3 Employment by occupation, employees and self-employed aged 16 and over

Major occupational groups	Women (%)	Men (%)
Craft and related	7	93
Plant and machine operators	18	82
Managers and administrators	33	67
Professional	40	60
Associate professional and technical	51	49
Sales	64	36
Personal and protective	67	33
Clerical and secretarial	74	26

Source: EOC (2001) analysis of Labour Force Survey Spring 2000, Office for National Statistics.

Table 1.4 Occupational segregation, employees and self-employed aged 16 and over

Selected occupations	Women %	Men %
Drivers of road goods vehicles	2	98
Production, works and maintenance managers	7	93
Warehouse and storekeepers	15	85
Technical and wholesale reps.	19	81
Computer analysts/programmers	21	79
Marketing and sales managers	29	71
Sales assistants	72	28
Bookkeepers and financial clerks	74	26
Computer and records clerks	76	24
Waiters and waitresses	77	23
Counter clerks and cashiers	80	20
Retail check-out operators	81	19
Cleaners and domestics	81	19
Catering assistants	82	18
Primary and nursery teachers	86	14
Nurses	90	10
Care assistants and attendants	92	8

Source: EOC (2001) analysis of Labour Force Survey Spring 2000, Office of National Statistics.

Thus, in the UK, most men and women are concentrated in occupations that employ workers of predominantly the same sex; 52 per cent of women and 54 per cent of men are employed in occupational groups in which more than 60 per cent of workers are the same sex. These statistics are reminders that gender is a fundamental feature around which the UK labour force is fragmented. Also, even when women do make some inroads into traditional male domains they still run the risk of reverting to enforced stereotypes. In 1996, women made up 31 per cent of all hospital doctors, yet at the consultancy level, the highest level of medical staff, only 19 per cent were women. Women are segregated further within consultancy, leaning heavily towards the field of children's medicine (35 per cent of paediatric consultants), whereas only 0.4 per cent of consultant surgeons were women (ONS/EOC, 1998).

In the UK women still bang their heads on the glass ceiling when it comes to top positions. In a wide range of occupations and professional contexts, management has been seen to constitute a significant career hurdle for women, with it being especially difficult for them to reach middle and upper management (Bagilhole, 1994; Davidson and Cooper, 1992). Nine out of ten men and half of all women employees had a male boss, reflecting clearly the predominance of men in management. Men account for two-thirds of employees in the managerial and administration field and fewer than one in twenty directors are women (ONS/EOC, 1998). Also, men predominate in most professional occupations at the senior levels, despite all top five occupational orders showing an increase in the number and proportion of women (ONS/EOC, 1998).

The EOC (1997) regards the proportion of women in management as one of the central indicators of progress towards equality between women and men. Therefore, it is significant that considerable gender differences in the distribution of management remain. During the 1980s and 1990s, women's share of managerial and professional occupations rose, suggesting a reduction in vertical segregation. However, many studies show that these trends were accompanied by new patterns of segregation, such as the concentration of women managers into service occupations or particular specialist functions where these women tend to hold lower-level positions and are in positions with less authority and responsibility than men, and in different occupational fields (Coe, 1992; Crompton, 1994; Savage, 1992).

According to the EOC (1997) one-third of all managers are women. The numbers of both women and men employed in managerial occupations, particularly as corporate managers and administrators, have risen rapidly since 1981, and women have increased their share of managerial employment by about 10 per cent. However, as the EOC (1997) points out, women and men tend to be employed in different kinds of managerial occupations. The average profile of the female manager compared to her male counterpart has hardly changed over the past decade. She earns less, even at director level, and there is still continued managerial segregation by gender, with the most popular jobs for women being in marketing and personnel, in both of which women make up about 35 per cent of managers. Female managers more often occupy specialist or support roles or positions of high expertise, rather than generalist line management positions.

There are also different levels of job segregation within particular managerial occupations. For example, men make up 90 per cent of general managers (managing directors, chief executives and other senior managers) in large organisations, but women form the majority of local government officers in management positions. The glass ceiling still exists, with the majority of women concentrated in the lower levels of management. In fact the percentage of women directors went down from 4.5 per cent in 1997 to 3.6 per cent in 1998. Since 1994, the increase in the overall percentage of women directors has been less than 1 per cent. 'Whilst there has been some progress in the position of women in management, this tends to be slow. There are still relatively few women in line positions, few women among the highest corporate ranks, and few women in industrial as opposed to service companies' (Davidson and Burke, 2000, p. 5).

The USA

Sex segregation of the labour market also has a strong grip in the USA. To desegregate occupations in the USA, estimates of workers who would have to change jobs range from 38 to 63 per cent, depending on the occupational classifications used (Renzetti and Curran, 1999). However, when workers do move jobs they predominantly move to those dominated by their own sex, even if they have previously been in other sex-dominated or evenly segregated jobs. There is also evidence that workers who hold sex-atypical jobs leave them at a greater rate (Wright, 1996).

This phenomenon is represented as the concept of 'revolving doors' with social pressure from both within and outside the occupational environment for continued segregation (Jacobs, 1989). Also, where women do enter men's jobs they predominantly do so as a gradual but continuous process of 'feminisation' or as Reskin and Roos (1990) name it 'resegregation' of the job into women's work. Reskin and Hartmann (1986) raise the intriguing issue of 'occupational resegregation'. They argue that: 'Perhaps after reaching some "tipping point" integrated occupations become resegregated with members of one sex replaced by members of the other' (p. 31). This often occurs when a shortage of male employees, as a result of men deliberately leaving or avoiding a particular occupation because they perceive it as declining in skill, prestige, salary and good working conditions, leads employers to look for alternatives (Wright and Jacobs, 1995). Historical examples of this in the USA are bank telling and teaching, whereas more recent examples include the occupations of bartender and psychologist (Roberts, 1995). 'Thus, the gender composition of blue-collar, white-collar, and professional occupations sometimes reverses, but gender segregation persists' (Lorber, 1994, p. 195).

The striking lack of overlap in the jobs held by women and men in the USA is illustrated in Table 1.5 which shows in which occupations women and men are concentrated.

Women are primarily in clerical and other service occupations. About one in every four full-time working women holds a clerical position and the service sector continues to be an area of high job growth for women. Men, in contrast, are concentrated in the skilled trades and operative jobs. Also, men tend to be in supervisory positions, even in areas that are predominated by women, such as sales and clerical work. About 40 per cent of clerical supervisors are men, although 98.2 per cent of clerical staff are female. An interesting feature of Table 1.5 is the extent to which jobs are either seen as 'women's work' or 'men's work'. Of the occupations that employ the largest number of women, four were more than 80 per cent female. Of the occupations that employ the largest number of men, five were more than 90 per cent male. Therefore, in the top female occupations, there is less sex segregation than in the top male occupations.

Nevertheless, there are indications in the USA that women have had some success in moving into a small number of male-dominated professions. For example, between 1962 and 1997 female engineers increased from 1 per cent to 9.4 per cent of the total engineering workforce, female medical doctors from 6 per cent to 30.1 per cent, and female college and university teachers from 19 per cent to 36.4 per cent (Renzetti and Curran, 1999).

However, Renzetti and Curran (1999) suggest caution in reading the signs of decline in occupational segregation. The number of women in

Table 1.5   Top occupations for women and men in the USA

Women

	Occupation female (%)
Secretary	98.7
Registered nurse	92.5
Nursing aide	88.6
Miscellaneous administrative support worker (for example, office clerk, bank teller)	82.8
Sales counter clerk	77.1
Health technologist or technician	76.7
Teacher, except college and university	74.3

Men

	Occupation male (%)
Vehicle/mobile equipment mechanic or repairer	98.6
Construction worker (for example, carpenter, dry wall installer)	98.3
Truck driver	95.9
Material moving operator (for example, crane operator, bulldozer operator)	95.4
Engineer	90.7
Protective service worker (for example, police officer, detective, guard)	84.3
Janitor or cleaner	73.9

Source: Adapted from Renzetti and Curran (1999, p. 26).

many occupations has historically been so low that even what appear to be quite substantial percentage rises do not mean that large numbers of women now hold these jobs or that they are no longer male-dominated. For example, even though the number of women employed in skilled trades increased by almost 80 per cent between 1962 and 1997, women still comprised only 1.3 per cent of carpenters and plumbers, 1.5 per cent of auto mechanics, 2.2 per cent of electricians, and 3.5 per cent of painters.

Although apparently contradictory phenomena, occupational sex segregation has declined slightly overall, while at the same time women's likelihood of sharing the same job as men has declined. This is because the numerical increase in women's labour force participation, mostly into 'women's work', has offset the decline in occupational segregation. In fact, some female-dominated occupations have become more female-dominated. For example, 77.7 per cent of bookkeepers in 1950 were women, but this was 90.6 per cent in 1997 (Renzetti and Curran, 1999). Therefore, the labour market in the USA continues to be a dual labour market, largely characterised by one set of jobs employing almost exclusively men and another set of jobs, largely lower paid and of lower status, employing almost exclusively women.

Another familiar feature of occupational segregation in the USA is where an occupation becomes more evenly balanced between women and men (a reduction in horizontal segregation), but is accompanied by the establishment of vertical segregation with women typically concentrated in the lower-paying, lower prestige specialities even if they hold the same job titles as their male colleagues. This occurs in both professional and non-professional occupations. Wright and Jacobs (1995, p. 339) give the example of bakers, where 'women mostly work in supermarkets baking prepackaged dough, whilst men continue to monopolise the more skilled positions in bakeries'. Also, in law firms women tend to be concentrated in the family law division, while men dominate the more lucrative corporate and commercial law department (Kay and Hagan, 1995). In the USA, 42 per cent of all managers are women, but again they hold very few top positions (less than 1 per cent) (Northcraft and Gutek, 1993).

Conclusion

It can be seen that women's and men's positions in the labour market remain pervasively segregated. Even with the introduction of sex equality legislation women have not moved in any great numbers into areas of employment which have traditionally been associated with men. Rather they have consolidated their position within a narrow range of stereotypical female occupations, which are generally low paid. As Lane (1993, p. 297), in drawing comparisons between the German, British and French labour markets, argues: 'Despite some reconstruction of the gender regime, particularly in the division of labour in paid work, the power relation between men and women has not been fundamentally affected. This is manifested in an only marginally changed pattern of vertical occupational and organisational segregation.'

What emerges from an analysis of where women and men work in Europe and the USA is a pattern of slow horizontal desegregation, but it is difficult to know whether in particular occupations it is really desegregation, or the introduction of vertical segregation, or even resegregation with occupations gradually switching from domination by one sex to domination by the other. One important point is that sectoral, occupational and job segregation need to be studied separately. Also, we need to go beyond mechanical calculations and look at how jobs are defined in order to study how the degree of segregation in different occupations changes over time and space. There is a need for studies of the position of women in various occupations, and on opportunities for women to break out of existing segregation patterns in order to reach better positions. Also, the organisational level of occupations needs to be studied to try to reveal the tacit or unspoken strategies that create and recreate segregation. It is this meso-level approach that is adopted in the later chapters of this book, which recount qualitative empirical studies undertaken by the author into women's experiences in four male-dominated occupations.

2

Explanations of Continuing Occupational Segregation and Identification of Potential Levers for Change

The statistics examined in Chapter 1 are reminders that gender is a fundamental feature around which the labour force is fragmented. The horizontal segregation of labour markets into male-dominated and female-dominated occupations, and the vertical segregation of occupations, with women generally concentrated at the bottom of occupational hierarchies, continues. Therefore, the first section of this chapter analyses various key theoretical and ideological explanations for this international pattern of sex segregation. The second section of the chapter examines potential levers for change.

Explanations

A wide range of explanations have been offered to explain the phenomenon of occupational segregation. At one end of the spectrum, inequality is explained by claiming differences in preferences and choices between women and men, most of which concentrate on women's lack of desire or inability to compete on equal terms with men in the labour market (see Bagilhole, 1994). At the other end, studies analyse segmented labour markets and gendered institutions to demonstrate how current inequality reflects a male-dominated and male-centred view of society. These explanations argue that the labour market in general and organisations in particular fail to acknowledge all aspects of gender inequality, in particular women's role in unpaid work (Platenga and Rubery, 1999). Underpinning these explanations of gender segregation in the labour market are issues concerning male power, and gendered assumptions about the division of labour (see Bagilhole, 1994; Reskin and Padavic, 1994; Crompton, 1999).

Thus at both ends of the spectrum of explanations, one of the main areas of debate over women's position in the labour market is the relationship between women's role in paid and unpaid work. There is general agreement that women's integration into the labour market has come about despite the persistence of the double burden of both paid and unpaid caring work in the family. For some analysts, women's subordinate position in the labour market reflects their choice to allow unpaid work to dominate and subordinate their role in paid work. However, this notion of free choice has been challenged by a range of studies and approaches. For example, for the dual systems theorists, women's position in the labour market is the outcome of both capitalism in the labour market, and patriarchy in the home; for other analysts, women's work in the home is seen as constituting a central and integral element of the overall productive system. Thus it is seen as axiomatic that to understand continuing sex discrimination and gender inequality the segregated workplace should be regarded as an important site of power relations between men and women.

Many women have family or domestic responsibilities that largely preclude them from following men's employment patterns. This is because women face many problems combining their socially allotted dual roles of homemaker and paid worker. The separation of production from the domestic domain prescribes that women's participation in paid work is affected by their need to provide childcare and housework. Much research has used this conflict between the contradictory demands of paid work and the demands of the female life cycle to explain women's segregation in the labour market.

It is true that for women the demands of home and a career can be seen as being in conflict. For some women it is accepted wisdom that they should put their families first. For other women the decision to delay or even eschew having children seems the only possibility of reconciling their desire for a career (for an example see Bagilhole, 1993a). These women assume that it is inevitable that those who leave work for any length of time to have and to care for children find this detrimental to their career. Therefore, in the UK, the traditional continuous male-oriented career and women's career breaks provide the basis for prejudice.

Many women managers have had little choice but to take this double standard for women and men into account in their career strategies, avoiding the responsibility of family commitments wherever possible. Research in the UK by the British Institute of Management (cited in Vinnicombe, 2000) shows that only 58 per cent of women managers are married compared with 93 per cent of male managers. Of the married women, half have children, compared with nearly 90 per cent of their married male counterparts. Male managers are three times more likely to have children than their female colleagues. One in five women in Britain can now expect not to have children. This childless rate has doubled in a generation. The situation is much the same in other parts of Europe. Vinnicombe (2000) shows that in the former West Germany, and in France, low numbers of women managers are mothers, and they usually have only one child, whereas almost all their male colleagues are married and have an average of two children. Also, they are more likely to be divorced or separated than the men.

Usually women do the greater part of, and take the major responsibility for, housework and childcare even if they have a strong career commitment (see for example Bagilhole, 1993a, 1993b, 1993c, 1994). Men generally do not make alterations in their personal and working lives to permit women to have careers. It is one thing to subscribe to a theoretical state of equality for women, but another to take half shares in housework or to relinquish the power and status of being the main breadwinner. While it has become the norm for many men to espouse the view that they should share household duties, their behaviour falls short of this. In the UK, 73 per cent of women still do 'nearly all the housework' and men with working partners have an average of six hours more free time at the weekends than their partners (Vinnicombe, 2000). In the Netherlands women spend 15 per cent of every working day on housework, whereas men spend 4 per cent. In France employed women devote 48 out of every 100 hours to domestic work and 52 to professional duties, while men devote 28 to domestic work and 72 to professional activities (Vinnicombe, 2000).

The major source of concern for most women in the UK labour force is the long-recognised and continuing problem of inadequate childcare. There is an anomalous situation where mothers work in increasing numbers but adequate childcare is conspicuously lacking, thus forming a major stumbling block to occupational achievement. Therefore, the 'burden of parenting has been moderated as much through a reduction in fertility rates as through a move to equal parenting' (Platenga and Rubery, 1999, p. 3). Women who are successful in paid work have often made the choice not to have children. For example, Bagilhole (1993a) finds that very few women university lecturers had children and many had felt that they could not have a 'normal' woman's family responsibilities.

Therefore, a key question that has to be addressed is whether women's domestic responsibilities are the basis of their position in paid employment or whether labour markets are active agents in women's occupational location. Also, what is the interrelationship between these two spheres; the private and public domains of women's work. Cockburn (1988) suggests that, while neither of these areas of explanation is invalid and each contributes some information to the analysis, they were insufficient to explain women's position in the labour market on their own. Therefore, a 'theoretical pluralism has emerged over the decades, with emphasis being laid on different explanations for different facets of gender segregation in the workplace' (Rees, 1992, p. 13). Gonas and Lehto (1999, p. 10) list these factors as 'structural (organisational structure), cultural (gender identities) and psychological variables (women's ambitions)', which they see as mutually reinforcing segregation.

The following sections of the chapter look at some of the various theories that make up this 'pluralism'.

Explanations at the 'choice' end of the spectrum

These explanations for the sex segregated labour market focus on labour supply. They look at the social, cultural and structural constraints on women which affect their orientation and commitment to paid work, sometimes years before they enter the labour market. It is assumed that these are transmitted through socialisation into traditional gender identities and roles, corresponding to their primary responsibility of home management and childcare. This in turn is seen to lead women to choose to accrue less human capital than men in terms of marketable qualifications and skills.

The human capital theory emerged from orthodox economics with its concentration on labour supply. It explains occupational segregation by citing the nature and particular qualities of female labour supply. Women workers are seen as bringing special orientations to paid work, which play a large part in their own underachievement. Women are perceived as less motivated towards paid work, focusing instead on children and the home and fitting paid work around their domestic responsibilities. Thus they end up in traditional women's jobs. These views are still extremely influential in the everyday actions of many men and women, as both employees and employers (Collinson et al., 1990).

Gender role socialisation is seen as facilitating the sexual division of labour, with the family as women's primary role obligation. This influences women's attitudes to, and choice of, paid work and also importantly affects employers' attitudes and actions. Girls and women learn that they are supposed to have certain qualities that belong to their role of homemaker. An extreme example of this orientation may be women who, because their husbands have highly demanding occupations, take on their homemaking role enthusiastically. They become married to their husband's job as well as to him. For example, Finch (1983) argues in her study of clergy in the Church of England (then all male) that they are an example of an occupational group where 'constant availability is considered essential' (p. 30). She also finds that clergymen's wives, because they believe in their husband's 'noble endeavours', take on even more responsibility than usual for family and home responsibilities to give him more space to get on with 'the great work'. 'A wife who sees work taking over her husband's whole life, and who endorses the legitimacy of its claims upon him, may well respond by taking *all* responsibility for domestic tasks' (Finch, 1983, p. 28).

Women are also discouraged from having other qualities, without which they are disadvantaged in the labour force. It is argued that this socialisation is reinforced through discrimination within the educational process itself. Although the level of academic achievement of girls and young women in the UK now exceeds that of boys and young men, the disciplines studied are divided by gender. Even today women are mostly not educated or trained in subjects or areas which would open up male jobs to them (EOC, 2001). Rees (1992) shows that the anticipation of a career break or a return to work part time is taken as read in many girls' decisions about careers. They are far more likely to choose arts and humanities rather than science and engineering and therefore are excluded from a range of possible careers. They are not prepared for employment in the generally more lucrative scientific, engineering and technical jobs.

Many arguments have been raised against human capital explanations of women's underachievement in the labour force. Overall it has been shown to be inadequate on its own in explaining occupational segregation. Walby (1990) criticises the human capital theory as tautological and argues that it was flawed in both empirical and theoretical terms. She argues that the arrangement of work into gender segregated sectors offers a better explanation for women's and men's position in the labour force. The idea that women have low aspirations was challenged early on (Kanter, 1977). Female aspirations may be restrained in part by what appears attainable. It is not possible to evoke the idea of women's orientation to work as an isolated explanation of their employment patterns. It does not exist independently of their work experience in the restricted labour market. Also, the idea that women have an 'attenuated commitment' to paid work has been disputed. The vast majority of women are strongly involved in paid work.

Finally, the human capital approach makes the assumption that workers are rewarded in proportion to their skills. However, women who have equivalent amounts of human capital to men and even work in the same occupations receive lower pay and are segregated into different specialisms and hierarchical positions (see for example, EOC, 1997; Institute of Management, 1994; Bett, 1999). Bourdieu (1986) talks about 'habitus' and Atkinson (1983) the 'indeterminate' knowledge of professional and organisational life. Using these concepts, the problem for women is not their human capital, that is, women's investment in technical knowledge and expertise. Rather, the problem is professional contact, style and legitimacy, 'their perceived failure to behave in ways which reveal their mastery of the indeterminate, that is, their failure to share the habitus' (Atkinson and Delamont, 1990, p. 107).

Clearly, women's dual role in society, with their allocation of the majority of domestic tasks, has an important impact on choices they make about the labour market. Working mothers, with their present responsibilities, need the expansion and normalisation of day care for children and dependants to begin to transform domestic ideology, and to gain greater employment opportunities. Until this happens, the employment of mothers in particular, and women in general, will continue to be considered as a problem to be explained, justified, or condemned. Therefore, it is tempting to look no further than this for an explanation of the gender division within the workforce. However, the evidence that most women have prime responsibility for housework and childcare can deflect attention away from and camouflage the role that the labour market plays in structuring sex segregation. As Lorber (1994, p. 200) argues: 'Low pay and uninteresting jobs encourage single women to marry and married women to devote energy and attention to child rearing and domestic work. Better job opportunities for men encourage them to devote their energy and attention to paid work.'

This identified deficiency has led to the consideration and analysis of the effects of the labour market, which are addressed in the next sections.

Explanations at the 'power' end of the spectrum

Structural constraints on women's achievement exist within both the external and internal labour markets. The labour market has active consequences for women rather than being merely the recipient of women's attenuated commitment to work outside the home. Explorations of these areas lead researchers to ask what factors in the mechanisms of the external and internal labour markets limit and restrict women's achievements and aspirations.

The dual labour market theory sees the external labour market as divided up into primary and secondary sector occupations. The primary sector consists of jobs with high wages, good promotion prospects, fringe benefits, security and trade unions. The secondary sector consists of jobs that lack these advantages. This theory was originally used to explain race segregation in the USA, but was imported to the UK to try to explain the inequality of women in the labour force. If women can be shown to be confined to the disadvantaged secondary sector, where rewards are low and promotion unobtainable, then the dynamic of the labour market itself can help to explain women's segregation. A worker's earnings and career success can result from the jobs or job ladders to which they are permitted access.

The external labour market is certainly split into men's work and women's work, as was demonstrated in Chapter 1. Women are concentrated into what are considered to be women's jobs despite possessing a variety of skills and aptitudes. The nature of this occupational segregation is twofold; the absence of men in women's occupations, and the concentration of women into relatively fewer occupations than men. Reskin and Roos (1990) take this idea of a dual labour market further by proposing the more complex idea of a 'queuing' perspective that views labour markets as comprising labour queues (employers' ranking of potential workers) and job queues (workers' ranking of jobs). This results in 'a matching process in which the top ranked workers get the most attractive jobs and so forth, so that the lowest workers end up in the jobs that others have rejected' (p. 307). They argue that these labour queues are gendered. Men (particularly white, non-disabled, heterosexuals) are placed highest in the queue with women at the bottom. However, women are further ranked by marital and parental status, ethnicity, disability and sexuality. Therefore, if an employer cannot recruit his ideal men, he will look next to suitably qualified white, young, single, non-disabled, heterosexual women.

Various studies offer different reasons for this consistent prioritising of male workers over female. Most simply, Oppenheimer (1968) argues that traditional labelling of jobs into either men's or women's work influences employers' perceptions of the appropriate workers to recruit. Also, stereotypical notions of men's superior productivity have been shown to continue and influence employers' decisions. Men are perceived as stronger, more rational, more mechanically adept, whereas women are perceived as having higher absentee and turnover rates (England and McCreary, 1987; Kanter, 1977). Another reason put forward for the ranking of these gender queues is employers' fear of male workers' negative responses to the hiring of women, in the form of demanding higher wages as compensation or organised resistance such as strikes (Bielby and Baron, 1986; Milkman, 1987). Finally, it is acknowledged that some employers even accept having to pay higher male wages as a price worth paying to favour men. As Cockburn (1988, p. 41) argues: 'Behind occupational segregation is gender differentiation, and behind that is male power.'

This male power has been conceptualised as patriarchy. Patriarchy is defined as a 'system of social structures and practices in which men dominate, oppress and exploit women' (Walby, 1990, p. 20). Advocates of the 'dual systems' theoretical approach see the position of women in the labour market as a consequence of the interrelationship between capitalism and patriarchy. The pioneer of this approach was Hartmann (1976) who argued that the patriarchal relations of male dominance and female subordination have been sustained within capitalism. In 'patriarchal capitalism', male power is based in both the family and the labour market. Occupational segregation has secured male dominance in the labour market, and secured women's unpaid domestic services within the family. However, Walby (1986), while supporting the dual systems approach, argues that the relationship between capitalism and patriarchy is more complex and sometimes in conflict and tension. She argues that the struggle between men and capitalists have produced particular sets of gender relations in the workplace at different times.

Hartmann (1976) adds to the concept of patriarchy the dimension of some men's domination over other men, by defining it as 'a set of social relations which has a material base and in which there are hierarchical relations between men, and solidarity among them, which enable them to control women' (p. 232). Patriarchy is seen as operating throughout society including the labour market, and, although it changes over time, it substantially remains the same (Maddock, 1999). Cockburn (1991) argues that because of its systematic nature, even a woman who gains access to a male occupation cannot escape its power, 'since she will modify her own subordination [but not remove it] only at the expense of that of other women' (p. 8). For men, likewise, membership is compulsory, 'being male they continue to be seen by others as members of the patriarchy, and they are bound to share, even if unwillingly, in the benefits it affords men' (Cockburn, 1991, p. 8).

In summary, then, the dual labour market theory argues that because male employers place greater importance on a job's traditional sex-label, rely on stereotypes of productivity, and have a preference for men workers, they operate gendered labour queues that favour men.

However, the dual labour market theory can be criticised, because although it offers some insights into the structuring of the labour market it cannot provide a watertight explanation of either the operation of the labour market or sex segregation. In attempting to explain vertical or hierarchical segregation within occupations, the dual labour market theory suffers from tautological dangers. On the one hand, employers are seen as perceiving women as lacking in commitment and will not consider them for primary sector jobs. On the other hand women who are confined to monotonous, low-paid jobs suffer from a lack of motivation, thus reinforcing employer's prejudices.

While it is true that a higher proportion of women than men will find themselves in the disadvantaged secondary sector, it is also true that women are to be found in the primary sector and men in the secondary sector. The theory cannot explain divisions and sexual segregation within each sector. There is in fact, substantial segregation of jobs within both market segments. Certainly there are some sectors of women's employment, such as shop working and clerical and secretarial work, which clearly fall into the secondary sector. There are, however, some areas of low-paid employment (construction labourers provide a good example) where men form the vast majority of workers, and where employment is highly insecure. At the same time there are certain categories of professional work for women, particularly in the public bureaucracies, that would fall into the primary sector.

Clearly, men and women are found in both the primary and secondary sectors of the labour market, and segregated within the sectors. Therefore, it is possible that the notion of an internal labour market within occupations may provide a more useful insight into the mechanisms through which occupational segregation is accomplished. Most analysts now place more emphasis on the role of institutional and organisational factors in sex segregation of occupations, and of roles and specialisms within occupations. Thus they introduce the recognition of the concepts of gendered organisations and regimes.

Cockburn (1988) suggests that much could be learned by looking at small-scale, local mechanisms in the workplace itself and in particular at the relationship between women and men in the workforce. The formal structures of the internal labour market can place barriers in the way of female achievement. Also, informal processes perform a vital role in the functioning of organisations and can facilitate occupational segregation. Organisations are divided into higher and lower-paid jobs, with restricted mobility across the boundary. Higher-paid jobs are more likely to be occupied by men, linked to promotional or career ladders and more secure. The organisational structure of work has a major influence on the careers of women, and the concept of occupational assignment reflects reality more than the concept of occupational choice. The location of workers in the internal labour market is the major determinant of their occupational rewards, irrespective of their qualifications.

The designation of the skill level of a job and its grading within an organisation is gender biased. The study by Crompton and Jones (1984) of clerical workers in insurance, banking and local authorities confirms this. Women are more likely than men to be in relatively demanding jobs using a range of technical and social skills, but placed in lower clerical grades. Also, in manual work, women are more likely to be segregated into labour intensive jobs and men into more mechanised, capital intensive jobs. This has been highlighted by a series of studies of factory work with a distinct division between women and men on the shop floor. Men are concentrated in craft work, women in semi-skilled assembly work, women's skills are unrecognised and women are classified as less skilled than men.

Within organisations more than one internal labour market may exist, with women and men having different kinds of career ladders open to them. Crompton and Sanderson (1990) examine different professional internal labour markets and argue that women have been historically excluded from access to career structures. For example, although there is a considerable overlap between upper level secretarial and middle management skills, secretarial positions are rarely linked to managerial openings. Positions of authority are a male preserve and even when women are included in managerial and professional positions they are absent from high levels of power. For example, there are more male heads of social service departments and head teachers of primary schools. Even in nursing, where men are a clear minority within the profession, men dominate the top management (MacDougall, 1997; Evans, 1997a).

Crucial to understanding why men dominate managerial positions in nursing, for example, is the impact of gender on promotion-seeking opportunities. Male nurses are encouraged to apply for promotion, while some women's domestic commitments are interpreted by interviewers as constituting potential difficulties (Evans, 1997b; Villeneuve, 1994). Commenting on men's gender advantage in nursing in the USA, Williams (1992) pointedly reworks the metaphor of the 'glass ceiling' to that of 'glass escalator' in order to reflect men's smooth and inexorable rise to senior management.

Managers act as either sponsors or gatekeepers for individual's careers, depending on their views. Lipmen-Blumen (1976) argues that men prefer to associate and interact with other men and power allows them to enforce this 'homosociability' by segregative patterns in the occupational structure. Witz (1992) sees these as processes of social closure. Atkinson and Delamont (1990) argue that the core sets of male professionals responsible for selecting candidates for promotion looked for professional contact, style and legitimacy. This is what Atkinson (1983) calls 'indeterminate' knowledge and Bourdieu (1986) calls the 'habitus' of professional and organisational occupations.

Crompton and Sanderson (1990) find evidence of direct and indirect male exclusionary practices in accountancy and building societies, which have been of prime importance in keeping women out of the higher levels of their hierarchies. Williams (1993) argues that occupational sex segregation is a symptom of men's desire to differentiate themselves from women and maintain domination over them, and Rose (1994, p. 69) sounds a similar note of caution to women academics, that 'we should never underestimate the extent of the resistance we will encounter'.

When analysing the workings of gendered organisations and organisational processes, Connell (1993) introduces the concept of 'hegemonic masculinity', which he adapts from Gramsci. In this case, hegemony does not mean 'total cultural dominance; the obliteration of alternatives. It means ascendancy achieved within a balance of forces, that is a state of play. Other patterns and groups are subordinated rather than eliminated' (p. 184). Connell (1993, p. 186) argues that to survive the increasing influx of women into the labour market hegemonic masculinity had to 'embody a successful collective strategy in relation to women. Given the complexity of gender relations no simple or uniform strategy is possible: a "mix" is necessary.' Gramsci (1988, p. 211) interpretes hegemony as dynamic and argues that 'hegemony presupposes that account be taken of the interests and the tendencies of the groups over which hegemony is to be exercised, and that a certain compromise equilibrium should be formed – in other words, that the leading group should make sacrifices'. Therefore, it is argued that this 'accommodating' masculine hegemony is found in organisations and internal labour markets, and that it subordinates women, and some groups of men as well.

Connell (1993, p. 183) argues that 'the interplay between different forms of masculinity is an important part of how a patriarchal system works'. All men do not necessarily conform to the dominant cultural ideal of masculinity, but many cooperate with each other in supporting these images. One example of a subordinated male group came from Cockburn (1983) in her study of printing workers where hegemonic masculinity involves ascendancy over young men as well as over women. Also, Whittock (2000) suggests that male manual workers may constitute a further form of subordinated masculinity given their relative powerlessness in relation to high status professional workers. Thus, Connell (1993, p. 185) explains that hegemonic masculinity 'is not necessarily what powerful men are, but what large numbers of men are motivated to support. This complicity ensures that men as a group benefit from the subordination of women.'

Men in positions of power use informal control mechanisms over women. Sexual harassment at work is a common and serious problem for women. The US Equal Employment Opportunities Commission guidelines define sexual harassment as 'verbal or physical conduct of a sexual nature' when submission to it is linked, either explicitly or implicitly, with the victim's employment, or the harassment interferes with a person's work performance, or creates 'an intimidating, hostile or offensive work environment' (Stanko, 1988). A survey by the Industrial Society in the UK shows that 57 per cent of women have been sexually harassed at work (*Guardian*, 1991). In a similar vein, a study of women academics shows that 24 per cent say they have been sexually harassed, and a further 42 per cent go on to describe incidents which came under that category of behaviour (Bagilhole, 1993a).

Sexual harassment has structural causes stemming from the inequitable power among men and women and is an expression of this power. It is one of the ways in which gender segregation of the workplace and hierarchies within it are reinforced (Stanko, 1988). By treating women as sexual beings rather than workers they are kept in an inferior position. Sexual harassment undermines women and prevents them from being treated on the same terms as men in the workplace.

Conclusion

Organisational-level analysis has been an important development in labour market theory and has great potential for increasing the understanding of women's occupational segregation. It confirms the evidence of the role of labour market experience and, in particular, the characteristics of employing organisations in determining a worker's career. Both formal and informal processes within organisations mitigate against the equality of women. While neither the 'dual labour market theory' nor 'internal labour market theory' are sufficient to explain sex segregation they are both valid and contribute some information to the analysis of occupational segregation.

It would seem that occupational sex segregation can only be explained by reference to broad interdependent forces that come from all the areas outlined in the first part of this chapter; women's socialised choices and preferences, the segmentation of the external labour market, and from within internal labour markets. An understanding of women's position in the labour market must take account of the terms under which they enter paid employment, with regard to domestic responsibilities and the distribution of finances within the household, as well as the job opportunities available to them.

An interplay between ideology and structure at all these stages determines the pattern of female participation in the labour force. Rees (1992) highlights the importance of the ideology of the family, the material realities of women's lives, and the exclusionary mechanisms employed by men in the labour market. The reality is that most women still have the prime responsibility for childcare and home management, and many have given priority to family responsibility. Also, there is evidence of the division of the external labour market by employers, and exclusionary and segregating practices by both employers and male workers within internal labour markets.

The first section of the chapter has identified where change needs to occur to effect a desegregation of occupations. The second section goes on to look at some of the potential levers for change that have been identified.

Potential levers for change

Negative levers: economic downturn and men no longer wanting certain jobs

Reskin and Roos (1990) argue that potential levers for change in horizontal occupational segregation could be established by identifying the properties of gendered labour and job queues. They show that the structural change in labour queues that have contributed most to women's inroads into male occupations is where these occupations, through changes to conditions of service, have lost status or power. Therefore, men abandon them to women. Women entering into traditionally male occupations has been linked with declining earnings and prestige, diminished occupational authority and requisite levels of skill, and sharp decreases in young men interested in occupational or professional training and entry. They argue that this cause of occupational feminisation is the one most likely to contribute to at least nominal desegregation in the future. In some occupations employers totally transform the work process. In others, the work process changes only slightly, but workers perform it in altered settings. In still others, both the work process and the work setting remain unchanged, but workers' rewards (autonomy, task diversity, and career prospects) deteriorate.

Technological innovations have often created jobs for women in male occupations when they reduced skill requirements (Hartmann et al., 1986; Bagilhole, 1994). As Hartmann (1976, p. 160) observes; 'In several cases [an occupation's] shift to women was accompanied by technical innovations which allowed increased output and sometimes reduced the skills required by the worker.' Scott (1982, p. 45) agrees: 'Machinery that extended the division of labor, simplified and routinised tasks and called for unskilled workers rather than skilled craftsmen was usually associated with [a change] to the employment of women.' However, as in the case of Bagilhole's (1994) study of the introduction of the typewriter into clerical work as the catalyst for its feminisation, we should be cautious about concluding that typing is less skilled than the manual methods men formerly used to produce the same products. This is because there is a strong tendency to devalue women's work primarily because it is performed by women. This latter case fits more closely into Rotella's (1981) idea that technological change can also foster feminisation by providing employers with the opportunity to re-label male jobs as women's work. In this way, changes can circumvent the stereotypes of appropriate workers.

Reskin and Roos (1990) also show that employers have set aside their biases and ignored possible adverse reactions of male workers when their firms' survival was at stake. 'In periods of economic flux, firms' willingness to donate profits to the support of white male privilege went by the wayside, and they struck a bargain with women workers that led occupations to feminise' (p. 311).

Kanter's 'critical mass' theory

Kanter (1977), in her classic study of women and men in corporate management, considers the experiences of, and consequences for, women who enter this male-dominated field. She identifies the problem of 'tokenism', the marginal position and status of women in a minority, and its serious detrimental consequences for women workers (these are discussed in more detail in Chapter 7). She sees the potential lever for change as a matter of numbers. In her 'critical mass theory', she argues that once women become a large enough minority, they will succeed in a previously male-dominated occupation. Reskin and Roos (1990) also argue that although exclusion of women may be possible when their numbers are small, once women reach a 'critical mass', unions usually try to organise them and advocate equal pay to keep employers from using women to undercut wages.

However, there are disagreements as to the required number of women for a critical mass. Although Kanter (1977) suggests 15–20 per cent as a critical mass that can change the culture of an organisation, Reskin and Roos (1990) cite 30 per cent as a 'tipping point' threshold, and Gale (1994a) suggests 35 per cent is necessary in the UK construction industry. It is very unlikely and rather simplistic to assert that a definitive, quantifiable target for women can be established as a change mechanism. The different nature and organisation of occupations must be taken into account in assessing the potential for change. Also, not just the quantity of women, but also the positions they hold within hierarchies are another important factor. Women must be in positions of power and decision-making within organisations to effect change, rather than accumulated at the lower end of hierarchies.

Byrne (1993) develops the critical mass theory beyond rather crude quantifiable figures. She sees 'critical mass' as the proportion which forms the threshold beyond which a minority group need to move in order to achieve 'a sense of normality, a transcendence of identity beyond "the rubric of exceptions"' (p. 35). Thus the critical mass theory asserts that organic long-term and sustained change will only occur above a threshold point. Critical mass is a mass of significance. The theory is thus developed to the idea of a level of influence and potency as a change agent, and not one of numbers as such, and the threshold for change can be seen as varying from one organisation to another.

Lantz (1982) postulates that for success (that is, self-sustaining and self-perpetuating change) the effect of passing over a threshold into normality (away from atypicality) has to be evident or felt in the relevant community. However, other researchers claim that men's negative behaviour towards women in the workplace is not primarily motivated by their being in a numerical minority. It is based on 'notions of inferiority rather than scarcity' (Zimmer, 1988, p. 72), and the crucial factor that determines their behaviour is 'the social status of the token's group not their numerical rarity' (Williams, 1992, p. 263).

Kanter's (1977) theory suggests that as women in organisations move from a small minority to a bigger minority the 'critical mass' will help their power and position. However, the opposite has also been shown to occur. Bagilhole et al. (2000) show that, as the number of minority or subordinate members in proportion to dominant or majority members increase in the UK construction industry, tensions and hostilities increase rather than decrease. Greed (2000) also sees the critical mass theory, despite being one of the most frequently advocated in the construction industry when discussing equal opportunities, as being highly optimistic and over-simplistic and not acknowledging the immense cultural and structural obstacles present. Burke and McKeen (1996) argue against the critical mass theory, the effect of which they claim is mediated by the culture of an organisation. The workplace culture can be defined by a small number of men who have power or control over the work environment and who can marginalise women's participation (Rasmussen and Hapnes, 1991).

Greed (2000, p. 183) points out that 'more [women] does not necessarily mean better'. She argues that women have had different experiences of class and life, which can distance them from each other and prevent the build-up of a supportive critical mass. Women working in strongly male occupations are more likely to deny difference between the genders (Ledwith and Colgan, 1996). Bagilhole (1993b) describes how women academics act in an ambivalent way. Like the women in Ledwith and Manfredi's (2000) study, they respond to women students' pastoral needs, but also show strong commitment to the male model of the profession and do not want to be suspected of 'exaggerated' identification with women. As Cockburn (1995) points out, having more women in positions of power by no means guarantees a change in culture and attitudes. Women should not necessarily be expected to speak for women and their concerns.

Role models and mentoring

One factor that has been advocated as a way of provoking women out of a conventional stream of low achievement is a female model of success to follow. It is argued that women make judgements about their work in relation to other women's careers. This role-modelling concept suggests that in the process of shaping vocational aspirations in adolescence or adult life, or of forming occupational goals, members of each sex are reinforced more securely in decision-making by seeing same-sex role models ahead of them in the power structure. The belief in role modelling is widespread in most countries and cultures concerned about sex-role stereotyping and about women's under-achievement in non-traditional areas. There is an entrenched belief that the existence of more women role models would automatically and, by itself, increase female enrolments in the area represented by the female role models. In the UK active policies for encouraging girls and women to enter engineering, the technical trades and applied sciences have been heavily based on traditional role-model theory (Bagilhole et al., 2000).

However, Byrne (1993) argues that role modelling is an inappropriate policy approach. She claims that there is an almost total lack of empirical evidence that it works. Much of what has been described as role modelling is no more than the actual, passive presence of a woman. She questions the assumption that aspiration alone will be translated into motivation and then into decision-making, merely by the visible but passive presence of women in non-traditional settings. Also, she argues that this widespread belief in role modelling as a policy direction is detrimental because it allows and justifies male inactivity and responsibility, and active role modelling wastes women's scarce time.

As opposed to role-model theory, mentorship has had a relatively low profile in terms of research investigation, and is almost non-existent in policy-making. Mentorship can be distinguished from role modelling because it is an active process of positive sponsorship by older 'patrons' towards younger or less experienced colleagues. There are suggestions that, hypothetically, for women a mentor who is both female and a role model will be doubly influential. Collins' (1983) review of professional women and their mentors identifies five generic criteria for a true mentor. They must be higher up the organisational ladder; an authority in the field; really interested in the protégée's development; influential; and willing to invest more extra time and personal commitment than mere interest. However, the current pattern of occupational segregation makes it unlikely that many women will find themselves in suitable positions to act in this way for other women. Mentors will, therefore, in most professions, more often still be male.

Byrne (1993) argues that in contrast to role modelling mentorship has been shown to have a significant influence in women's retention and progression in non-traditional areas of study and employment. In business, some key writers on mentorship in management, including Kanter (1977), identify it as having and using the power to help someone through a form of patronage or individual personal sponsorship to move upward by bypassing the usual hierarchical process. It involves providing a generalised sponsorship which enables the person receiving it to achieve progress through a form of reflected power.

Agency

Connell (1993) argues that a social theory of gender relations must go beyond a narrow focus on social structures. The power structures of capitalism and patriarchy should be analysed in terms of the practices that compose them, thus requiring an exploration of subjective experience, agency and resistance. 'By emphasising the constitution of social structures through human practice, the potential for social transformations within gender relations and various labour processes that are the result of the agency of women and men can be acknowledged' (Collinson et al., 1990, pp. 50–1).

As Cockburn (1991, p. 61) queries about the Civil Service: 'How is it then, given the disapproval of many men, that women have been admitted in such numbers to the fraternal hierarchy of the Service?' She answers herself by highlighting women's agency. As she shows, some women seek higher status positions and careers. 'To a degree the social and sexual contracts that are the basis of modern society are being autonomously rewritten by women in their own hand' (Cockburn, 1991, p. 61). Thus any understanding of potential levers for change in occupational segregation should incorporate an account of human agency and social practice.

Conclusion

Various potential levers for changing and desegregating the labour force have been investigated. Some of these potential levers can be seen as rather negative, like economic difficulties for organisations. Changes to the remuneration and conditions of an occupation may mean that men desert it leaving opportunities for women, albeit less favourable than previously enjoyed by the men. The idea of a lever of a critical mass, either numerical or incorporating the more sophisticated ideas of achieving a threshold of acceptability and normality, may affect change. Also, role models and mentorship have been advocated, and finally attention was drawn to women's own agency in affecting change. However, on a rather negative note, it must be pointed out that, given the evidence of persistent occupational segregation in the first chapter, none of these identified potential levers for change have as yet been effective strategies for desegregating the labour force.

The next chapter moves on to investigate the various gendered concepts, language and symbolism around both women's and men's occupations, which are also important in the process of maintaining the status quo of a differentiated labour force.

3
Concepts and Themes around the Difference between Women's and Men's Work

This chapter investigates some explanations of how different occupations and jobs get labelled as either 'women's work' or 'men's work'. Generally two theoretical perspectives are identified. The first looks at the supply-side of skills that women and men bring to the labour market, and the second looks at the demand-side of the labour market, which is seen to designate jobs as female or male. Using the first perspective, some researchers have cited psychologically innate differences and skills that women and men possess, whereas others look at the socialisation process whereby women and men learn different competencies. The second perspective investigates the power of employers and male workers to determine men's superior position in the labour market and the ways that they exclude women from the better paid, higher-status jobs and positions.

In both perspectives gendered concepts, discourses, language and symbolism are important in the process of the differentiation between the types of jobs and occupations that are seen as suitable for either women or men. This complex process culminates in general categories of occupations and jobs being seen as suitable for men, that is, leadership, managerial positions and technical occupations, whereas caring and emotional work is designated almost exclusively to women. At the end of the chapter, a brief consideration is given to the consequences for women of contravening these conventions and entering male-dominated occupations.

The gendering of jobs

Many jobs are sex-segregated, and women and men continue to be allocated to them according to past conventions. The persistent gendering of jobs in which managers and workers emphasise the gender-appropriate aspects of individual jobs has been well documented (see, for example, Cockburn, 1991). It seems that, once established, the pattern of occupational segregation by gender becomes fixed. Purcell (1989) observes that the initial condition which produces segregation might be as simple as a shortage or availability of female or male labour. However, once a job becomes associated with one sex or the other, the perception of it as a potential job for members of the opposite sex is less likely. Thus its gendered character is consolidated by custom, and jobs are constructed either as masculine or feminine in a manner which becomes accepted as normal by both men and women (Glucksmann, 1990). Lorber (1994) goes further and argues that the gendering of jobs can be seen as so natural that it takes on a moral quality.

> The assumption is that the skills, competence, strength, and other qualities needed to do a job are tied up with masculinity and femininity ... femaleness and maleness are stereotypically linked to certain capabilities, such as finger dexterity and physical strength; gender then becomes the discriminant criterion for hiring and not what potential employees can actually do with their hands, backs, and heads.
>
> (Lorber, 1994, p. 199)

Milkman (1983, p. 160) describes this sex typing as subject to cultural inertia: 'Once a job becomes "male" or "female", the demand for labour to fill it tends to expand or contract as a sex-specific demand.' It has been argued that the professions are especially attached to these gendered attitudes. Each profession is seen as having its 'gender tag', for example, medicine is male and nursing is female (J. Acker, 1992). Therefore this gendering of occupations and jobs, often part of a post hoc rationalisation, is persistent even to the point where if some women enter men's work or vice versa, this does not necessarily affect their designation as 'women's work' or 'men's work' (Packer, 1996).

Wilson (1995) shows that all round the world, men and women perform different types of work. Even where men and women work in the same industry sexual demarcations are rigidly maintained. This sex typing of jobs, the specific allocation of tasks to men and women, even exists when men and women are working side by side. For example, 'men will be cutting corn and wheat while women gather, women sew what men cut out, women run machines that men service' (Bradley,

1989, p. 30). However, which tasks and occupations are defined as men's and women's do vary according to time and place. Some tasks, even those that seem typically masculine to the Western world, are carried out by women in the East. However, whatever work women do is habitually viewed as less important, and women are the assistants to men's work. For example, women are predominantly represented in the heaviest manual work tasks in the construction industry in India, whereas in the UK and the rest of Europe they are virtually excluded from these tasks. In the West, it is argued that women are not strong enough for these jobs even though they are more mechanised than in India. However, Indian women often do this work as unpaid assistants to their husbands who carry out the more skilled crafts (see Bagilhole, 2000a).

There are, broadly, two different theoretical perspectives to explain the international demarcation of jobs and occupations as suitable for one sex or the other (see Rubery, 1999). They are split into either those that emphasise the supply-side of labour or those emphasising the demand-side of the labour market. Firstly, supply-side theories lead researchers to investigate the difference between women's and men's skills, either assumed to be natural and innate, or learnt. Feminist researchers, who tend to reject any psychological explanations for differences between women's and men's talents as essentialist and oversimplistic, argue that through early socialisation and later reproductive unpaid work at home women learn and develop skills which are oriented towards activities involving human and social relationships and are different to those developed by men. This approach is associated with a theory of 'difference', according to which the different worlds in which men and women live structure their ability, skills and choices in the labour market.

Alternatively the demand-side theoretical perspective is based on the concept of hierarchy and the power of exclusion or inclusion. This highlights employers' and male workers' labelling and designation of particular occupations and jobs as female or male, and their power to exclude the 'wrong' sex. Rhetoric concerning gender-typing of occupations and skills is seen as a means of legitimising exclusion rather than as relating to specific female skills. This approach has been used in the investigation of occupations where both women and men are present, but where men have risen to the top of the hierarchy into managerial positions, thus showing how the possibility of career progress for men has been premised on large amounts of routine work being done by women who were in positions not eligible for promotion (Crompton, 1986; Crompton and Jones, 1984; Bagilhole, 1994).

Based on a comparative US–UK study, Webb and Liff (1988) argue that the concept of suitability for a job is complex and includes both the supply-side and demand-side theoretical perspectives; the skills women 'supply', and the power of demand and exclusion by employers and male workers. They argue that the labour supply is gendered because men and women are differentiated by experience. Then the way in which jobs are specified means that women and men will appear differentially suitable for certain ones. Thus aspects of masculinity and femininity become established as indicators of suitability. This differentially impacts on women who come to be concentrated in a very few occupations as they are seen as unsuitable for many jobs by virtue of their sex, regardless of their demonstrable skills or experience.

Hirdman (1990) also introduces to this idea of segregation the principle of hierarchy where women and men workers are not only segregated, but also male activities are valued more than the female. Women's work is more likely to be labelled as unskilled and women's skills used in employment, such as caring and dexterity, are seen as innate and natural for them, and therefore not even labelled as skills. Also, Ferguson (1984) focuses on the links between femininity, bureaucracy and power and notes that femaleness gets inscribed onto jobs which involve little control or power, and these jobs are simultaneously labelled as 'unskilled' work requiring feminine traits. Hence, the concept of skill is often an ideological category imposed on certain types of work by virtue of the sex and power of the workers who actually perform it (Philips and Taylor, 1986).

Thus these processes create clear distinctions between women's and men's work; women's work is always lower paid, lacking in craft tradition, has weaker union organisation, and is of unskilled status. There is an undervaluing of jobs done by women relative to those performed by men, and women's work is low paid because it is done by women. It is well established in all countries that even when women work in different jobs which are comparable to men's, in terms of skills, effort, responsibility and working conditions, their pay is very often less on average than men's (Rubery and Fagan, 1993). Many feminist commentators have explored and exposed the ways in which, historically, male workers have managed to have their work defined as skilled, even when the content resembles women's work, which is invariably defined as unskilled or semi-skilled (Cockburn, 1983; Game and Pringle, 1984; Phillips and Taylor, 1986). The wage structure is related to the social construction of the occupational classification, which tends to devalue female activities and women's jobs. The characterisation of a job as female or male is a decisive factor in explaining the wage rate, and the work is often deemed inferior because women do it. In this way a hierarchical gender structure is reproduced in the workplace, with men's work carrying more status than women's.

'Men's work'

There is a belief that women's 'nature' makes them inherently unsuitable for certain work, notably that involving leadership, managerial or technical skills. This is because men have been historically considered more rational than women, who were thought of as intellectually weaker because of their emotional natures.

Leadership, management and power

According to Judeo-Christian tradition, leadership has been equated with masculinity; and management as an occupation has been historically and culturally associated with men. It was seen as intrinsically something men do (Wajcman, 1998).

> The dominant symbolism of organisations is suffused with images of masculinity such that a successful organisation is lean, mean, aggressive and competitive with a tough, forceful leader. Managerial work itself is conceptualised as involving constant action, the image is of a fire-fighter dealing with constant pressure, doing rather than thinking – 'action man'. Thus the social construction of management is one in which managerial competence is intrinsically linked to qualities attaching to men.
>
> (Wajcman, 1996, p. 262)

Powell (1988) shows how the job of manager has been defined as masculine, aggressive, independent, competitive, ambitious, unemotional and self-confident. Managerial jobs have also been defined as a matter of instrumentality, autonomy, and result-orientation (Billing and Alvesson, 2000). This image is intrinsically and conventionally masculine and produces a close identification between men and management. In this way, women are marginalised and out of place, and management is a foreign territory for them (Marshall, 1984).

Mant (1983) identifies this conception of leadership as the 'raider' style, which he argues has become the predominant leadership style in many Western organisations. This form of leadership is characterised by an emphasis on competition and the ability to be entrepreneurial.

This not only favours and is more compatible with the image of men, but also places women in a no-win situation. If they display strong 'raider' characteristics, they are felt to be excessively hyperactive and too assertive. On the other hand, if they do not they may be characterised as too 'passive'. Thus 'women are permitted to exercise leadership only in styles that are considered to be "appropriate" to their gender – but that when they actually do this many men (and some women) will think less of them' (Billing and Alvesson, 2000, pp. 172–3). Rubin (1997) argues that this emphasis on the aspects of management which are appropriate to the existing gender, means that there has been little or no recognition of the interpersonal skills, perceived as feminine, that are actually required for managing people.

Good managers are perceived as having masculine characteristics, and until recently adjectives such as 'competitive', 'aggressive', 'rational' and 'strategic' were associated with 'good' managers. All of these characteristics are conventionally seen as undesirable traits in women. Women are seen as being socialised into feminine patterns of behaviour not suited to a managerial role. Women are supposed to lack confidence, drive, ambition and competitiveness. As Wajcman (1996, p. 261) argues 'women are socialised into feminine patterns of behaviour which are ill-suited to the managerial role. They lack the confidence, drive, and competitiveness which are seen as key to effective performance as a manager.'

However, this view of management can be seen as a stereotypical and oversimplistic, and widely discredited. Firstly, some women have been shown to possess the qualities and skills required of management (Crompton and Le Feuvre, 1992; Crompton and Sanderson, 1990; Davidson and Cooper, 1992). These researchers argue that the explanation for women's lack of success in gaining managerial jobs lies not in their innate characteristics, but rather in family structures and the domestic division of labour such that women's life cycle patterns of work and childbearing and rearing roles do not fit them for a career in management. In the UK, women with families are not considered suitable for senior management positions whereas men with families are. Also, ironically, 'female' characteristics have now been cited as 'good' for management; intuition, empathy, and cooperative team working. There seems to be a broad interest in leadership being more participatory, non-hierarchical, flexible and people-oriented. These new ideas are often seen as indicating a feminine orientation. However, women in management still have a perception problem, they are either seen as 'insufficiently authoritative (but therefore normal women) or too authoritarian (because this is abnormal for a woman)' (Wells, 2001, p. 45).

Interestingly, the argument of 'which comes first, the chicken or the egg' may be a useful tool here to analyse women's position. It has been suggested that women do not display managerial characteristics because they are excluded from management positions, and men do because they are included. It has been shown that both a woman's and man's view of their gendered attributes will vary according to their position in the organisational power hierarchy (Fagenson, 1993; Kanter, 1977). Those occupying positions at the upper corporate levels have power and are in an advantageous position. Those in the lower positions have little power. Those located high in the organisational hierarchy think of themselves as more instrumental and masculine; forceful, strong, self-confident and independent. In contrast, those outside this hierarchy are inhibited from acting on their own behalf and are dependent on others to meet their needs. They then see themselves as being more feminine (Kanter, 1977). Leventhal and Garcia (1991) also show how male and female employees perceive their female bosses, and female bosses perceive themselves as high on the masculine scale and to have characteristics related to managerial success.

Less conventional ideas about feminine leadership and claims about women having advantages in managerial work due to their feminine skills (for example, Lipmen-Blumen, 1992) may be seen as a progressive force. This force could facilitate women entering senior positions in harmony with their female identities and values, as well as transforming organisations into more humane, relations-oriented, flexible, participatory and caring institutions. Nevertheless, a warning bell has to be sounded. Men's numerical dominance, and deeply rooted cultural ideas and current processes of social constructions still give leadership a masculine image in most countries (Collinson and Hearn, 1994; Hearn and Parkin, 1987). As Billing and Alvesson (2000) argue, the world of management is still strongly dominated by men, and leadership is still conventionally constructed in mainly masculine terms. Also, importantly, the transformation of organisations is not achieved necessarily by more women in management. Predominant values and ideas in society embraced by both men and women are firmly anchored in the material operations of capitalism and the market economy, and the dominance of instrumental rationality.

Technical skills

Scientific, engineering and technical occupations exhibit among the most persistent and extreme patterns of gender segregation. In studying this phenomenon, Cockburn (1992) looks at what is understood as being technical (for example, engineering but not cooking, saws but not sewing machines) and considers how artefacts and practices admitted into this category are seen as masculine, and the effect this has on women's and men's choices about the activities in which they want to be involved. In reality, women have always been engaged in certain types of activities that could be considered technical. For example, they make containers, clothing and various domestic artefacts. However, as Kirkup and Keller (1992) point out, their exclusion from industrial technical processes has caused them to be seen as non-technological and their technological activities to be redefined as art and craft. Thus girls and women are not expected to know about conventionally defined technical matters. As Benston (1992, p. 34) argues:

> There are machines and tools 'suitable' for men – saws, trucks, wrenches, guns and forklifts, for example – and those 'suitable' for women – vacuum cleaners, typewriters and food processors ... Most often, women are excluded from control of large or powerful pieces of equipment. More importantly, women are excluded from an understanding of *technique* and of the physical principles by which machines and tools operate.

Dominant, masculinised discourse around technology is implicated in the under-representation of women in technical occupations. Lie (1992) approaches this aspect by attempting to identify the elements that technology symbolises: activity, mobility, knowledge, control, challenge, danger, independence and freedom. She sums these up in the words 'strong, hard and vigorous, which alludes rather directly to male potency' (p. 10). However, Packer (1996) challenges the stereotypical view of women as 'technophobic' and men as 'technophilic'. In fact she shows that women scientists in laboratories enjoy working with machines and find the experience empowering to a greater extent than their male colleagues, who seem to be indifferent to the technology they work with. Thus we see there is a need to question and problematise the assumption of the equation that technology equals masculinity. This exploration needs to expose both the processes whereby technology is constructed as masculine, and how masculinity is constructed through technology.

It has been shown how technology and technical skills are implicated in the very construction of gender identities so that it has become widely accepted, though not empirically proven, that men are good with technology whereas women are technically incompetent (Cockburn, 1985; McNeil, 1987). Keller (1982) argues that the numerical preponderance of men in technical occupations has resulted in male bias in the choice of the methods of investigation and how they are defined. Thus objectivity, rationality, logic and impersonality is perceived as masculine and then endorsed as scientific. This makes it difficult for women to join without fear of loss of gender identity and self-esteem. Hence women who choose these occupations risk a loss of femininity, at least by imputation.

In dominant discourse, gender is symbolically constructed – in relation to technology and technical skills – in oppositional terms, so that the acquisition of technical skills by women is perceived by many as a threat to the masculinity of men and to the gender order more generally. As Newton (1987, p. 186) argues in her study of engineers:

> The boy who chooses engineering is seen as following his natural talents and interests. He is typically encouraged in a single-minded pursuit of engineering-related hobbies and his narrow interests are seen as congruent with his developing 'masculinity'. In contrast, the girl choosing engineering is seen as defying gender-role expectations and as seriously lacking in 'femininity'.

The end result has been identified by feminists as the wastage of virtually 50 per cent of the population's talent to science, engineering and technical occupations, the construction of these occupations and processes in male terms, and inevitably a shortage of skilled workers as these occupations become less popular with men (Bagilhole et al., 2000).

'Women's work'

There exists a traditional belief in a difference between men's and women's capacities, where women are assumed to be good at interpersonal relationships and to focus on people and emotion. The counter to this is that they are viewed as less rational, less capable of abstract and 'objective' thought than men (Benston, 1992). Thus what is classified broadly as caring and emotional work has been virtually exclusively reserved for women.

Caring and emotional work

Supposedly individual characteristics of women and men are often used as explanations for the occupational segregation of women into work conventionally classified as 'caring'. This approach utilises psychologically based theories of differences in personality traits.

> There is an assumption that women are innately gentler, more caring, and more 'people-oriented' than men. This seems to be a comprehensive derivation from the kinds of unpaid domestic servicing activities of men, children, the elderly, and the ill traditionally undertaken by women in the home, that is assumed to be 'innately' women's work.
>
> (Spencer and Podmore, 1987a, pp. 125–6)

Crompton and Sanderson (1990, p. 28) show that women's paid work 'closely parallels women's work in the household – cooking, cleaning, caring for small children, and the sick, etc. – in short, nurturing and supportive ... Clearly, occupations such as nursing and primary school teaching, and working in old people's homes and in the school meals service, are congruent with feminine stereotypes.'

During an investigation of this type of explanation, Gonas and Lehto (1999) discuss the heated debate that has taken place in West Germany about the relevance of supply-side factors, including women's individual preferences, socialisation and rational choice in explaining their predominance in caring work. The initial hypothesis is that, since women are responsible for reproductive work at home, they develop a specific 'female human capital'. The skills women acquire from caring work in the home make them particularly suited to jobs for which such skills are required. However, this is subsequently disproved. It is shown not to be the specific characteristics of women that explain this segregation. Instead a whole variety of factors are seen to be part of the process, such as selective recruitment, working conditions, career structures and organisational culture, in which 'female human capital' did not play a significant role. This is demonstrated by the fact that young women and unmarried women also end up in women's jobs, despite their lack of acquired 'female human capital' in the form of traditional feminine skills.

Maddock (1999, p. 200) argues that: 'The "care and cope" response is common in female professions while those in male professions are encouraged to question, decide and think.' Also, female professions tend to be those with less prestige, whereas the male professions have more status in almost all communities. For example, in medicine, nursing has a caring public image because it is a female profession. The ethics of care, selflessness, passiveness and martyrdom are enshrined within nursing more than any other profession. By contrast, doctors make decisions and are not traditionally managed, but guarded by professional bodies and monitored by peer review. Also, on the essentialist predication that women are good with people, and good at caring, women academics consistently report that they are under pressure to take on more pastoral care than their male colleagues, and heavier teaching loads (Bagilhole, 1993c; Eggins, 1997; Morley, 1996).

While 'natural' aptitudes and learned abilities are used to justify women's disproportionate participation in those jobs that express aspects of 'femaleness', such as nursing, caring and service to others, simultaneously these jobs are devalued because they are women's work (Legge, 1987). As a contributory part of this process of undervaluing, Platenga and Rubery (1999) show that typical characteristics of women's jobs such as caring and social skills are usually omitted in job evaluation systems.

> The skewed gender perspective in the formulation of the points scoring system has been revealed. For example, there are several indications that heavy physical work such as lifting and carrying objects scores higher on the factor physical effort than lifting and carrying people, be they elderly, handicapped or very young.
>
> (Platenga and Rubery, 1999, p. 8)

Caring work is closely aligned with emotional work, but also some emotional work is not conventionally or so closely identified as aping women's unpaid domestic responsibilities, but often assigned and seen as suitable for women. According to Hochschild (1983), emotional work requires the worker to generate emotions in herself and others during social interaction within the labour process. This is not gender neutral. 'The term "emotional" was frequently used by men to describe women and formed a central part of their stereotypes about what women are like' (Spencer and Podmore, 1987b, p. 126). As Lorber (1994, p. 232) argues:

> Many working women are expected as part of their job to smile, be cordial, sympathetic, agreeable, and a bit sexy. The qualities men want in women in the workplace as well as in the home – sympathy, looking out for the other person, understanding the nuances and cues of behaviour, caretaking, flattering them sexually – keep women out

of the top ranks of business, government, and the professions. Such qualities are gender-marked as 'womanly'; they are also subordinating.

Forms of employment that demand significant amounts of emotional labour are dominated by women, for example the airline service industry (Mills, 1998; Taylor and Tyler, 2000). Again, gendered assumptions are made about the 'natural' abilities and 'personalities' of women. 'The work of flight attendants is deemed to involve skills which women possess simply by virtue of being women ... The work is deemed to involve "caring", physically and emotionally, for others ... The skills are seen as "common-sense" ways of being a woman; that is, of anticipating the needs and (exceeding the) expectations of others' (Taylor and Tyler, 2000, p. 86). Also, Reskin and Roos (1990) argue that public relations jobs seemed to fit Hochschild's conceptualisation, hence their feminisation. Women are seen as expert at making amends and placating the public after mistakes made by their company. As Hochschild (1983, p. 159) argues: 'This transmutation of women's private "emotional work" into paid "emotional labour" locks women into servicing roles vis-à-vis men.' Similarly, as Ferguson (1984) argues in his investigation of the Civil Service, women are expected to be conforming, conciliatory and passive and to exhibit responses that reflect a sense of subjugation.

However, although emotional work is usually identified with women and femininity, Hochschild (1983, pp. 163–4) also suggests that men perform emotional work, albeit of different kinds, 'for each gender a different portion of the heart is enlisted for commercial use'. Women are more likely to be required to exploit qualities of 'sexual beauty, charm and relational skills' (p. 147), while for men 'it is more often the capacity to wield anger and make threats that is delivered over to the company' (p. 164). Hochschild uses the example of the male debt collector, who performs an act of 'escalating aggression' in order to extract money from the debtor to illustrate men's emotional work. In this conception both men and women do emotional labour, but women predominate in emotional work, and women's and men's emotional work are of fundamentally dissimilar kinds, with women being subjugated and men subjugating others.

Challenging conventions: women in non-traditional occupations

Reskin and Padavic (1988) argue that research into women entering non-traditional occupations is very important as it challenges the ideology of inherent differences that justifies male dominance. In other words, how can man's work serve as a rugged test of manhood if women are able to do it?

In fact, the alternative theoretical approach, opposed to the essentialist citing of innate differences between women and men, but rather based on the concept of hierarchy and power of exclusion or inclusion in the labour market, has been developed mainly in studies on women in male-dominated professions or occupations. It is argued that gender specific segregation in the labour market and within organisations is accompanied by (rhetorical) discourses on the gender typing of occupations, tasks and skills. These discourses have little to do with specific job skills, but serve to legitimise and provide a convenient justification for the persistence of segregation and gender hierarchies in the labour market and society at large. Thus using a set of cultural representations people construct their understandings of the gendered structure of work and opportunity in organisations (Gonas and Lehto, 1999; Wajcman, 1996).

Spencer and Podmore (1987b) provide the example of lawyers, where the numerical predominance of men, particularly in certain specialisms, has enabled a discourse of traditional masculinity to shape the form and nature of the job, and for it to be considered inherently unsuitable for women or at least for 'feminine' women. Practice at the Bar is an example:

> Interactions with clients was one focus for these qualities of aggression ... the need to be 'hard' with clients ... [also] the ability to dominate a situation ... [there was an] argument frequently advanced by men, that their greater size and superior physical strength are reasons why they should be regarded as innately superior to women ... These are very much attributes linked to the 'masculine' stereotype.
>
> (Spencer and Podmore, 1987b, pp. 114–16)

Cockburn (1985) endorses this polarised characterisation of certain occupations and has argued that when men and women, things and jobs, comfortably reflect such gender-differentiated values, order prevails. However, when women undertake 'male work', for example engineering, they upset a widely accepted sense of order and meaning. Thus, 'technology enters into our sexual identity: femininity is incompatible with technological competence; to feel technologically competent is to feel manly' (Cockburn, 1985, p. 12). This presents women with great conflicts and dilemmas.

Conclusion

Occupations and jobs are internationally designated as either suitable for women or for men. This chapter has identified the theoretical perspectives utilised to explain this persistent and almost total occupational segregation. They fall basically into two camps; either citing differences in labour supply from women and men, or different labour market demand for women and men. The first perspective looks at possible innate or learned differences in women's and men's skills and abilities. The second investigates the processes of exclusion and inclusion of workers of a certain sex through the power of employers and male workers.

The designation of occupations and jobs as either 'women's work' or 'men's work' is in fact a complex and involved process where both perspectives feature. Gendered concepts, discourses, language and symbolism are extremely important in the process of the differentiation of jobs that are seen as suitable for men, that is, leadership and managerial positions and technical occupations, in contrast to caring and emotional work, which is designated almost exclusively for women. Women who contravene these conventions experience conflicts and dilemmas, which are investigated in the latter chapters of this book.

4
Four Non-Traditional Occupations for Women

This chapter introduces the four non-traditional, professional occupations for women considered in detail in the latter chapters of the book. All of these occupations have been the subject of qualitative research by the author: managers in the Civil Service, academics, engineering professionals in the construction industry, and priests in the Church of England. Although they are all male-dominated, each of these occupations presents a different example of occupational segregation. The feminisation of the Civil Service was accompanied by the introduction of vertical segregation, with women remaining predominantly at the bottom of the organisation and excluded from managerial positions. Academia has not experienced feminisation. In fact there has been relatively very little shift in the numbers of women working in this profession. However, as with the Civil Service very strong vertical segregation exists, with men in numerical dominance at the top of the hierarchy. Both the Civil Service and academia would appear to have organisational structures that should allow the overcoming of obstacles to women's inclusion. Therefore, their continued gender segregation would suggest that informal mechanisms and the male-dominated nature of their organisational culture play an important part in their lack of change.

The construction industry presents the most male-dominated sector of employment in the UK. Women engineering professionals in this sector experience a very extreme case of both horizontal and vertical segregation, due to both structural and cultural factors. Finally, the Church of England has only relatively recently moved from a totally male priesthood, where women were prohibited, to a position where women can now be ordained as priests. However, vertical segregation is still maintained by their official regulations, which do not allow women to become bishops. Therefore, although all these four occupations can be considered to be non-traditional for women, they do vary in their historical and present distribution of women.

Kanter (1977) constructed a fourfold classification of occupations on the basis of the various proportional representations of the kinds of people within them: *uniform* occupations containing only one social type; *skewed* occupations with a large preponderance of one type over another (within such occupations the numerically dominant group invariably controls its culture and the minority groups are the 'tokens' since they can be regarded as representatives of their category, that is, as symbols rather than individuals); *tilted* occupations where minority members can affect the culture of the occupation; and finally *balanced* occupations with typically a ratio, of the majority group to the minority group, of usually at least 60:40. Using this useful classification for the four occupations under scrutiny, we can see that the priesthood in the Church of England has moved from a *uniform* to a *skewed* occupation, but only since the early 1990s when the first women priests were ordained. The construction industry presents an example of an extremely *skewed* occupation, and academia has stubbornly remained a *skewed* occupation, if not so extreme. Finally, although the Civil Service has moved over a long period of history from a *skewed* to a *balanced* occupation, it still remains *skewed* in its management positions.

This chapter highlights each of these four male-dominated occupations in turn. It examines the history of women's involvement in them, including dates when they were first allowed entry and under what conditions, numbers of women in them, and where they are in the hierarchy of the organisations.

Civil Service managers: feminisation and vertical segregation

The history of women's struggle for recognition and acceptance in the Civil Service has been 'ungracious and forbidding' and the moves towards equal opportunities were made in the context of 'bitterly contested' arguments over long periods of time (Bagilhole, 1994). During the latter half of the nineteenth century, the infiltration of the Civil Service by women was through the channel of clerical work. However, this work was formally segregated from men's jobs, not so much in the nature of its duties, as in rank, pay and possibility of advancement. Certain posts were reserved for men only and women were excluded from competitive examinations for admission to other posts.

It took a century of women's employment to break down three major barriers in the Civil Service. By the 1930s, the right was finally won for women to enter all grades in the Civil Service. The requirement that women retire on marriage was finally dropped in 1946, and finally, equal pay was agreed in 1955 and implemented in 1962 (for a detailed history see Bagilhole, 1994).

The First World War forced the Civil Service to employ large numbers of women. Also, women were placed in higher posts than before which undermined arguments against their competency in these positions. However, after the war the selection of women by the same methods as men was delayed until 1925, and only a small number of women were selected for higher posts. The formal segregated structure was dismantled during the 1930s, but a special grade of Clerical Assistant, right at the bottom of the hierarchy, was reserved exclusively for women (Kelsall, 1955). The Second World War labour shortages meant that married women formed a sizeable proportion of those recruited as temporary staff at all levels. Therefore, in 1946, the Treasury quietly dropped the marriage bar. Finally, in 1955 the Civil Service agreed to introduce equal pay in seven annual instalments (Civil Service Department, 1971).

However, the persistent concentration of women in the lower grades in the Civil Service has continued over the decades. In 1971, while women represented 75 per cent and 55 per cent of the two lowest grades, they only held 3 per cent of the top management positions. The proportions of women staff that reached the higher levels of the Civil Service were so small that they could be seen as a rarity. This was despite the fact that over the twenty years from 1950 to 1970 the number of women in the main Civil Service classes increased by just over 40 per cent, whereas the numbers of men increased by only 1.5 per cent (Civil Service Department, 1971).

The Kemp-Jones Committee, set up in 1970, found that several classes and posts were still reserved exclusively for men and that rates of promotion were unequal for men and women (Civil Service Department, 1971). The Committee argued that special arrangements were needed to enable women civil servants to combine family responsibilities and a career of a kind that made real use of their abilities and experience. The most important issue to be considered was the provision of part-time work. Only a very small proportion of posts were part time, and mostly in typing and the lowest clerical grade. However, in practice the report had little effect, and nearly a decade later, because of the growing dissatisfaction of women civil servants expressed by pressure groups and trade unions, a Joint Review Group of management and trade unions was set up to review the development of employment opportunities for women.

Fogarty et al. (1981) concluded that there had been no change in the top levels of the Civil Service from an earlier examination undertaken in 1968. They highlight the importance of informal processes in women's unequal treatment. They argue that these take the form of 'understandings, attitudes and morés [sic] which are part of the texture of the informal organisation of higher administration and which operate to steer women more than men away from the scenes of important action and hence lessen the likelihood of their being seen as candidates for top jobs' (pp. 280–1).

The Joint Review Group found that part-time posts were still very few, and concentrated in cleaning, typing and secretarial and clerical work (Management and Personnel Office, 1982). The maternity leave allowance for women civil servants had been increased and further unpaid leave was permitted at departmental discretion, but nursery provision had not developed. One area that was left completely to the discretion of departments was the issue of special leave, both paid and unpaid. Also, the Kemp-Jones Committee recommendations on the reinstatement of women after a career break had not been implemented.

In particular, the report highlighted two kinds of disadvantage that women experienced. Firstly, it argued that little account was taken in working conditions of the fact that women held the primary responsibility for the care of children and elderly relatives and the maintenance of the home. In fact, personnel systems and career paths were geared to a continuous career. Secondly, supervisors and managers held prejudiced attitudes and beliefs about the abilities of women and the types of work to which they were most suited (Management and Personnel Office, 1982).

The Joint Review Group made a series of over 70 recommendations, but few required major changes in Civil Service regulations. Most reiterated, or developed only slightly, proposals put forward in the Kemp-Jones Report, which had already not been uniformly or enthusiastically implemented in the decade from 1971–81. As Cockburn (1991, p. 52) points out all it really did was 'made public what women already knew; that women civil servants did most of the grafting and got few of the rewards'.

Progress was again assessed for the years 1984 to 1987 (Cabinet Office, 1988). Women were still clearly over-represented in the lowest two clerical grades (76 per cent and 61 per cent respectively), and there was still no change in the representation of women in top management. Promotion rates for women were still lower than for men. The use of seniority criteria was seen as an important reason for this, and it was felt that, in some circumstances, their use may constitute indirect discrimination against women. Some jobs were still perceived as unsuitable for women.

Further progress reports were produced (Cabinet Office, 1990, 1991, 1992). They continued to show an over-representation of women in the lowest grades, where women represented 70 per cent of new entrants. In 1992, while women still represented 74 per cent and 69 per cent of the lowest two grades, there were only 20 per cent in the lower managerial grades and even fewer above that, with no women in the top grade. Women's promotion rates remained lower than men's, and women working part time had lower promotion rates than full-time women. Each year a higher number of women than men resigned, just over 60 per cent of all resignations were from women. Twenty-six nurseries and over 120 holiday play schemes were running. However, these were mainly used by staff in the lower grades.

As Cockburn (1991, p. 50) argues the pace of change in the Civil Service is 'of geomorphological gradualness'. Women's segregated employment position within it continues. The Hansard Society Commission (1990, p. 6) expresses the view that: 'Women are seriously underrepresented in senior positions within the Civil Service.' They recommend that the Civil Service should take much more positive action. However, changes forecast by the Treasury for the year 2016 indicate an 'intractability of the obstacles facing women' (Hansard Society Commission, 1990, p. 34).

One of the major areas of concern remaining is identified as attitudinal barriers of managers (Hansard Society Commission, 1990). Cockburn (1991) reports men within the Civil Service claiming that, if women were not making progress within the organisation, it must be because of the 'handicap imposed on them by nature' or because they choose to give priority to their home lives (p. 66). Evidence suggests that line managers judge women's suitability for promotion more harshly than men. Cockburn (1991, p. 56) shows that for many male civil servants, 'the Civil Service hierarchy they belong to is, in their minds, every bit as masculine as that of a business enterprise or the army. Though women have penetrated up its ranks, at each step they have been considered intruders ... Even today the Service remains in men's minds a male hierarchy with women in it.'

Walters (1987, p. 14) shows that the Civil Service is ambivalent in its handling of the issue of women's employment: 'It is an occupation that opens itself to women and yet squeezes them out; which integrates them and yet marginalises them.' The bureaucratic organisation of the Civil Service that was built around the development of continuous lifetime careers works against the acceptance of women's broken careers, late starts, and periods of part-time working. Cockburn argues that in an organisation where institutional barriers to women's equality are challenged new processes are utilised by men to retain their control: 'men are found to be culturally active in creating an environment in which women do not flourish' (Cockburn, 1991, p. 56).

While women have increased their proportion in management positions they still have a long way to go. Women have found it difficult to make progress into the most senior positions. Although by 2000 women represented 51.4 per cent of all staff in the Civil Service, they only held 17.2 per cent of senior posts. Also, only 11.5 per cent of women were at middle and senior management level, compared with 31.4 per cent of men. The relative position of women and men in the grade structure was reflected in their pay level. While 46.5 per cent of men earned a gross salary of £20,000 or more, only 14.1 per cent of women did so (Cabinet Office, 2001).

Also, the lack of part-time work or job sharing at a senior level creates significant barriers for many women with caring commitments. Only 13 per cent of Civil Servants work part time; 23.8 per cent of women and 1.6 per cent of men (Cabinet Office, 2001). Working long hours has come to be seen as an indicator of commitment and stamina and reflects a 'masculine' work culture (EOC, 1997). It would appear that until women's extra domestic responsibilities are either lifted or shared by men, or positive action is taken by the Civil Service to change its work culture and accommodate them, then equality for women will remain elusive, and a lot of talent will continue to be wasted. A few women may break through chips in the glass ceiling, but it remains largely intact for most women.

Academics: maintenance of horizontal and vertical segregation

The history of women in universities is one of total exclusion until the end of the nineteenth century (ETAN, 2000). For centuries women were legally prohibited from studying in universities, obtaining a degree or becoming an academic. Women had to fight a hard and bitter battle to enter universities (see David and Woodward, 1998). Women were not admitted to degree programmes on equal terms with men in all UK universities until 1895. However, even after this date, women were not permitted full graduate status from Oxford and Cambridge universities. Oxford University did not admit women to full membership until 1921. At Cambridge women were not allowed to take anything but titular degrees until 1948. This was because the position of a full degree would have given them a seat on Senate and a say in university policy. Even then, both Oxford and Cambridge set quotas of 25 per cent and 10 per cent respectively on the proportion of women students. Even as late as 1970, women only made up 11 per cent of students at Cambridge (David and Woodward, 1998).

Many young women on both sides of the Atlantic faced opposition from society in their attempts to undertake a university education. In the USA, the best-selling book by Edward C. Clarke, *Sex in Education; or a Fair Chance for the Girls,* predicted that if women went to college their wombs would atrophy (Kimmel, 2000). In the UK, Vera Brittain's mother was criticised for allowing her to go to university in 1914: 'How can you send your daughter to college, Mrs Brittain! Don't you want her ever to get married?' (quoted in David and Woodward, 1998).

After the Second World War, all the universities in the UK allowed the entry of women undergraduates. By the time of the Robbins report in 1963, 7 per cent of men and 6 per cent of women went into higher education (David and Woodward, 1998). This has increased to about 30 per cent of all school leavers, and nationally women now constitute 52 per cent of all full-time, and 58 per cent of all part-time under-graduates. However, due to the time lag, still a higher proportion of men (16 per cent) of working age have degrees than women (13 per cent) (EOC, 2001). Also, importantly, there is a big difference in the disciplines that men and women study. Women constitute 77 per cent of education students, but only 15 per cent of engineering and technology students (EOC, 2001).

Women academics have not enjoyed the same success as women students. Their position has moved from one of exclusion to the main-tenance of relatively stable horizontal segregation, especially by disci-pline, and vertical segregation by grade. While the first woman was appointed as an academic in 1893 and the first woman appointed as a professor in 1894, since then there has been very slow progress. Rendel (1980) shows that even by the 1970s, the proportion of women academics was virtually the same as in the 1920s, and the proportion holding senior posts virtually the same as in the 1930s. She comments that 'individual women have learnt it is not enough to be better than men ... they are not perceived as scholars' (p. 143).

Women constituted only 12 per cent of academics in the late 1970s, and were disproportionately concentrated in the worst paid, lowest status and least secure positions (S. Acker, 1984). By the academic year 1991–92, they had increased to 22 per cent, but there was little change in the predominance of men at senior level. Women only held 5 per cent of professorships (S. Acker, 1994). Acker expresses her surprise at this: 'If there is anywhere that women professionals should be success-ful, it is in the universities. We think of teaching as a women's forté and universities as meritocratic institutions' (S. Acker, 1994, p. 125).

Despite the introduction of equal opportunities policies by many universities in the 1990s, their academic staff continues to be male-dominated. Overall, women hold only 35 per cent of full-time acade-mic posts (including both teaching and research), and account for only 10 per cent of professors (Universities UK, 2000). The figures are even more revealing if we look at different disciplines and grades. Whereas 24 per cent of education professors are women, only 2 per cent of physics professors are women, and there are none at all in civil engineering (Universities UK, 2000).

The proportion of women academics in the most prestigious and older established universities has always been lower than those in newer institutions. Rendel (1980) shows that the proportion of women holding university posts at Oxford and Cambridge was always far below the national average. This pattern continues with significant differences between the 'new' (post-1992) and the 'old' (pre-1992) universities. Women make up 42 per cent of academics at the former, but only 27 per cent in the latter. When higher education institutions are ranked by the percentage of women academics in the equivalent positions of senior lecturer in old universities and principal lecturers in new universities, the percentage ranges from 42.6 per cent at the top to only 4.2 per cent at the bottom. The old universities cluster predominantly at the bottom of the ranking (Universities UK, 2000).

Women academics are also in less secure and lower-paid positions than their male counterparts. The Bett report showed that women make up two-thirds of part-time staff. Also, the report expresses 'real concerns' about whether universities are meeting their statutory obligations to ensure equal pay (Bett, 1999, p. 26). Figures from the Higher Education Statistics Agency show that only 42 per cent of women academics had full-time permanent positions compared to

59 per cent of men, and that women are 33 per cent more likely than men to be employed on fixed-term contracts (*Guardian*, 1999a).

There is long-standing discrimination against women academics. Higher education institutions pay women less than men for doing the same jobs in the same subjects. A big pay gap exists in almost all subjects and at every grade. Topping the list is anatomy and physiology, with an £8,000 difference in male and female professors' pay. Even in nursing and paramedical studies, the subject with the highest proportion of women (70 per cent of lecturers), male lecturers earn £1558 more on average (MacLeod, 2000).

Interestingly, the disadvantaged position of women academics is a universal feature across countries in Europe, the USA and New Zealand (Brooks, 1997; David and Woodward, 1998; ETAN, 2000). Women students outnumber men in higher education with an average of 103 women for every 100 men across all European Union countries (European Commission, 1997). However, nowhere has women's representation in academia kept up with the increasing numbers of women university students. Even in the Scandinavian countries, which show the highest figures of women studying for degrees, the proportion of women in top academic jobs is low. For example, in Finland, which has one of the highest levels of women's participation rates in the labour market (over 50 per cent), women only make up 13 per cent of university professors and 22 per cent of associate professors (Academy of Finland, 1998).

Because of the position of women academics, Opportunity 2000, the national business-led campaign to increase the quantity and quality of women's representation in the workforce, has singled universities out as 'under-performing employers' who had 'signally failed to make enough progress in promoting women' (EOR, 1997). Stanley (1997, p. 5) strongly agreed that 'there are clear signs that higher education is becoming one of the last bastions against the recognition of "women's worth"'.

The original Hansard Society Commission Report (1990) hoped that the sheer numbers of women studying in higher education would bring changes to the academic workforce. However, their subsequent progress report exposes this as erroneous: 'generational change does not appear to have done the trick and the evidence suggests that waiting for it to do so may well take a long time' (McRae, 1996). Evidence shows that women still face a combination of structural and cultural barriers in academia (see Bagilhole, 2002a, 2001a, 2000b, 1993a, 1993c; Bagilhole and Goode, 2001, 1998; Bagilhole and

Woodward, 1995; Goode and Bagilhole, 1998a, 1998b; McRae, 1996; Hammond, 1997). These include discrimination in recruitment and promotion, lack of support for family responsibilities, pressures to maintain a continuous publishing career, and hostility and harassment from colleagues and students.

Although over 90 per cent of universities have formal equality policies, these initiatives are described variously as 'feeble' (Heward, 1996, p. 16), and 'too little too late' (Bagilhole, 2000b). Fewer than a third have action plans to back up their policies (Bagilhole and Robinson, 1997). As the Bett report observes, 'most HE institutions have yet to become model employers as regards equal opportunities' (Bett, 1999, p. 26). Universities remain persistent sites of inequality for women academics.

Construction industry engineering professionals: an extreme case of horizontal and vertical segregation

> On Wednesday, 7 December 1989 a man in his early twenties went with a gun, into the Engineering faculty of the University of Montreal, Canada. He ... shot dead fourteen women, and injured a further twelve ... the shooting was a planned massacre of 'feminists' ... He saw women engineers ... as archetypal 'castrating feminists', ... What many women saw in the Montreal massacre was the tip of the iceberg of hatred directed against women who were entering one of the most masculine professions: engineering.
>
> (Kirkup and Keller, 1992, p. 162)

As the engineering institutions and engineering trade unions developed in nineteenth-century Britain, they adopted a deliberate policy of excluding women (Drake, 1984). This certainly worked in the construction industry. Census data indicates that in 1871, there were only 171 female builders out of a total of 23,300 (0.75 per cent), and of the 5697 architects, only five were women (Powell, 1983).

However, during the First World War women replaced men in undertaking semi-skilled and unskilled work in the engineering industries generally. Also, a small number of instructional factories were set up to put educated women through crash courses to raise them to the level of professional engineers (Drake, 1984; Kozak, 1976). However, the Amalgamated Society of Engineers (ASE) had a government agreement that, despite women proving their ability in this skilled work, at the end of the war they would be removed and their special training stopped. Many thousands of women were ejected from their jobs because they were identified as potentially diluting the power and status of professional engineers (Cockburn, 1992). Therefore, by 1939 there were only 15,700 women employed in the building industry compared to 1.2 million men (Powell, 1983).

In the Second World War, women again replaced men in engineering, including skilled jobs. However, following the war, under the intense ideology of 'femininity' and 'domesticity', women were once more expected to leave the jobs for the men. Most did so, and those who stayed were reduced to unskilled or semi-skilled work. Since then there has been a steady, but small, rise in the number of women entering engineering in professional positions (Garner and McRandal, 1995).

Thus we can see that men have jealously guarded the engineering professions (see Cockburn, 1992). Prior to the Sex Discrimination Act 1975, this was relatively easy because it was perfectly acceptable and legal to offer separate curricula for boys and girls. Boys studied science and technology and girls did 'domestic' subjects (Whitelegg, 1992). Since the latter half of the 1970s, increasing numbers of women have been studying engineering and technology, but their numbers remain low.

In the late 1980s, with concerns over the so-called 'demographic time bomb' and problems associated with skill shortages in engineering, there was an increased interest in encouraging women to enter engineering occupations through initiatives such as the Women into Science and Engineering programme (WISE) launched in 1984. Despite the time and resources devoted to these initiatives, the number of women studying all types of engineering at degree level only grew to 12 per cent by the late 1980s. The number of women employed as professional engineers, scientists and technologists also remained low at 5.2 per cent (Devine 1992). The importance of opening up the profession to women was recognised by bodies such as the Engineering Industry Training Board (EITB) and the Engineering Council. In 1987 an EITB pamphlet concluded that 'it is imperative for the survival of the engineering industry that the talents and abilities of the female half of the population are not ignored' (EITB, 1987).

Accordingly, efforts were made by the construction industry to attract more women using initiatives such as targeted recruitment literature and insight programmes (Gale, 1991, 1994a). These helped to increase the proportion of women managers and professionals entering the industry throughout the late 1980s and early 1990s (Dainty et al.,

1999). However, an investigation by the Equal Opportunities Commission found that all parts of the engineering profession are still male-dominated (EOC, 1997). Also, the construction industry is an extreme case of the lack of women engineering professionals. Greed (2000, p. 181) sees the construction industry as so male dominated as to warrant the label of '"Planet Construction" upon which live a series of male-dominated professional tribes, each with its own culture and world view'.

At 9 per cent, construction has the lowest female representation in its workforce of all major industries and service sectors in the UK, and women are concentrated in clerical and secretarial positions, or other positions not directly involved in the construction process (EOC, 2001). Overall, women represent fewer than 6 per cent of construction professionals, with the majority working in architecture, landscape architecture, interior design or town planning. If these design, planning and support professions are removed from the analysis then fewer than 2 per cent of qualified construction engineering professionals are women, and they are not proportionately represented at middle and senior levels (Bagilhole et al., 2000).

Until the 1990s, the industry did little to facilitate women's entry to construction. Recruitment by the UK construction industry is virtually homogeneous, with a marked propensity for companies to attract, recruit and select white men (Greed, 1991; Gale, 1994b; Court and Moralee, 1995; Ansari and Jackson, 1999; Bennett et al., 1999; Fielden et al., 2000). This maintains a situation where women and ethnic minorities are virtually excluded.

A body of research exists on women's under-representation at the professional and technical levels of engineering (see Bagilhole et al., 2000; Carter and Kirkup, 1990; Evetts, 1996; Kvande and Rasmussen, 1993; McRae et al., 1991). This under-representation is commonly attributed to the effect on potential female entrants of the image of engineering as a traditional, male-dominated, heavy industrial environment. Also, women engineers experience problems in being accepted into their work environment, because the accepted professional identity in engineering is to be a white male. Therefore, aggression, competitiveness and hierarchical leadership form the institutionalised traits of engineering. The result is that women, being in such a small minority, are seen as being representative of their gender, as 'token' employees rather than as individuals. They experience prejudice and negative stereotypes, are more conspicuous, and likely to be the subject of ridicule, harassment and discrimination.

Thus, as Bagilhole et al. (2000) show, in the construction industry women continue to be excluded by the industry's poor image, the gate-keeping of construction education, male domination, lack of role models and knowledge, gender biased recruitment literature, informal recruitment, the requirement for high levels of geographical mobility, low flexibility in working hours, and potential conflict with family responsibilities.

However, the industry has begun to recognise that a diversified workforce offers a potential solution to impending skills shortages. Moreover, there is also a recognition in the sector that workforce homogeneity is detrimental to long-term growth and adversely affects the ability of organisations to adapt to new markets, tech-nologies and societal trends (see Bagilhole, 1997; CIB, 1996; Kossek and Lobel, 1996; Latham, 1994). A report *Constructing the Team* (Latham 1994) led to a working group with a remit to 'promote equal opportunities within the industry and to widen the recruitment base', with special emphasis on the under-representation of women. Their work carried on through the formation of the Construction Industry Council's Equal Opportunities Task Force, and the 'Change the Face of Construction' initiative which aims to promote the sector to all under-represented groups. The industry has been criticised for its failure to recruit women and ethnic minorities (*Building*, 1999), and for its lack of support for an initiative set up by the Department of the Environment, Transport and the Regions (DETR) aimed at promoting equality (Glackin, 1999). Diversity issues are now at the forefront of the government's drive for 'Respect for People' within the construction sector (Raynsford, 2000). The junior minister for construction, Beverley Hughes MP, has called for the industry to do more to combat the significant prejudice that women face (Hughes, 2000).

However, maintaining an upward trend in the number of women wanting to enter the industry proves to be problematic. Membership data from the professional institutions show women's representation has levelled out and has not increased since 1996 (Hampton, 2000). Concerns remain that barriers to women's career progression may threaten their continued presence in the future. Reports in the trade press indicate that women find developing their careers problematic (Finch, 1994; *Building*, 1995). If women enter the construction work-force in increasing numbers, employers will have to promote equality of opportunity more effectively in order to retain them (Khazenet, 1996; Yates, 1992).

Church of England priests: the latest to abolish exclusion, and a retention of formal vertical segregation

Women's ministry in the Church of England has always been and continues to be different from men's. They are given a lesser and subordinate position to men in the organisation of the Church. The Anglican clerical profession is divided into three orders: deacons, priests and bishops in ascending order. Women's history in this profession has seen them move very gradually and with bitter and acrimonious struggles, from the right to be ordained deacons to ordination as priests, but they are still denied the right to become bishops.

Until 1986, the highest form of women's ministry was limited to the role of deaconesses (not even women deacons). They were technically lay people licensed to carry out certain minor duties in the Church. Their role was largely determined by the goodwill of the all-male priesthood. As Aldridge (1987, p. 378) describes it, 'patronage is dispensed by men', despite these women taking on their role as 'a lifetime commitment' (Aldridge, 1994a, p. 144). Aldridge (1987) argues that the role of deaconess is 'compounded of anomaly, ambiguity and subordination' even to deacons. They are only allowed to wear a blue cassock (Mary's colour) and most positions of responsibility are denied them. Formal processes take little account of them and they are largely excluded from the organisation of the Church (Aldridge, 1994a).

In July 1985, the Church of England's General Synod finally allowed women to be ordained as deacons. Interestingly, while all 36 bishops voted in favour, 25 per cent of the clergy and 20 per cent of the laity voted against (Aldridge, 1987). Therefore, women gained the right to be recognised as religious professionals, and enter the lowest rank as deacons. Deacons are allowed to wear the clerical uniform of a black cassock and clerical collar. However, they are not permitted to perform the central functions of the Church; celebration, communion, pronouncing blessings and absolution, marriage and burial. Out of the 601 deaconesses in 1987, only 21 did not proceed to ordination as deacons (Aldridge, 1989).

By 1989, a national survey of deacons found 999 women, but only 51 per cent of these were in receipt of a full stipend (the salary a priest gets for the care of a parish) paid by the Church, 8 per cent were paid by non-church agencies, 9 per cent received a part stipend or honorarium, and 32 per cent were unpaid. Aldridge (1994a) argues they form 'a rich resource of human capital for the professional ministry of the Church', and, it could be added, a cheap resource. Moreover, whereas

for men deaconhood was normally a one-year probation before ordination to the priesthood, for women it was envisaged to be the height of
their career. Therefore, the admission of women to the role of deacons
was seen as a way of defusing the campaign to ordain women to the
priesthood. At the same time, it adds 'very little to their role or their
career prospects, and will not undermine but perpetuate their structured
subordination to the clergy' (Aldridge, 1987, p. 391).

Despite the inequality in opportunities for men and women deacons,
women's experiences in the role of deacons constituted a highly
symbolic advance and raised their aspirations. Aldridge (1991, p. 16)
reports that 'women's entry into the Diaconate has contributed to a
revolution of rising expectations'. He argues that fundamental change
had taken place with women gaining 'growing confidence in the place
of women's professional ministry in the Church of England, and in
their own vocations to priesthood'. They were beginning to view deaconhood as a probationary period within the promotion structure of
the Church, like their male colleagues. Although male deacons could
also remain as deacons and as assistants to their priest, few did so. As
Aldridge (1987, p. 16) argues it is the priesthood that is viewed as the
important stage of divide from the laity and as crucial to the practices
and functions of the Church, as priests are in control of the mediation
between humans and the sacred.

The ordination of women to the priesthood is one of the greatest
controversies in the Church of England. The Movement for the
Ordination of Women (MOW) was the main pressure group campaign-
ing for their ordination. Feminist Christians interpreted their exclusion
from the priesthood as symptomatic of deep-rooted sexism in the
Church of England and many came to the conclusion that feminism
and Christianity were incompatible (Aldridge, 1989). However, MOW
adopted a strategy of inclusionary, rather than revolutionary incorporation. It did not campaign for the overthrow of the clerical, professional structures, but for women to be included in them. Their demand
was for 'equal opportunity' and a career open to their talents (Aldridge,
1994b).

As pressure grew in the Church of England for the ordination of
women priests, so opposition was organised. Theological arguments
were cited against them, mostly by men, and primarily from the
organised opposition campaign, Forward in Faith. These included
assertions such as 'a woman could not be an icon of Christ'. As Aldridge
(1991, p. 143) argues, 'historically, theology has been ring-fenced as a
predominantly male discourse, one which has celebrated women's

subordinate role'. Also, more profane incentives were used in trying to stop the ordination of women to the priesthood. The Additional Curates Society, founded in 1837 to give financial support to deacons and priests working in poor parishes, announced that they would withdraw grants they had given to women deacons if they became priests. However, this threat of withdrawal of funds may not have had an important impact, as 'the amount given to these ladies is negligible, a mere £10,000 out of our total £350,000' (Aldridge, 1994a, p. 140).

Over the decade from 1978–88, patterns of voting in the General Synod in favour of the ordination of women priests showed an upward trend, but also some volatility. Bishops' votes ranged from 65 per cent in favour in 1978, up to 87 per cent in 1987, then down to 57 per cent in 1988; clergy votes in favour went from 39 per cent to a consistent 57 per cent in 1984 and 1988; the laity went from 53 per cent in favour in 1978, to 63 per cent in 1984, and down to 59 per cent in 1988 (Aldridge, 1989). However, after twenty-five years of hard and bitter struggle, in November 1992 the vote was won, by the required two-thirds majority, to ordain women to the priesthood. The final and decisive voting was: bishops 75 per cent in favour, clergy 70 per cent in favour and the laity 67 per cent (Aldridge, 1994b). This led to John Gummer, then Conservative Minister for Agriculture, to resign as a lay representative on the General Synod despite 13 years' membership, and the Conservative MP, Ann Widdicombe, to leave the Church of England and join the Roman Catholic Church, where women cannot become priests.

The first women priests were ordained in 1994, and entered an almost entirely male organisational structure and culture. Interestingly, while 2000 women priests have been ordained in the first five years, 450 male clergy have left as an issue of conscience over their ordination (*Guardian*, 1999b), and this has cost the Church of England £15.6 million in compensation payouts (Bates, 2000).

Women's ordination to the priesthood allows them to perform the sacraments of the church; marriage, burial and communion. In other words, as Charlton (1997, p. 600) so concisely points out allowing them to practice by giving them a 'union card'. However, at the same time the Church sets a concrete ceiling or 'lead roof' for women by building sex discrimination into its very structure in three important ways (Bagilhole, 2002b). Aldridge (1994b, p. 509) names these 'the managed institutionalisation of discontent'. Firstly, it denies women the right to become bishops. Secondly, it allows bishops to refuse to ordain women as priests. Finally, it allows parishes to object to women priests on the grounds of their sex. As Lehman (1987, p. 9) states: 'While in many institutions sex discrimination may be subtle and indirect, often part of institutional cultures rather than matters of rules or law, in the case of the Church of England it is direct and written in "tablets of stone". This is an example of institutionalised sexism "writ large" in two orders of priesthood; one completely integrated and male, and one on the margins and female.'

The first women 'pioneers' to be ordained by the Church of England experience difficulties with the male-oriented organisational culture of 'constant availability' often facilitated for clergymen by their wives. They suffer from exclusion and marginalisation into lower paid (or unpaid), less secure positions and by the often secret and informal processes of recruitment and selection. Finally, they have to cope with hostility and harassment from male colleagues and superiors, and their congregation members, both male and female (Bagilhole, 2002b).

Like other organisations, the Church of England has finally adapted to the greater and increasing involvement of women in paid work and other parts of the public domain. However, this was a gradual, strongly contested and painful process for the Church. Also, while gendered processes are often hidden or obscured in modern bureaucratic organisations 'through a gender-neutral, asexual discourse', the Church of England stands out by openly admitting to and retaining 'gender as a constitutive element in its organisational logic' (Acker, 1991, p. 163).

Despite continuing opposition and hostility to women priests, a campaign to gain women's acceptance as bishops is underway. In 1999, a private member's motion was tabled to the General Synod, which called for an official examination by the House of Bishops of the theological implications of admitting women colleagues (*Guardian*, 1999). This was the first attempt to gain women's right to be consecrated as bishops. Subsequently, the Church of England General Synod passed a motion in 2000 to begin a theological study on the implications of promoting women to the Church of England's highest offices. The motion was overwhelmingly carried, bishops voted 36 to one in favour, as did 80 per cent of clergy members and 77 per cent of the laity. However, more radical moves to speed up the appointment of women bishops have been thrown out, and it has been predicted that it will be another ten years before women are appointed as bishops. This will require not only the eventual approval of the Synod but also Parliamentary legislation (Bagilhole, 2002b).

Conclusion

This chapter sets out the historical and contemporary patterns of occupational segregation for women in four male-dominated occupations. It highlights each of the four occupations in turn, examining the history of women's involvement in them, dates when they were first allowed entry and under what conditions, numbers of women in them, and where they are in the hierarchy of the organisations.

Using Kanter's (1977) classification of occupations by the representation of different groups within them, it shows that priesthood, academia, and professional engineering all remain *skewed* occupations with men in the majority, and construction engineering being the most extreme. Also, while the Civil Service has moved from a *skewed* to a *balanced* occupation, it still remains *skewed* in its management positions.

All four occupations demonstrate a long, hard-fought struggle for the inclusion of women, with the Church of England holding out until 1992, when it first allowed women to be ordained as priests. Despite the feminisation of the Civil Service, it maintains vertical sex segregation. Academia remains both horizontally segregated by discipline and vertically segregated by grade. Construction engineering is virtually exclusively white male, despite some success in recruiting women as engineering students. The Church of England, with its very late acceptance of women as priests, still maintains a 'concrete ceiling' on women's progress up its hierarchy, by prohibiting them from becoming bishops.

What can be seen to be common across these four occupations is the continuing existence of both structural and cultural barriers that disadvantage women and limit their careers. Therefore, to investigate this phenomenon further, the following chapters use qualitative research to compare and contrast women's experiences of working in these occupations.

5
No Change at Home?

> At the moment women fight for personal improvement with one arm tied behind their back.
>
> A Civil Service manager

Using evidence from the author's qualitative research on women working in the four male-dominated professions introduced in the last chapter, this chapter investigates the relationship between women's paid work and unpaid work. It examines the way women combine wider and heavier responsibilities to their families and home with their paid work demands, and vice versa. This can be conceptualised as 'spillover theory', which hypothesises that there is a reciprocal relationship between paid work life, and home and family life (Caligiuri and Cascio, 1998). This relationship is a two-way process, therefore, firstly the chapter looks at the consequences of women's personal responsibilities for their paid work. Do they succeed less well in their careers because of either real or assumed, present and future outside responsibilities? Are they, as Cockburn (1991) argues, 'defined by domesticity' at work, and therefore disadvantaged?

Then the chapter goes on to investigate the effects of paid work on women's home role. Who does the care work and housework? Who takes responsibility for these? Does men's sexual contract of patriarchy in the workplace spread into and continue in the domestic sphere, as Cockburn (1991) suggests?

The impact of women's responsibility for unpaid work on their paid work

Assumptions about women's responsibilities

The unequal distribution of household work and care work between women and men is an important factor in the persistent inequalities in the labour market. Women as wives, partners, mothers, daughters, sisters, and even neighbours and friends are expected to be available for unpaid work and are therefore viewed as deviant in the labour market, which in turn makes them vulnerable.

Thus, it has been suggested by feminists that attention should be focused upon notions of 'equity' (valuing difference) rather than, as is presently the case, 'equality' (valuing sameness) (Cockburn, 1989, 1991; Phillips, 1992). One of the most obvious areas of 'difference' is women's reproductive role in terms of the capacity to bear children. Numerous studies have identified both motherhood (for example, Cockburn, 1991; Bagilhole, 1994) and the potential for motherhood (Collinson et al., 1990), as impacting detrimentally on women's opportunities for employment and career advancement. So we see that 'difference', far from being positively valued, serves as a major source of continuing disadvantage.

Cockburn (1991) uses the idea of women being 'defined in domesticity'. In this way, men represent women as a problem in the workplace, and

> what is being problematised is women's relation to the domestic sphere. The way women do or do not fit into the schema of paid employment and organisational life is seen primarily as a correlate of their marital status and, more important still, whether they do or do not have children. This is what women are to most men (and to most women): people who have domestic ties.
>
> (Cockburn, 1991, p. 76)

Their assumed domestic responsibilities affect paid work opportunities in very different ways to men's. For example: 'The assumptions made about the "wife" role act positively in relation to men's career progression and negatively for women' (Jones and Causer, 1995, p. 54).

Whether women have children or not, they are believed to bring 'problems' associated with their reproductive role into the workplace (J. Acker, 1992; Alvesson and Billing, 1992; Bagilhole, 1994). Their commitment to the male-dominated public sphere is thus constantly open to scrutiny and treated with suspicion. Women continue to be seen as potential mothers and as a risk both at the point of recruitment and during their career development (Collinson et al., 1990; Devine, 1992). 'By drawing upon the discourse of women as potential or actual mothers, their perceived commitment to their careers, and thus to the organisation, is assumed to be open to question' (Jones and Causer, 1995, p. 55).

Women Civil Service managers divine this assumption in their managers' attitudes, even though it is outlawed by equal opportunities policies and therefore mostly covert.

> When managers were writing annual reports, they used to ask the women if they're having babies or not. They've stopped asking, but attitudes have still carried on in their minds. They've not changed just because they don't ask the question.

> I went through three boards to get my promotion. I felt there was an attitude that because I was married and at childbearing age they wondered if it was worth giving me promotion.

Because this attitude is covert it is difficult to prove any unfairness, although one woman sitting on a promotion board did experience an outburst by a male manager: 'On a recent board I sat on, a man turned round to me and said any woman with children stood no chance as far as he was concerned.'

Jones and Causer (1995) find that women engineers are also aware of the extent to which they are defined in relation to the 'discourse of domesticity'. They implicitly know that 'by consciously emphasising their potential as mothers, they would at the same time devalue their status as professional engineers' (p. 56). Therefore, for women in professions 'actual or potential motherhood continues to serve as a disqualifying capacity, to be obscured as much as possible' (p. 60). Career structures and patterns of work continue to be premised on the norm of the 'male full-time continuously working' model where family responsibilities impinge only marginally if at all. However, as Pascall et al. (2000, p. 66) argue 'most women cannot have the male-oriented career, aimed at high personal achievement, with a wife who is married to his job and manages his family'.

The invisibility of the family remains central to the demands of the workplace. Therefore, the assumed primacy of women's domestic commitments leads to prejudice against them, detracting from the notion that women can be committed professionals and this damages their prospects for promotion (Homans, 1987; Spencer and Podmore, 1987b; Acker 1991; Fraser, 1999; Maddock, 1999).

Also, it is worth emphasising, as Cockburn (1991, p. 76) points out, that 'the influence of domestication is not limited to married women ... Even if the woman in question is celibate or childless she is seen and represented as one of the maternal sex.' In a similar vein, McAuley (1987, p. 70) found that in academia 'many men had a negative view about the "reliability" of women. This was particularly directed towards women with children, but could also be directed towards women generally on the grounds that women are less committed to their careers.' The following comments from women academics illustrate this.

This is a disadvantage of being a woman. You are categorised. Women with families are put in the worst category. We're expected to be somehow less intelligent and less able to achieve.

I do get comments from staff, particularly my HOD [Head of Department] as I am a mother. He says things like – 'We can't expect her to do this as she's got to leave early. That's what happens when you become a mother'. I try desperately hard, and feel very pressurised as a woman.

Effects of family-friendly policies

In the late 1980s, with concerns over the so-called 'demographic time bomb' and problems associated with skill shortages in many sectors, organisations began to devise specific measures to attract and retain female employees. Some companies, developed family-friendly policies in terms of career break schemes and enhanced maternity packages, and began to explore the feasibility of alternative patterns of work organisation, as a means of reducing high turnover rates among female professionals with family commitments (Rees, 1992). Also, in the late 1990s, European Union Directives on extending maternity leave and introducing parental leave came into force in the UK.

However, despite the intentions, this policy focus on 'helping' women combine paid and unpaid work can reinforce traditional gender roles. It can confirm women as deviant workers and maintain the invisibility of men's families. It is clear that the organisational context within which policy development and implementation occurs reflects gendered assumptions about women's role in the family and can prove contradictory for women's opportunities (Jewson and Mason, 1986a; Collinson et al., 1990; Alban-Metcalfe and West, 1991; Cockburn, 1991; Alvesson and Billing, 1992; Bagilhole, 1994). As Jones and Causer's (1995) study of female engineers shows, such policies and practices therefore continue to function essentially as a concession to the deviant status of women in general and mothers in particular, rather than as broader tools of equal opportunities.

Thus, while greater flexibility in working hours and work organisation undoubtedly assists many women in practical terms, it also proves to be a 'double-edged sword' (McRae, 1989). Lorber (1994) identifies these policies as compiling the 'mommy track' which justifies women professionals and managers being in the lower-paid, and lower-prestige ranks.

> This exclusion from top-level positions is considered legitimate because they are mothers. The assumption is that women could not possibly handle the responsibility of leadership and the responsibility for their children's welfare at the same time, but they are never given the chance to try ... 'Mommy tracks' thus reinforce and legitimate the structural glass ceiling, the processes of exclusion, and the justifying stereotypes.
>
> (Lorber, 1994, p. 235)

Jones and Causer's (1995) women engineers recognise how vulnerable women are to manager's views about women's domestic responsibilities, and the way in which these could influence the operation of family-friendly policies in practice. It therefore becomes clear that, even where formal policies exist, their actual application frequently involves the exercise of a significant degree of discretion on the part of individual managers. This can undermine initiatives which, on the face of it, might be expected to promote greater equality within the workplace. For example, in the Civil Service, despite the fact that maternity leave was available many women had experienced a great deal of hostility from managers when they sought to use this right.

> Managers are not happy about maternity leave. They tend to be antagonistic towards it. They find it annoying, messing up the running of the office. They see it as disruption by silly women who decide to have babies.

Attitudes come through, odd remarks made by managers, for example, not encouraging women to take maternity leave. Remarks such as, 'These women are a bloody nuisance'.

The actual effect of women's unpaid work

So far we have examined the effect of women's assumed domestic responsibilities for their paid work opportunities. In other words, the ways women are condemned without trial. However, it has to be acknowledged that women's disproportionate burden of unpaid work does have a real effect on their ability to carry out paid work responsibilities, in the light of the male model that is demanded by employers. 'For some women at some times in their lives, however, the truth is that the combining of childcare, husband-care and housework with a demanding paid job is very difficult. ... perhaps most women, will put the family first if it comes to the crunch' (Cockburn, 1991, p. 86).

Caligiuri and Cascio's (1998) spillover theory conceptualises the responsibilities and demands in one domain (home life) carrying over into the other (work life), and vice versa. However, these two directions of spillover are not gender neutral. For men, paid work makes demands of their home responsibilities and diminishes them, while for women the reverse happens (Alban-Metcalfe, 1987; Maddock, 1999; Linehan and Walsh, 2000). Women work a 'second shift' at home, in addition to their first shift at work (Hochschild, 1989).

The Civil Service managers' domestic responsibilities are very important active contributory factors to their careers, ambitions and aspirations. Both the role of wife/partner and the role of mother carry their own ideologies which influence women's choices, and they both present practical difficulties when they are combined with being a paid worker

For many of these women having a partner affects their desire for and expectations of promotion. They are less likely to want or expect promotion than the women without partners. Also, women without partners are more likely to want higher promotion. The women with partners often display contradictions, ambivalence and confusion around their dual roles of paid worker and homemaker.

We've moved from a situation where women's prime role was housework. We've gone from the differentiation of roles into breadwinner and homemaker. Men now expect women to work. Women are expected to work and look after the home. This puts strain on women. It's a very confusing role. My partner now expects me to work and look after the home, but he would still really like to be the breadwinner.

People of my generation are in a dilemma. We were the first women who were able to make a decision about whether to have children or not. We didn't have children and our mothers told us how lucky we were to be able to make this choice. This has created a great dilemma for me and many of my friends. In fact my husband and myself are now considering whether we made the right choice and are thinking of now changing our choice and having children instead of my career.

Their comments on the level of support they receive from their partners are again sometimes ambivalent, and certainly it is clear that this support was often conditional on the couples not changing their established division of domestic labour.

My husband's glad I work. He doesn't object, now. He has very traditional views, but he's accepted it and settled into a routine. It was completely my decision to return to work and he does nothing in the house.

He's quite happy about me working now. He didn't particularly like it at first and certainly wouldn't have approved when the children were younger. But he realises now though, that I would be bored and unhappy. He's never got round to helping in the home much, although he's better than he used to be.

My husband is happy about me working as long as my interest is at home when I'm there. So home must not be dominated by work.

I'm married to an unskilled worker. Initially his ideas were that once we'd put our house together I would take the role on of wife at home bringing up the children, but this wasn't my idea of married life. I made it clear I wanted a career. I've taken maternity leave twice. He's supported me with every decision I've made, but he doesn't necessarily agree. It was new in his family for a wife to work. But my job's well paid and secure.

One woman said her husband's views had in fact changed in the opposite direction and, after supporting her in her career, he was now changing to a view which was opposed to her working. He is putting pressure on her to give up work and have children. This is beginning to make her have doubts and question her own ambition.

> My husband's views about me working have evolved. He thought at first it was great to have two pay packets and he was pleased when I was promoted. He didn't mind that I became part of management. But now he would prefer to change to the traditional way of life with him as breadwinner and have a wife at home with two children. With the stress that we both bring home from our jobs, he thinks it would be therapeutic for him to have us in traditional roles. He never wanted children, but now he's keen on having them. He's got on in his career and now he wants to look for something else. He's looking for something extra. He's done all his achieving.

Even the one woman, who had swapped roles with her husband, so that he stayed home and looked after their children, voices a suspicion that really her husband would prefer a conventional role at work supporting her.

> We've swapped roles. My husband was a miner, now he's a house-person. It just finished up like that. We always accepted my Civil Service job came first and we readjusted round to my job. I think secretly my husband would like the old-fashioned way with the man as the breadwinner. However, he knows it never has been, or could be, possible with me. He's proud of me, but he would like it to be him really.

For these women their partner's views are important and influential in determining their own ambitions and aspirations. In fact, women with partners in favour of them working, however conditionally, had gained more promotion and are more likely to still want promotion, and more of it. It is interesting to speculate whether women who are ambitious chose partners who would approve and support them, or whether partners' support actually increases women's aspirations.

On the other hand, wives and female partners make a substantial contribution to their men's careers (Acker, 1980). For example, Wajcman (1996) shows that male managers are highly dependent upon the domestic input of their wives in terms of the practicalities of running a home, but also in any entertainment which is required to be given to customers or colleagues. As Evetts (1996, p. 102) argues: 'Men have ideological support and confirmation for career development and progress whereas women developing careers are path-finders in an, as yet, relatively unsympathetic and underresourced world.'

Finch (1983), in her study of clergymen's wives, finds that, because they believe in their husband's 'noble endeavours', they take on even more responsibility than usual for family and home responsibilities to give him more space to get on with 'the great work' (p. 28). It is interesting to investigate whether the same support comes from husbands of women priests, and what happens to this relationship when they are both priests.

One woman priest comments that as a clergy couple it is: 'Difficult, because I also have to be the vicar's wife!'

Higginbotham (1993) uses a story of a woman Baptist leader to demonstrate the continuing traditional expectations of men married to women clergy in the USA. Her response to her husband's request to spend more time at home is: 'I belong to God first, and you next, so you two must settle it' (p. 132).

Also, the advantage of support given to male vicars by their wives, and the disadvantage of lacking this support for women clergy is recognised: 'Men have unpaid servants and secretaries in the form of wives. Women could do with a vicar's wife.'

Very real practical problems are attached to women's maternal role. Hantrais (1990, p. 166) argues that: 'Since women do not have wives, and only very few husbands are prepared to accept role reversal or the delegation of the majority of household and childcare tasks, most women working full-time need to find a substitute who can deputise for them when they are away from home.' This is confirmed in the study of Civil Service managers where nearly three-quarters of the women who have worked full time before their children reach school age have to seek help from their families.

Childcare provision for school age children is even more inadequate and scanty than that for pre-school children. Therefore, the mothers with school age children have to rely totally on family support for childcare during the school holidays, when the child is ill and outside school hours. The most difficult and frightening time for mothers is when their children are sick. Even the woman who had swapped roles with her husband felt the need to be present when her children are more seriously ill.

If it was anything serious I would be there. This is where role reversal doesn't quite succeed. The children want their mother if they're ill. Recently my son went into hospital for a tonsilectomy. I took him in and stayed with him for a few days. The two year old's been with my husband since she was ten weeks but she still wants her mother.

Some mothers admit to the need to have a 'diplomatic' illness themselves to get time off to care for sick children: 'When my kids are ill I have to pretend to be ill myself. I get a doctor's certificate for flu coming on. This is quite common amongst mothers.'

Therefore, it is perhaps not surprising that the role of mother also has a negative effect on women's ambitions and expectations of promotion. In this group of women civil servants, mothers are more likely to turn down the opportunity of promotion than women without children. Also, less than half want promotion compared with four-fifths of those without children.

Maddock (1999, p. 111) argues that 'women continue to be viewed through the prism of the domestic roles of mother, housewife and carer, not just by men but also by women'. Interestingly, nearly a quarter of these women managers in the Civil Service are against women with very young children working. They feel that job will suffer because mothers' minds would be elsewhere and they would not be able to concentrate on the job. In contrast, some of the women who had taken time off for maternity leave are even more determined to work now: 'I enjoy going out to work. I wouldn't want to stay at home. I see it as prison. But I'm not domesticated. I was desperate to get out to work again. If I had a child now I would go back sooner, if I had my time over again.'

Therefore, it is important to signal up and recognise the heterogeneity of women. In the UK, women's decisions on working hours are heavily constrained by the presence of children. Certain women resort to shift work and part-time work to fit in with domestic commitments (Brown and Charles, 1982; Dex and McCulloch, 1995). Hakim (1991, 1993) suggests that part-time work can act as a proxy for working women's commitment to work. She describes those women who accept part-time work and its poor conditions as 'grateful slaves', with a low commitment to work and a 'marriage career'. However, this can be seen as rather too simplistic an analysis. Women's choices are influenced and restricted by discriminatory structures and cultures, which both work against women taking part in paid work equally with men, and men taking part in unpaid work equally with women.

The impact of women's paid work on their unpaid work

Demographic changes

It is well established that while a relatively minor contribution is made by men to domestic work, women undertake the double shift of paid and unpaid work, suffering work overload especially if they have dependent children (Bagilhole, 1994; Brannen et al., 1994; Gershuny et al., 1994; Glucksmann, 1995). As Lister (1992, p. 25) points out the 'greater acceptance of women's right to work outside the home does not appear to have translated itself into a sense of egalitarianism in the allocation of tasks, either actual or prescribed, within the home'.

Instead women's increased involvement in paid work has led to important changes in demographic patterns. Chafetz and Hagan (1996) find changes in married women's employment reflected in changes in family structure and relations; marriage rates have decreased, most notably among young women, divorce rates have increased, total fertility has fallen, and first births have been increasingly deferred to the late twenties and beyond.

The trend of 'economising' on domestic demands is most pronounced in women in managerial careers over and above professional occupations (Scase and Goffee, 1990; Alban-Metcalfe and West, 1991; Crompton, 1995). Wajcman (1998) finds that women in the UK who reach senior managerial positions are far less likely to have children than their male peers. 'In relation to family structures and the domestic division of labour, the contrast between the situation of men and women could not be more stark ... The marital status of the men and women managers is very different' (Wajcman, 1996, p. 25). As Liff and Ward (2001, p. 32) show, the old adage 'think manager, think male' has changed with the increasing numbers of women managers, to the new image of 'think female manager, think childless superwoman'.

Particular occupational contexts make particular employment/family combinations more or less likely for women. Crompton and Harris (1998) find family behaviours vary between women in the two different occupations of medicine and banking. Women doctors plan their domestic careers ahead, choosing family-friendly specialities, which offer both regular hours of work and wide availability of flexible and part-time work. In contrast, banking careers do not have a long period of training, expertise is acquired in employment and part-time working is only available in non-managerial positions. Thus few women managers have domestic responsibilities.

Looking at the four occupations in this book, the Civil Service managers, academics, and engineers have fewer partners and even fewer children compared to other groups of women and their male colleagues. Many women have given up the idea of having husbands/partners and families, in order to be successful. The only exceptions are the women priests. Zikmund et al. (1998) find that American women clergy are usually either divorced or women who have never married. Whereas the UK women priests show a mixture of marital status. The majority of the women are, or have been, married and most of these have children. They have a total of 46 children between them with seven women having three or more. The women themselves acknowledge that this was because they had a long hard struggle for their right to be ordained, and therefore got on with fulfilment through their family 'careers'.

In the Civil Service, the encouragement given to some of these women managers by gaining promotion contributes to, and in some cases provokes, their decision not to have children so as not to inhibit their careers.

> Once I started to go on I became keen. I've made the decision now to have a career and try until I can't get any further. I've made the decision now not to have any children. When I first started I never really gave promotion a lot of thought, but as I progressed through it has become more important to me. I'm not bitter though. I wasn't that keen to have children. If my husband had earned more and I'd earned less, we probably would have conformed to a normal pattern.

> I prefer working to staying at home. I need to work. I assumed when I got married that I would work for five years and then retire with a family. This was a widely held expectation. However, this changed over the years. I made a choice with promotion. My will to have children has diminished. The will to have children goes down when you realise what you will lose.

However, some of the women who had made conscious decisions not to have children show signs of a constant quandary in their minds between work and family roles.

> I used to know what my ambitions were. I don't any more. I feel I've achieved in work. But now I'm seeking, asking what I want. I've got

the job right. What do I want now? More social involvement? A family?

I want a career myself. I couldn't ever envisage staying at home with children. I enjoy the challenge of work and meeting people. Occasionally I fall prey to some of the propaganda and wonder what I might be missing at home. Then I sit and think about it and decide I'm not missing anything.

These women have put in long years of continuous full-time service, to ensure their promotion success, throughout the years when most women are having children. As one woman without children puts it: 'Women lose a lot of experience by having children. The loss of time when women have children is definitely damaging to their career.'

Again relatively few of the academics are married or have a partner, and only a third have children. Many have chosen not to have a conventional family life, in favour of their career. Thomas (1990) demonstrates that women can succeed in higher education, but that they do so at a price. This is the price that these women academics feel they have to pay.

I haven't had a normal woman's life because I am an academic. This has involved a lot of moving around and this has broken up relationships, because men won't pack up and come with you.

There is a difficulty in combining the conventional role of a woman, family, children, with the expectations of a successful academic. Successful women academics have to demonstrate that they are more committed to the task in hand, and better, which involves no domestic distractions.

In construction, the women perceive that they have to make a choice between a career or a family-oriented lifestyle. Construction work and particularly site-based roles in nationally based divisions are seen as demanding and time consuming and to impinge on social activities and family responsibilities. The result of this is that women adopt career focused lifestyles.

I would think twice about getting married because I don't think that they would take it very well. They would see it as a signal that my career was over.

When I joined the company, my two year relationship just fizzled out within weeks. He became possessive when I started working, because he knew that I was working with men all day, in the end we just couldn't carry on ... I think with retrospect it has worked out for the best in the end, because you can't have the same line of conversation that I have with the lads here if you are married I don't think.

I don't know why anyone would want to leave the industry to have kids. I mean, four years at college, two years at work, get married and that's the end of it. I certainly did not spend four years studying to give it all up ... if you're the type that wants kids you've chosen the wrong industry ... I'm pushing my career, no kids and no husband. My social life suffers enough from my work at the moment without the burden of a family.

Some women have changed their outlook, but realised this would involve leaving the industry.

If you had asked me five years ago the answer would have been that I'll never have children, but I have realised that I will never make it ... I look at the company, the pressure, the hours, the pay. I am not going to do it for the rest of my life. I would rather have a good life and be happy than become a complete career woman. I have already seen myself change to become harder than I used to be and I'm not sure if I want to become hard and horrible. I don't want to end up being like that every night to my family.

Small changes at home?

Acker (1990, p. 61) argues that: 'Until the symbolic man-as-citizen has his mind on the cooker, his eye on a toddler and a hand on granddad's wheelchair, no constitution will guarantee social equality ... Men have to be domesticated and in the workplace ... the rhythm and timing of work must be adapted to the rhythms of life outside.' All the evidence points to the fact that we are far away from this position, but there are some signs that women's continuing involvement in full-time demanding occupations may be making some small changes.

Time-use studies show that there are still considerable differences in the nature of time use by gender, with women spending a larger part of their time on unpaid work, especially when there are young children in the household. However, historical series of time-use diaries suggest that over a long period consistent changes have occurred in the amount of time that both women and men devote to domestic labour, such that women are doing on average proportionately less, and men proportionately more. Platenga (1999) shows that the gap between the length of men's and women's total workload has narrowed, although distinctive patterns remain. Men do more housework than before, but although women have reduced their household work they still do more than men. The surveys also indicate that men and women have different responsibilities in the household; while the daily housework chores primarily remain women's responsibility, men spend more time on repair and maintenance.

Also, evidence suggests that views change more easily than actual behaviour. Jowell and Witherspoon (1985) show that during the 1980s there was a shift in ideology around the domestic division of labour. It was widely held that existing or traditional gender divisions were unfair, and attitudes began to be more inclined towards egalitarian relationships and sharing. Bonney and Reinach (1993) find that in households where the woman is in full-time employment, there is more likely to be discussion about the division of household chores which results in changes over time. This confirms Martin and Roberts' (1984) earlier evidence that full-time employment for women increases the likelihood that domestic duties will be shared between partners.

Benjamin and Sullivan (1996) present some qualitative empirical findings that point to the existence of a long-term process of change in the realm of domestic division of labour in some households. Also, Gershuny et al. (1994) show that as the amount of time women spend in the labour force increases, there is a clear decrease in their proportion of domestic work, and a corresponding increase in that performed by their male partners. This trend is found to be most significant for couples who are both in full-time employment. It seems that the longer women spend in the full-time labour force, the more likely their male partners are to contribute a greater proportion of domestic work.

Therefore, there is some evidence for a change in the domestic division of labour at the household level associated with women's labour force participation. However, this change seems to be occurring particularly for a specific category of women; long-term, employed women in full-time, demanding jobs. Benjamin and Sullivan (1996) argue that although no clear-cut transformation of gender ideologies is necessarily involved, nevertheless some couples seem to be working towards new ways of performing gender roles.

Certainly, the majority of the married women priests feel that becoming a priest has positively changed their relationship with their partner, in terms of more equality, sharing and support. This is often attributed to their improved confidence or assurance.

It has created a sense of equality and unity. Personal affirmation.

It has improved. The work inequality made life impossible when I was a deacon. Psychologically, we are now clear equals, and this is creative and helpful.

Since priesting I have felt more myself. I'm sure that this must have changed our relationship.

Some women feel there has been quite a radical change in their relationship, and that it had demanded change from their partners.

Complete mind change, we've both had to let go of our previous identities.

He is aware of people's expectations towards me, which are different to their expectations prior to my ordination. This makes me 'different' to before.

A few other partners are less sympathetic or willing to change with accompanying negative consequences: 'His expectations remained the same, causing additional pressure. I think my commitment to vocation was one aspect that contributed to my divorce.'

However, in terms of practically doing the housework only three women feel that there is a completely equal sharing between her and her partner, and even one of those has reservations: 'We've always shared responsibilities, for "the home". My husband would say it's a seamless relationship. I would say ... almost!'

The Civil Service managers' partners' contribution to housework seems to lag behind their positive views on their wife working. The following comment from a woman on her partner's attitude to housework is an example of this phenomenon: 'He likes one side of me working and that's getting the money but the other side he doesn't like which is helping with the housework. He thinks it can all be done on a Saturday and ignores the rest of the week.'

Many of these women feel frustration at having to take responsibility for getting the tasks done, even if it is just 'nagging' their husbands or leaving explicit instructions for them.

> My husband begrudgingly helps me with housework. He begrudges everything he does and I end up doing most of it.

> My husband doesn't seem to see what needs to be done.

> He does help, the problem is sometimes he doesn't notice what is to be done. I moan a bit sometimes. I have to leave him a list of things for him to do.

Even in the couple that have 'role-swapped', she still feels responsible, and that she is more effective at doing the housework: 'Although he does a lot of the housework he gets less out of more effort. He's not as effective as me. I organise things and plan ahead. I'm more economical although he's the houseperson.'

Paid help

Therefore, the extent of sharing of unpaid work should not be over-estimated. Newell (1993) finds that women in full-time employment are more likely to believe in the equal sharing of tasks than men. Also, Gregson and Lowe (1993) shows that in dual-career households women's full-time employment does not necessarily result in a re-negotiation of domestic labour. Often there is instead a transfer of household work to paid individuals outside the household, such as cleaners and nannies. Women pay other women to do their unpaid work. Wheeler-Bennett (1977) argues that one reason that women who hold high-level jobs can be successful is their economic ability to buy in other women to replace them in terms of housework and childcare, plus their amazing organisational skills. Also, Wajcman (1996) notes that the majority of women managers are in fact reliant to a greater or lesser extent on paid domestic services to enable them to do their job.

Most of the married women priests have resorted to paid help with the housework: 'A cleaner does quite a bit for us, I do most of the rest.'

Some of the arrangements are quite complex but well planned: 'A paid help does the cleaning, and my ironing. I wash the clothes. He does the gardening, the car and his ironing. We both do the shopping, cooking, and washing-up.'

However, the responsibility for ensuring that someone does the housework, even if they have to be paid, falls mostly on the women themselves, even in three cases where their partners are at home as a househusband or retired.

> I do, and I pay. I also take responsibility for shopping, cooking, washing, ironing, remembering the children's birthdays, buying presents, taking the dog for a walk and to the vet – as before – only now I pay too!

> It does tend to be me who 'hires and fires', and who plans for tasks to be achieved. My husband does what's needed when the need is pointed out to him, and sometimes regards it as a bit of an imposition.

Nearly four-fifths of the Civil Service managers think their husbands do about enough housework, but this again is connected to the fact that they employ paid help.

> I have paid help, a woman three mornings a week. She approached me because she was at home with three children. I used to think I could do all the cleaning and it was my responsibility. Since I got this job with more travelling my husband helps a little bit more. He helps wash-up and shares cleaning the car.

Conclusion

To conclude, this chapter looked at the relationship between unpaid and paid work for women. There certainly seems to be a spillover from one domain to the other, but it has to be said that for women the real and assumed impact of unpaid work on paid work is greater than the other way around.

The chapter began by looking at assumptions about women's 'domesticity' and how this constrains their performance at work. There is an assumption of women's homogeneity, and the primacy they will all give to family responsibilities, even if they do not have one. The mirror image to this is the assumed primacy men will give to their paid work, and thus their families and family responsibilities remain invisible.

Some companies introduced family-friendly policies in the 1980s and 1990s. In very practical terms these policies are focused on helping women combine their unpaid and paid work. Therefore, despite being well intentioned, they reinforce traditional gender relations. They have the combined effect of labelling women as deviant workers, who need special treatment, and reinforcing the invisibility of men's family responsibilities. Also, the relative discretion that managers have in implementing these policies may discourage women from utilising them when they discern disapproving managers, both men and women.

It must be acknowledged that there is a very real effect on women of taking on a disproportionate amount of unpaid work. The spillover theory shows how work affects home and home affects work. However, this two-way process is not gender neutral. Women's unpaid work impinges on their paid work, limiting their chances, whereas men's paid work impinges on their desire or ability to take on more unpaid work. The roles of wife, or partner, and mother carry their own ideologies for women and also practical problems, which act negatively on their careers, ambitions and aspirations. Most of the women acknowledge that their partner's support for their careers was ambivalent, and often conditional on them maintaining responsibility for the lion's share of the domestic division of labour. They also acknowledge their own doubts, contradictions and ambivalence in their own relatively uncharted role as professionals with home responsibilities.

The second part of the chapter looked at the contrasting issue; the effect of women's paid work responsibilities and demands on unpaid work. The first thing to note is that women's perception of the reality of often being required to 'choose' between paid work or a family has led to demographic changes. More women, especially young women are choosing their careers. The Civil Service managers, academics and the engineers have all 'economised' on domestic demands. They have relatively few partners and children, compared to other groups of women, and their male colleagues. Many have conformed to full-time continuous working to achieve success, and their subsequent success reconfirms their decisions not to have traditional, female, family responsibilities. Although it is important to note that some were still questioning their decisions. The exception to this pattern is the women clergy, but they formed their families before they had won the struggle to be ordained, and acknowledge this as a reason for their relatively bigger families.

Finally, the chapter investigated whether there may be some change, if only small, in these women's partners' contribution to unpaid work. International statistics are beginning to show some overall quantitative changes in women's and men's use of time. While the overall gender pattern remains, women are spending less time in unpaid work and men more. The women report that some of their partners had increased their contribution to unpaid work, but it is important to note that sometimes this is begrudgingly done, and that women still retain, on the whole, the responsibility for getting it done. One major way that these professional women have eased their burden of unpaid work is by paying other women to do it for them, and here again we see them having to take the responsibility for organising this and often paying for it too. So perhaps we can sum this section up as, 'small change within continuity'.

6
Structural Barriers

> It's very hard to get in with the 'old boys network' when you're not old and you're not a boy!
>
> A construction engineer

This chapter examines the effects on women of the structures in these male-dominated occupations. It demonstrates the consequences of the structural difficulties and barriers they face. These begin with entry into the occupation through the recruitment and selection processes. Then, on a day-to-day basis, structures and procedures adversely affect their career development and opportunities, chances of promotion, pay and working conditions. The chapter directly examines this structural discrimination through women's voices, which also allows them to express their views and feelings on these issues.

Internal labour markets

Institutional structures impede women's success in paid work. Structural approaches see women's work experience as shaped by patriarchal practices in the family and at work (see Bagilhole, 1994; Ginn, 1996). This is not to deny women's agency, but the approach is set in opposition to others that cite women's choices as the key element in patterns of work.

Hakim (1995) takes the latter approach in explaining women's position in paid work as determined by their choice to become either 'career women' or mothers. In contrast, it is suggested here that any choices that women make are shaped, and to a large extent determined, by the structural environment at work. The structures within which women make decisions are seen as largely shaped by men, with men's interests as paramount (Walby, 1990). Therefore, 'it is the context which constrains and limits women's achievements, not women themselves or their career strategies' (Pascall et al., 2000, p. 66).

However, these structures are not set in stone. The women priests feel that change is occurring in the Church of England, but it is coming from below, where most of their influence exists, rather than higher up the hierarchy.

> We are not yet part of the establishment, i.e. the upper echelons – so our influence is from below. Gradually – very gradually – we are moving the Church of England towards an equal opportunities policy.

> Very slowly at grass roots level, we are producing a less stuffy, more accessible God and Church.

However, this can be a long and hard-fought process. Even when women enter previously male-dominated occupations, we can identify internal segregation of these occupations, with women consigned to different jobs to men. As Wajcman (1996, p. 262) states: 'The central argument ... is that gender relations are constitutive of the structure and practices of organisations and that this is key to understanding how men define and dominate organisations.'

There have been a number of studies that explore the interrelationship between gender and organisations and highlight the barriers that women face if they want to reach senior positions. Women's power both individually and collectively remains less than men's. There are many women workers whose needs and concerns remain hidden behind a workplace agenda controlled by men and dominated by male interests.

The study of construction engineering professionals gives an example of internal segregation constructed in male interests. Most of the women see an initial period of site-based work experience as a prerequisite for eventual progression to senior positions. This is because significant levels of responsibility can be held at relatively junior levels on site, which facilitates rapid vertical advancement later in their careers. In reality, however, women are encouraged by senior male managers to enter supporting roles, which tend to be office based. Such positions, removed from the production function, are widely acknowledged not to afford as many opportunities for rapid advancement.

Evetts (1996) argues that hierarchical organisations have accommodated the entrance of women by encouraging them into skill specialisation, while leaving men to use the mainstream route into positions of power and authority. 'In these ways organisations have changed to incorporate women professionals but organisational power is retained for men' (p. 33).

As Reskin and Roos (1990, p. 307) caution: 'Society's self-congratulations on women's advances into male occupational titles are premature and must await women's entry into the jobs men still dominate.' In fact, women are seen to be disproportionately segregated into lower-level positions as their concentration increases in previously male occupations (Almquist, 1991; Nesbitt, 1997). Nesbitt (1997) gives the example of priesthood in the USA, where systematic discrimination prohibits 'women from attaining positions of authority and leadership beyond token representation ... [and] religious organisations headed and dominated by men effectively have accommodated the influx of women clergy in a manner that poses little challenge to the organisational power and the resultant influence on religious doctrine, polity, and practice' (Nesbitt, 1997, p. 596).

In bureaucratic hierarchies men occupy positions at the top and women are concentrated at the bottom. The effects of gender are not simply eradicated, however, if women get higher positions that is, achieve powerful positions. 'Bureaucracies are not neutral but are gendered organisations which reproduce prevailing notions of masculinity' (Platenga and Rubery, 1999, p. 6).

Thus, the dominant contention seems to be that women tend to 'do better' in small, dynamic organisations (Reskin and Roos, 1990) than in large bureaucracies. In those sectors where work organisation is more highly regulated, such as the Civil Service, the probability of progression through the career structure is much lower for women than for men. The Civil Service is a prime example of a formal hierarchy, with bureaucratic and explicit rules. As Cockburn (1991, p. 50) argues, the Civil Service is a 'near-classic bureaucracy'. Also, it is a classic example of the introduction and use of women in subordinate jobs, which began in the mid-nineteenth century and continues today. As Witz and Savage (1992) argue there is a separation of intellectual and mechanical labour tasks. When this bureaucracy was reorganised away from nepotism and patronage, women were employed to carry out the routine white-collar work. This constituted the 'white blouse revolution'. The modern organisation still depends on cheap, flexible female labour and this helps to define women as subordinate workers to men.

While new and different forms of organisation can increase women's career opportunities, there is also contradictory evidence. Organisational renewal leads to flattening of the internal structure which means thinning out the ranks of middle management. This may have a negative impact on career prospects for women as they face greater competition for fewer higher level jobs (Platenga and Rubery, 1999).

Thus, the concept of a glass ceiling for women has gained currency in attempting to explain women's concentration at lower levels of hierarchies. However, in their study of banking Pascall et al. (2000) argue that the picture is more complex than this as most women do not even get anywhere near the glass ceiling. In their explanation, they put forward the concept of a 'pyramidal crystal maze'. Where 'women in hierarchical organisations meet invisible barriers at every turn and every level. Most are making laborious progress through clerical grades, up blind alleys through which there is no route to the top' (Pascall et al., 2000, p. 71).

Full-time continuous employment model

The accepted and dominant pattern of a career is still built around continuous lifetime service, working hard at all times, making oneself available at all times, working long hours, and with no career breaks. Only men can succeed within these gendered processes, because they are relatively unencumbered by domestic and personal responsibilities and can fulfil professional duties and achieve career potential.

This pressure for a continuous career is seen in three of the non-traditional occupations studied here. Academics are under pressure to ensure a continuous publishing record. Time consuming family responsibilities distract and divert women from research activities and the traditional research-based career path, often normalised and formalised through the process of performance appraisal (Heward, 1996; Thomas, 1996). In the Civil Service, having children holds women back in their career, so that male peers overtake them. In construction, women largely find it impossible to deal with the responsibilities of a family and stay within the profession. The women clergy are the exceptional case, with many having had children before becoming priests, as discussed in Chapter 5. Any consequences of this for their careers will only be measurable in the future.

However, it is important to point out that even when women conform to this male, continuous career model they still encounter problems. Crompton and Le Feuvre (1992) find that women managers in the finance sector whose employment patterns are similar to men face problems when trying to progress through organisational career routes and paths. This leads them to conclude that processes within work organisations rather than within families are probably the most crucial influences on women's careers.

Recruitment

Crucially, the very first obstacle that women face with male-dominated occupations is making it through the recruitment process, be it formal or informal.

The four occupations under scrutiny in this book are prime examples of Lipmen-Blumen's (1976) 'homosocial' institutions, having been established for and being run by men. Therefore, the rules pertaining to appointment are male driven and are evaluated according to male standards. Chapman (1991, p. 2), when examining interviews for chief librarians in higher education institutions, identifies that 'inexpert, irrelevant, inaccurate and illegal practices usually ensure the "right man for the job"'.

Nearly half of the women academics in the study had heard about their posts through personal or informal contacts: 'The Head of Department (HOD) had a chat with my HOD.'

Informal recruitment processes are recognised as one of the major areas where discrimination and prejudice can creep into an organisation. Obviously they have worked in favour of these women, but there is no way of telling how many women have been discriminated against because of the same processes. Also, importantly, being in small minorities in higher education women are less likely than men to have access to informal professional networks and contacts which can assist their career (O'Leary and Mitchell, 1990). Lipmen-Blumen (1976) offers a useful conceptualisation of this in the 'homosocial theory of sex roles', where men are dominant in sex-segregated institutions and act to exclude women from participation.

The women priests feel very strongly that there is not fair and open recruitment in the Church of England, because of the secrecy and informality of the system. Also, they think that this unfairness in appointments works against some men as well.

> No – it's word of mouth. The old boy network prevails and is very powerful. Most jobs are not advertised. Criteria are not disclosed, decisions are made secretly.

It varies – method of recruitment is so varied in the C of E. Even where posts are advertised, it is more difficult for women to be appointed because of reluctance on the part of parishes. I think women are very much discriminated against. Some parishes and Diocesan staff are enlightened, but not all. Family considerations are thought about for women.

Recruitment in the construction industry is often informal and through personal contacts (Druker and White, 1996). Sommerville et al. (1993) show that informal practices, such as internal recruitment, employee referrals and casual call-in by applicants are all prevalent. Also, Wilkinson (1992) finds that some 20 per cent of employers believe that construction work is 'unsuitable' for women. Greed (1997) attributes women's under-representation to men blocking the entrance of people and ideas that are seen as different and/or unsettling.

Women construction engineers face a rigorous and discriminatory selection process, which is facilitated by a lack of formal recruitment guidelines: 'Recruitment works very informally. I think it's a personality industry and so you are recruited by people you know, and then by default by how good you are.'

The effectiveness of networking for informal contacts is gender specific, with many women discussing difficulties they have experienced.

Although informal recruitment processes are most likely to lead to discrimination, formal processes can also work against women. Over a quarter of the women academics have problems with the unsophisticated nature of application forms. This is because nearly two-thirds have not come to their career through the standard research route and have varied work experience outside the academic profession.

I had to decide whether to include a curriculum vitae or not. I did in the end because there was not enough room to include everything. I had a block of previous experience, which I felt was relevant, but there was nowhere on the form to detail it.

Interviews can also create problems for women. The women construction engineering professionals generally find they experience more rigorous recruitment and selection techniques than their male colleagues. In interviews, they are subjected to an in-depth examination of their commitment and professional competence.

Men do not experience such a rigorous process or a questioning of their commitment.

> I had two interviews, the first with the head of department, the second with the director and the two principal engineers. I then had one of those psychometric tests where they fed the results back. They asked me very probing questions, I was wondering when it was all going to end.

> There is no consistency in the way they approach recruitment. Some people get a real grilling, others especially the men seem to waltz in without so much as an informal chat.

There is also a connection between the depth and rigour of the recruitment process and women's ages. Women in their late twenties and early thirties had encountered particular difficulties. Several had been asked about their personal relationships and many feel that this stems from assumptions that they would have families at this age.

> As the interview went on they began to ask me some very pointed questions about my future plans with regards to having children and getting married. I tried to fend them off as much as possible, but it was clear that they would not back down until they had an answer on my future plans ... needless to say that I didn't want children.

However, discriminatory questioning is not always overt, with tacit questioning of women's long-term commitment often being made through questions regarding the candidate's personal status.

> I think he only offered me a short-term contract because he knew I was a woman who had been married for four years, and I was getting to that stage when I may decide to have children ... several of the questions were directed in that way, towards areas which did not seem directly relevant to the position, things about my social life and long-term plans, but nothing that appeared too obvious.

In the group of women academics, 42 per cent make negative comments about their interviews. The panels are criticised for being too large, intimidating and male, and there is evidence of inappropriate and discriminatory questions being asked.

> I felt that there was a token woman there. It was a panel of men with one woman from another department. There was an inappropriate question. I was asked if I wanted to come to the university because my husband was here. This question was disallowed by personnel, but I answered it anyway.

Also, many women experience confusion between the formal and the so-called informal part of the interview process.

> It was strange. I came to the department for a 'chat'. But that was the actual interview rather than the formal one. It was a three-hour lengthy session. I met all the staff and they were in on the decision. I was unprepared for that. The formal interview that came later was only scheduled for 30 minutes.

Career development

The first period of any career development begins with the induction process of new staff into the organisation, and this period is also problematic for women. The women construction professionals complain of inadequate supervision and assistance during this stage.

> The first few months were a nightmare because I was assigned to this guy who was never in his office. I arrived on the first day and they told me where to go and I met him, we went to a meeting and I didn't have a clue what was going on. Then he disappeared for two weeks.

> It's a bit embarrassing when you start on site because you don't want to ask people for help every five minutes. I sometimes feel it's left to me to go and find out about how things work without really being told who I should be speaking to ... I think it's easier for men because if they make a mistake everyone on the site isn't going to pick up on it. Sometimes I don't feel that I could ask. Or I will just make myself look stupid.

For women academics their probationary period is a crucial time for establishment within the profession. In an American study of women academics who had left the profession, the major reason identified was linked to their probationary period (Johnsrud and Atwater, 1991). Over half of the women academics report problems with the process, involving insufficient and inappropriate advice and support, and confusion over the regulations.

> I am given very little advice or support. I was told to take on anything and everything. I took on too much. My probationary supervisor loaded everything on to me. It was ages before I said no.

> My supervisor had to be changed. He was a bad choice in the first place. The second one is better. But the whole structure is not very organised or professional. It was assumed that I had a lot of previous knowledge about the university and the department. I was constantly having to ask about things.

It would appear that probation has long been a problematic area for many women. Over two-thirds of the established women report that they had problems during probation.

> I was extremely unhappy for my first two years. Everyone was very helpful if I went and asked, if you didn't ask you were left to get on with it. I had an enormous teaching load with no time to establish my research. I was not protected by my probationary adviser.

When these women academics are asked more generally about the advice they had been given on career development, the vast majority report that they had received none. This is particularly detrimental for women because they are in a minority, and, therefore, have fewer role models and informal networks to turn to for advice. They lack 'sponsors' or mentors; that is supportive relationships where older and experienced professionals contribute to younger colleagues' career development.

> I mentioned it recently to my HOD and he said regard the last five minutes conversation as advice.

> No, not in a definite way, casually in conversations picked up things. I'm only told to publish more, but I'm given no support or encouragement.

Training is an integral part of professional career development. However, the women Civil Service managers point out that being sent on courses was certainly not automatic and not necessarily concomitant with promotion. Persuading supervisors to put one forward for courses is seen as part of showing oneself to be keen and ambitious for promotion: 'You have to have the knack to get on courses. It's easier if you've got a good boss. You have to ask and insist that you want to go on courses.'

A reputation for comprehensive formal training by companies attracted women construction professionals, but many are disappointed. Many women describe training provision as 'ad hoc', or as being used only to meet minimum legislative requirements: 'When I joined they really sold the training side of things to me, but since then I've only been on a health and safety course. None of my requests have been answered, and I've been left to pick up what I can from my colleagues on site.'

Appraisal processes are also an important area of career development. They are seen as the principal mechanism for monitoring performance, assessing training needs, and allocating staff development opportunities. However, Tuck (1992, p. 5) shows that women are doing badly out of appraisal: 'For women, appraisal does not provide anything "value-added"; it is more an exercise in asset stripping.' This is because appraisers often reflected prevailing social expectations and attitudes which reinforced stereotyped expectations and assessments of women.

In academia, given the lack of seniority of women, both women and men will more often be appraised by men. For most of the women academics in this study appraisal is a negative experience because they feel they have different perceptions of their job to their male appraisers.

> I tried to push forward the fact that what women do cannot be measured in the same way; caring for students. I managed to give this more status but it took time to convince my male appraiser of this. Measured against male successes and other things it doesn't seem to count as much. Women have more contact with students at the coal-face. They take account of the needs and expectations of students. They are involved more with explaining what they're doing and why, because they can't hide behind male authority. I give more individual supervision. The students know I'm always here.

> It's all done by men. The senior staff are all men. I mentioned the fact that I pick up a lot of pastoral care. Students come to me with problems that their personal tutors should be sorting out. This was dismissed by my appraiser as exaggeration.

In the construction industry, women feel that appraisal is used by some male managers as a vehicle to undermine women's careers. They give women lower appraisal scores, make unfair assessments of women's training needs, or use appraisal assessments as a way to restrict women's intra-organisational mobility: 'This performance appraisal system is a joke. What you get depends completely on who does your assessment – if you don't get on with your line manager they could make it difficult for you.'

Also, as women are more likely than their male colleagues to be in support positions, they feel that their performance cannot be fairly assessed as they had less tangible outputs: 'It's fine if you're a project manager and you have control of your project ... but if you're doing business development ... how on earth can you appraise what I'm doing?'

Selection and promotion

There is evidence of the persistence of certain work practices relating to promotion, which are discriminatory towards women (for example see Bagilhole, 1993c; Cockburn, 1991). In the American clergy, Nesbitt (1997, p. 596) concludes that by maintaining these discriminatory mechanisms 'men are unlikely to surrender their dominance of religious leadership'. However, the position in the UK is likely to be even more stark with the prohibition of women becoming bishops, as explained in Chapter 4.

The majority of the women priests feel that there is not equity between women and men priests in terms of selection and promotion.

> No – and it's not a 'glass' ceiling more a lead roof! Women are generally passed over for 'plum' parishes. Sometimes a job is said to be too big for a woman.

> No. Old boy network prevails. It depends whether you have a tick by your name! Most women and some men don't. I've no idea how it works.

When asked about the future prospects for women of becoming bishops, the women vary in their confidence and optimism of it happening, and its timing: 'No chance at the moment. A big shift of opinion is needed, but miracles can happen!'

Also, they give warnings of the political struggle it will take.

> The voices against it are small in number, but strategically placed in the structures to make a lot of noise about it. Needs care and political 'moves'.

> Women will inevitably become bishops, but only after a significant fight. The process will be tough and bruising. More blood will be spilt.

The women Civil Service managers recognise the phenomenon of women's greater likelihood of leaving the Civil Service, having contributed very efficient work at a low level. They see this as extremely useful to the working of the system.

> If women stayed in the Civil Service things would be more equal. Pressures of numbers would force the promotion issue. It's easy for the Civil Service at the moment, when so many women leave and drift off. Therefore, the Civil Service doesn't have to face the problem of their promotion.

> The Civil Service will do nothing about pushing opportunities for women as the situation at the moment suits them nicely. Perhaps this is why they employ so many women. They expect and want a lot to leave to have a family despite their abilities or qualifications as there aren't enough promotions to go round. They get very good, efficient workers that are expendable. If the women were as ambitious as the men they'd have the problem of coping with promotion.

The vast majority of this group of women Civil Service managers want promotion. However, they report that they are confused as to what is needed for promotion. This suggests a divergence from set procedures. One woman describes it as 'floundering in the dark'. There are complaints of lack of information and misinformation.

> Different people say different things. It's difficult to know, there's no rhyme or reason to it. If I knew what was needed for promotion I would do it, but I never know. It depends who is writing the report. They look for different things.

Thus promotion boards are a stage where discrimination may occur. Most of the interviewers on the board will be male because they are in a large majority in the top grades. One woman found her experiences at promotion boards changed her mind about wanting promotion: 'I've been for three promotion boards and failed them all. I was offered a fourth, but I turned it down because I'd had enough. I was a career girl but now I'm not particularly ambitious. I find the boards horrifying.'

There is a high level of ambition in the group of women academics; 71 per cent of the probationers and 62 per cent of the established staff want promotion: 'I hope to rise up the hierarchy of the department and the university. I'm ambitious. I ultimately want a chair. I'll be very disappointed if I don't make senior lectureship.'

However, in contrast to their high aspirations, their expectations are much lower. Only 30 per cent of the probationers have positive views about their promotion chances and even fewer established staff expect advancement; only 23 per cent. These assessments dovetail with the view of the Association of University Teachers (AUT, 1992, p. 13) 'that the combination of secrecy, subjectivity and amateurism which surround too many promotion procedures, is lethal to the objectives of equal opportunities'.

> I try to look at it positively but looking at the statistics it's not very hopeful. There is an unofficial agenda. If you publish enough papers you'll get on, even if you fail at teaching students. It helps if you're male. Being a woman is a disadvantage.

Pay and remuneration

Has moving into customary male occupations brought women the economic rewards that male colleagues enjoy or has there been only limited progress towards economic equity?

Reskin and Roos (1990) caution that a healthy degree of scepticism should be used when looking at women's entry into male occupations. Although these women increase their earnings relative to women's average earnings, they do not reach equity with their male colleagues. They argue that 'researchers do women a disservice if they let some women's progress relative to other women overshadow the distance women of all backgrounds have to travel to achieve an equitable return on their labour' (p. 307).

As women enter new fields they rarely close the wage gap (see Chapter 4 for evidence that women academics earn less than their male counterparts, and women clergy are less likely to be paid than men). Zikmund et al. (1998) compare American men and women clergy, and find that women experience discrimination, being paid 9 per cent less than their male colleagues, after controlling for all other variables. In Walrond-Skinner's (1998) research, clergy couples in the UK report that the Church often finds them a problem, and sometimes responds to them quite punitively. Some couples are offered only one full and one-third of a stipend for two full-time jobs. Others are told that the Church will never pay the woman in a joint clergy couple team, although they are happy to give her a job for no remuneration.

The majority of the priests feel that women are not getting the same financial rewards as male priests, often being non-stipendiary, and having less security of job tenure. This is seen as a particular problem for women priests in clergy couples.

> Many are on short-term or 'end-able' contracts – many are non-stipendiary (not paid). I run two parishes on a half stipend.

> There is some evidence that some dioceses encourage women to be non-stipendiaries, particularly if they are married to clergy. Those women, who are married to incumbents and are also ordained, they get a raw deal and are often not paid, even in diocesan posts.

> All the part-time, short-term contracts are in clergy couples with the women less well off. These women are more likely to be denied a stipend for stipendiary work.

Working conditions

Working conditions disproportionately impact on women to their disadvantage. They can be seen as indirect discrimination, when a requirement or condition which cannot be justified on grounds other than sex is applied to men and women equally, but has the effect of disadvantaging a considerably higher proportion of one group than the other (Bagilhole, 1997).

This may occur in physical working conditions in certain occupations which are predominantly if not exclusively male. For example, the Service Women in Non-Traditional Roles Study (Park 1985, 1986; Phillips and Park 1986) challenges gender-exclusive job requirements in the Canadian forces. There are systematic barriers in areas such as physical standards, clothing and equipment.

The women construction professionals also identify some physical working conditions as a problem for them. For example, they mention sites with no female toilets, and safety clothes and gear that are the wrong size.

> I find toilet facilities on site are horrendous because they don't think about women and the problems they go through once a month. You're sitting on the toilet with holes through the ceiling and no lock on the door, and that's the case on nearly every site I've been on.

The culture of long working hours in the UK is also a problem for women. The construction industry is a prime example. Because of the high investment cost, economic considerations usually require the shortest possible construction period, so sites work long hours (Neale, 1996). These characteristics have a great influence on the management principles and processes of construction project management, and obviously make the application of good employment practices very difficult. It is self-evident that most people employed in construction projects, and their families, will find these characteristics difficult to cope with, and they will disproportionately affect women who still bear the major proportion of these responsibilities.

The culture of long working hours is seen by many women as being ingrained within the work practices of the industry.

> When I was working on the tunnel, I was down there at seven and rarely got out before eight, six days so I saw virtually no daylight for 18 months. That's the way it is though, and it will never change. Either you accept it and work with it or leave, it's as simple as that.

This is also a problem in terms of the clergy. Charlton (1997, p. 608) finds 'lack of privacy, lack of differentiation between workplace, community, and home, and emotional labour intensified by blurred boundaries' are often cited by women as reasons for leaving ministry. The vast majority of the women priests report that the working conditions for priests are not equally compatible for women and men. In terms of the hours demanded of them, most feel that this is difficult for women and men in being too long, but that this disproportionately impacts on women priests who are wives and mothers, because of their extra responsibilities.

> There is no perceived end to work. It's difficult in setting boundaries for both men and women.

I have to do home and work. It's complicated by the fact that work is at home too. I am good at preserving my days off, but have been made to feel guilty if doing so, especially by male clergy!

Some parishioners expect six days and an infinite number of hours. Need to be strong to set limits.

Also there is some indication that women clergy may even work harder and even longer hours than men: 'A lot of women have very high standards and choose to work extremely hard. Also in family crisis and illness it's still usually the mother who deals with it. I think on the whole women in ministry tend to work more hours than men.'

Geographical mobility

The requirement for geographical mobility, either as a condition of doing the job, or for promotion, is a particular problem for women with family responsibilities. For this reason, many academic women report that they have decided not to get married or have a partner. The women priests find it difficult to get parishes geographically compatible with their families, and women Civil Service managers have given up promotion because of the requirement to move.

The construction industry has excessive mobility requirements. Construction projects are transitory. Construction companies arrive on site, build, and leave for the next project. The project site may be far distant from the headquarters of the construction company, and in the case of major international construction projects, it may be in another country, operating in a social, economic and physical environment that is quite different from that within which the construction company is based. No other industry sets up a new factory, in a new place, for every product it produces.

Therefore, a significant problem, which directly affects women's careers, concerns the geographical allocation of staff, which is seen as being carried out with little regard for employees' personal needs. Many of the women placed in national divisions for example, find it difficult to combine work with their family lives. On the other hand, this does not present a significant difficulty for men, as their partners often bear the burden of domestic responsibilities and support their careers.

In an attempt to remain geographically stable, several women travel long distances to work: 'The hours aren't too bad but I have to travel so far to get here, it's so far away from home. It adds four hours to my day. It's my choice, and I know it could be worse, but in the end it's worth it to maintain my career, and my relationship.'

Most women feel that they had little choice of where they worked.

> I like being close to home. They sent me to Scotland on the last job, and although it was a beautiful place, I really missed being close to my family ... they know I want to stay in London, but they keep telling me there's no work. One of the directors had me in to give me some friendly advice, that by saying I wouldn't move, I was harming my career, so I suppose in the end I am just going to have to go really.

Women perceive that allocation of staff is political and there are hidden agendas. It is felt that companies think that they get more work output from employees working away from home. They generally believe they have little say in where they are allocated.

> I don't believe you get a choice. You either go or you don't work for the company. If I said 'no' to coming up and working here I would have been laid off ... this guy came up from training and said 'you start in Manchester on 1st May, any questions?'.

> I think it's the uncertainty that gets to you, particularly if you have kids. We were sat around last week talking about this, I mean this job finishes in two months and we don't know where we are going next. We have heard on the grapevine that a new job is starting in Leeds, but if I get sent there I don't know what I'll do about childcare.

The possible requirement for geographical mobility for promotion is also identified by the women Civil Service managers. The mobility requirement creates problems for women with family responsibilities because of the necessity of considering their family's willingness or ability to move: 'It's a problem. I'm waiting for a posting. If I'm offered London I can't move because of my husband's job.'

Many married women have already turned down promotion because of the difficulty with mobility: 'I was offered a London posting, but couldn't take it and had to come off the list.'

The mobility requirement becomes an increasing problem for women the higher up the grades they go: 'It's virtually possible to go anywhere between offices. Yesterday I picked up the phone at nine in the morning, Thursday, and was told to report to London head office for three weeks starting on Monday.'

Conclusion

This chapter looked at women's disadvantage and lack of success in non-traditional occupations from a structural perspective. Evidence has been provided of discrimination against women, some appears to be intentional and some is indirect. Indirect discrimination is where there is formal equal treatment between women and men, but where this treatment impacts disproportionately on women. We can see that these institutional structures follow women from recruitment processes, both informal and formal, through career development, selection and promotion procedures, and finally into their day-to-day working conditions. These include physical facilities, particularly in the construction industry, the culture of long working hours and, importantly, the requirement for geographical mobility.

It was not the intention of the chapter to claim that these structures are the only reasons for women's relative lack of success in hierarchical terms in these occupations, but it is argued that they are very important contributory factors. The next chapter will go on to investigate the cultural environment of these occupations, which also makes a significant contribution to women's problems.

7
Hostile Reactions: Male Culture

> It's a man's world, and if you don't f***ing like it, don't f***ing come in to it.
>
> A construction engineer

This chapter examines the question: are women in management, the UK construction industry, academia, and the Church cultural discords? It investigates the cultural environment of these male-dominated occupations and organisations that prevent women achieving 'like men'. This environment involves issues of discourse, language and symbolism. The chapter examines women's experiences of relationships with colleagues, managers, clients, customers and the community, which can and do impact on their achievement and feelings of competence and confidence. When women enter these occupations they encounter hostility, both overt and covert opposition, and resistance to their success.

Organisational culture as an influence on women's careers

Generally, there are two approaches to the definition of the concept of culture within organisational literature; either as something an organisation 'has' or something an organisation 'is' (Liff and Cameron, 1997). The former approach is criticised for being over simplistic, presenting culture as the collective consensus of the organisation. In the second approach, culture is seen as more complex and as the outcome of social interaction. It consists of symbols and meanings, which are negotiated and shared. Drawing on the second approach, there is now widespread acceptance of the idea that gender is an essential aspect of organisational culture (see Morgan and Knights, 1991; Ledwith and

Colgan, 1996), and that women are prevented from progressing in their careers in parity with men by the cultural environments they encounter (see Davidson and Cooper, 1992; and Chi-Chang, 1992).

Work in this area has produced some recurring themes that are all particularly prevalent in male-dominated occupations. They basically relate to men's exclusionary behaviour, where men tend to share information predominately with other men, recruit in their own image, ostracise and undermine women, and generally act to perpetuate ways of working and forms of interaction with which they feel comfortable. Itzin (1995) characterises 'gender cultures' in organisations as hierarchical, patriarchal, sex-segregated, sexually divided, sex-stereotyped, sex-discriminatory, sexualised, sexist, misogynist, resistant to change and as encompassing gendered power structures. Marshall (1995) shows that masculine work cultures feature strongly in women managers' accounts of why they leave their senior jobs. Also, Maddock (1999) finds that women managers became tired of managing gender relations and a highly gendered culture. Women in male-dominated occupations and organisations are described as 'visitors' to another culture (Kvande and Rasmussen, 1994). When women enter occupations that were previously seen as the preserve of men, they encounter hostility, both overt and covert opposition, and resistance to their success.

Recruiting in one's own likeness

The 'gendered power system' is another concept used in studying women as a minority in male-dominated workplaces. Powerful individuals (mostly men) can influence or even define values within an organisational context by influencing the recruitment and promotion of those whom they consider to be similar to themselves (Kanter, 1977; Sharma, 1990; Bagilhole, 1993b; Kvande and Rasmussen, 1993; Lorber, 1994; Alimo-Metcalfe, 1995; Kettle, 1996; Walton, 1997; Dryburgh, 1999). Liff and Ward (2001) find that women in banking have problems presenting themselves as plausible candidates for promotion since the dominant organisational model of those that will succeed is strongly sex-typed male. Morgan and Knights (1991) find a rationale among male managers as to why women are not good sales representatives, which includes the idea that women will disrupt the 'esprit de corps' based on male gender identity and will not fit comfortably within the ethos and culture of the sales force.

Kanter (1977) in her classic study of managers in a large US corporation finds this culture of homogeneity. Men like working with those they are most sure of, that is other men. Lipmen-Blumen's (1976) 'homosocial theory of sex roles' also offers a useful conceptualisation of the problem, where men are dominant in sex-segregated institutions and act to exclude women from participation. Academia, the construction industry, Civil Service management, and the Church of England are prime examples of homosocial institutions, being established and run by men who prefer people like themselves. They reward those most like themselves and exclude and marginalise women.

This preference for men similar to themselves is confirmed in the study of women construction engineering professionals:

> A lot of the directors are very fierce men, they like to see that quality in the people following them up. But this is something which is unlikely to be found in most of the women managers ... if I see a potential conflictual situation when I'm negotiating a payment to a sub-contractor, I would rather work a way around the problem. My line manager would rather go in shouting and hoping to force them into submission.

> Managers assess people in terms of how they see successful managerial style, which in reality will mean who gets closest to their own style. It is a concern for women I think, because the male managers carrying out the assessments may overlook the particular skills that women bring to the job, and look for carbon copies of themselves. The problem is that it is these assessments that dictate where you develop within the company.

Dominance of the male career model

Women are expected to fit into a dominant career model, which is full time, with an ordered vertical progression, and requires a high degree of career focus. The most obvious effect of this patriarchal model of paid work is that it encourages discriminatory practices, which undermine, devalue and subordinate women's contribution (Gutek et al., 1996; Nicolson, 1996).

In assessing women for recruitment or promotion, managers assume women's commitment to paid work is reduced by their domestic responsibilities. The following is a comment from an academic, which confirms this idea: 'Women are not taken seriously as academics or, if they are mothers, not seen as interested in a career, academic or otherwise.'

This attitude towards women is also evident in the Civil Service.

> There's an ingrained attitude that women will leave to have children especially among the older members of the Civil Service and higher grades. They think women will not make a career of it, but they'll never admit to having that attitude. One manager said to me when I got pregnant that he expected me to leave, as I couldn't do two jobs at once.

The impact of these expectations on women is palpable.

> Five years in the Civil Service have changed me from a career woman. I think, like most other women, I have realised that unless I am prepared to make quite disproportionate sacrifices, I will not succeed in the Civil Service. Having accepted that you can seek satisfaction elsewhere, in the home, or in your family.

In construction, women have to accept the demands of an extreme male-oriented work pattern, which is even seen as damaging to men's family lives. Employees tend to arrive early, work late, sacrifice their holiday entitlement and social lives, and remain geographically flexible.

> You look at the top directors and their wives have all left them at some point. Our project manager has just cancelled his holiday because he was told to, and his wife and kids went without him, so I suppose it won't be long before he joins the divorcee list! ... you have to accept that if you are going to work in this industry that you must make sacrifices if you are going to get on, and so I have resigned myself to not having children.

In contrast, the following comment from a women priest shows that men carrying out family responsibilities were viewed differently:

> A lot of my male colleagues structure their day in the parish around collecting children from school because mum works day time ... no different from the women priests, but there is a different view of it, somehow indefinable.

Men's networks: men's clubs

Organisations are political cultural systems that promote competition and cooperation simultaneously, and form arenas for the manifestation of the power and interests of their members (Handy, 1993; Kvande and Rasmussen, 1994). Only those who understand this organisational power and politics are likely to progress (Hunt, 1992; Kvande and Rasmussen, 1993). An essential way of obtaining this understanding is being included in powerful networks, from which women are largely excluded in male-dominated occupations. Liff and Cameron (1997) find that the senior women managers in their study state that a predominant barrier they face in their careers is the 'men's club'. In universities, women tell of being outsiders in homosocial male territories and the existence of an influential 'old boys' club' (Sutherland, 1985; Kerman, 1995; Powney, 1997; Mavin, 1998). Greed (2000) in looking at the construction industry utilises the concept of 'closure' against women entering or remaining within the industry. Men control who is included or excluded. 'This is worked out on a daily basis at an interpersonal level. Some people are made to feel awkward, unwelcome and "wrong" others are welcomed into the subculture, and made to feel comfortable and part of the team' (Greed, 2000, p. 183).

Two women explain the problem for them, the first an academic and the second a construction engineer.

> Going over to a group of men at a conference and joining in their conversation is difficult. When I start talking to a man, it never occurs to me that he might think I'm making a pass at him, but it has happened and it is embarrassing. I try to be professional with them and not be aware of this, but it's a problem.

> I haven't met other women at my level in the company ... it's hard to develop the kind of relationships with men where you can keep it informal without creating rumours. I've found that the hardest thing being a woman in this industry.

This exclusion means that women find it very difficult to accrue the necessary resources to perform valued professional activities. Lorber (1994) describes men's circular proliferation of prestige, resources and power as the 'Matthew effect'. 'For whosoever hath, to him shall be given, and he shall have more abundance: but whosoever hath not, from him shall be taken away even that he hath' (Lorber, 1994, p. 29; quoting the Bible, King James version).

Even when women try to network themselves this is discouraged. The following is an example from the construction industry:

> A few women got together to attempt to arrange some kind of informal networking meeting, but we were told by the director to stop. It was perceived as a threat. We were only trying to bring something to the workplace instead of oppressive behaviour, but it was shot down in flames.

Male workers are well aware that important business and contacts are made, not only in formal work situations, but also at social and sporting events. However, it is these sorts of informal social activities from which women are easily excluded (Sutherland, 1985; Couric, 1989; Cockburn, 1991; Davies-Netley, 1998; Scott, 1996; US Department of Labor, 1997).

Many women academics comment on their exclusion from their colleagues' social life: 'There's a heavy male drinking social life. You're barred from meeting them outside the university because they're involved in sport, bars, things I can't participate in.'

In construction, the problems of women's workplace isolation is exacerbated by their deliberate exclusion from social events, which are regarded as an effective way of networking within organisations.

> I am about 400 miles from home here, and I sometimes feel quite lonely, but not once in that time have I been invited to 5-a-side football, or for a drink after work. They even ask each other if they are going for a drink in front of me. Sometimes I feel like asking them what is it about me that makes them want to exclude me.

Socialisation into the profession

Included in the resources needed for successful occupational performance is the 'indeterminate' knowledge of professional and organisational life. 'It is the indeterminate aspects of occupational performance in elite jobs which prove elusive to women' (Atkinson, 1983). These aspects are the 'distinctive modes of perception, of thinking, of appreciation, and of action ... the taste of a group, its characteristic taken-for-granted view of the world ... tacit, indescribable competencies' (Delamont, 1989, p. 29). Thus the problem for women is not their human capital; women's investment in technical knowledge and expertise. Rather, the problem is professional contact, style and legitimacy (Atkinson and Delamont, 1990; McIlwee and Robinson, 1992).

These essential performance skills of a profession are never explicitly taught, but are communicated via male networks. Thus we see the further marginalisation of women in male-dominated occupations.

Another side of socialisation into most jobs is the experience gained from doing particular tasks and having particular responsibilities, which is very important for promotion. In construction, women find themselves competing unsuccessfully for the necessary career experience.

> I've asked for the opportunity to do some international work but there's a guy there now who does it all. He knows that if I get this experience it will help me get my promotion and that's why he won't let it go, and he is so in with the boss that he is unlikely to make him share it. It seems so unfair, it's not anything that I've done wrong, it's because our boss is so biased towards men that he wants to see progress.

Also well over half of the women Civil Service managers feel that their jobs do not offer them opportunities to improve their skills and show their potential. Often the experience needed for promotion is reserved for their male colleagues: 'Men get the jobs which are important for promotion. They try to give most of the men at least a chance at them. This isn't true of the women.'

Two-thirds of the women complain about the amount of routine work they are expected to do. They feel that having such a heavy workload does not allow them 'scope to use their initiative' or to show their true worth: 'At the moment I can't think of promotion. My workload is too heavy and there's too much pressure.'

Also, in construction, some women find that they are allocated low-level tasks, or that they are overloaded to the extent that their failure to complete tasks leads colleagues to question their competence.

> My site manager asked me if I would temporarily look after the site safety inductions ... that was five months ago and I'm still doing it. There are so many other tasks that would better utilise my skills and experience, and I keep telling him that I'm finding it soul destroying, but it's the way that he sees the role for women on site.

> I complained so much at the mundane work that I was given that in the end they started to give me tasks, but then it got ridiculous, I had work coming out of my ears. In the end I just couldn't cope any

more, I thought that I was going to have a nervous breakdown ... if your manager gets it in for you there's not too much you can do but grin and bear it.

In contrast, one woman in the Civil Service notes that the amount of work was reduced to allow the full potential of male colleagues to show through: 'Managers have been known to lighten the workload of men so that they can shine and push themselves.'

Around half of the women do not expect promotion. The major reason they give is the feeling that their 'face does not fit'. They perceive a level of subjectivity in promotional procedures and a lack of a strict adherence to formal rules and regulations.

I suppose the Civil Service made me realise not to hope too much for promotion. I feel rejected in a way. It's who you know. You have to get on with the right person, get on well with your supervisor. It's not what you know but who you know. 'Wheeling and dealing goes on, wheels turning within wheels'.

Women given difficult jobs

Marshall (1994) finds that women are made vulnerable by being given difficult management roles, and 'generally held in low esteem until they proved otherwise' (Maddock, 1999, p. 168).

The following woman Civil Service manager gives her experience of this.

When I was first in my grade I had to doubly prove myself, especially with the nastier side of the job, for example, disciplining staff. When I became a manager first I was given an extra load of the nasty jobs, more than the men who were managers. It was as if I was on trial. I didn't realise this until later.

Also, in construction, male project staff are encouraged by managers to test women's commitment and competence.

The atmosphere on site is dictated by our project manager. You can see it reflected in the other managers ... I have found that quite often he'll encourage some of the other managers to test me out a bit, see how I'll take it. They have a dig at me, make a rude remark, try to undermine decisions and things like that. That's why the first few weeks are often difficult on site, until you prove that you are capable.

The stress on a woman in male-dominated occupations to perform well for herself, for her colleagues, and as a role model is immense (Powney, 1997). Several priests feel that being a woman marks them out as different and risky, and their visibility opens them up to being judged for their mistakes.

> It marks one out as being different. A priest who is a woman – there is a sense in which we can't be an individual because all women priests are judged by our mistakes.

> To be a different 'species' to the male priests, and therefore not 'real priests'. Risky!

In construction, women feel under pressure to perform better than their male colleagues.

> It's bad enough being a woman, but the opportunities for promotion are so few and far between, that we all know that we have to be one step ahead of our rivals to have any chance of promotion. The problem is that as a woman you already start ten steps behind, and that's before your colleagues have stabbed you in the back at every opportunity going!

Role models and mentors

Male networks also provide role models and mentors, whose sponsorship enhances men's self-esteem, self-confidence and careers. Less than a quarter of the women academics have a mentor, although they do feel a need for them and their benefits are appreciated. Success in the academic marketplace requires a high level of educational attainment, but moving through the system of rewards and status requires knowing colleagues who can provide guidance, support and advocacy to the apprentice.

Male colleagues' greater access to the benefits of role models and mentors is perceived.

> They come off the walls at them, don't they?

> Particularly in research, you see it going on. Men giving advice to other men in private. Sporting activities bring them into contact with staff from other departments, which gives them opportunities that I don't have. Then they make more of the right decisions about

research and so on. I've no access to the grapevine. They intertwine well and it helps their work.

In construction, most women have no female colleagues working with them on a daily basis, and, if they try to break down gender barriers in an attempt to find a mentor, they experience unfortunate consequences.

I wish that I had someone I could ask advice from, just someone I could get on really well with informally that would listen to me and get to know me and give me a bit of advice really. Everybody needs some advice about things now and again. It's just some recognition that the way I am doing things is OK and that I am going in the right direction. Sometimes I go home at the end of the day with no one to talk to and I feel so down, but I don't know any senior women and the men either don't seem interested, or think I'm after something else!

Chilly climate

For women to perform effectively in non-traditional roles, they must form good relationships with their male colleagues. However, they experience difficulties in forming such relationships (Johnsrud and Atwater, 1991; DiTomaso et al., 1993; Bagilhole, 1993a). Kanter (1977) finds that women entering male-dominated occupations experience 'boundary heightening', where men exaggerate the differences between themselves and the tokens and treat them as outsiders. Zimmer (1988) argues that these effects of tokenism actually increase as women increase in number, as they present a greater threat to men. This leads men to tighten boundaries and to increase their opposition.

Thus men are found to be culturally active in creating an environment in which 'women don't flourish' (Kanter, 1977). This can be oblique and subtle. Lorber (1994) identifies the 'Salieri phenomenon' named after the composer who allegedly sabotaged Mozart's career. 'Salieri's damning with faint praise is one way women are undermined by their male colleagues and bosses, often without being aware of it' (p. 237). Also, men generate a masculine culture in and around their work, whether this is technological or managerial, that can make women feel, without being told so in so many words, 'you are out of place here' (Cockburn, 1991, p. 65). This is identified in many studies as the 'chill factor'.

Only one of the women priests has not experienced any hostility or open opposition to their priesthood. In fact, although one woman points out that that there has also been 'lots of positive approbation', many report serious and upsetting negative reactions from male colleagues.

> The male priests wouldn't shake hands and threatened to walk out of a service, if I was robed as a priest. They won't take communion from me. They make me feel responsible for their discomfort. Also, vocal opposition to women clergy in general is expressed.

> I have had rudeness and downright brutish behaviour from male colleagues. I had to be removed from the parish where I served my title because I was bullied. I have been bawled at down the phone by male clergy who cannot bear the idea of women priests. There are still constant battles – or at least bitter pills to be swallowed.

A woman priest sums up her feeling of not belonging.

> I've had insulting and aggressive remarks. Because I am fairly high profile, I am the target for some animosity. I do recognise male bonding, an unwillingness to open a 'closed club' to females, a feeling that women must play by the men's rules, etc. I'm given a sense that I'm an intruder, a disturber. It is surprising how often women are spoken of in terms of being a problem.

While only one academic reports a positive, supportive relationship with male colleagues, nearly half report negative relationships.

> I was told by a male colleague that I only got the job because they wanted a woman. Their wives have looked after their children while they've concentrated on their career, and they're very macho about it. I spend most of my time with the secretaries. It's a common idea that you get through the door first, but if you do you get a knife in the back.

> It's more like non-communication rather than different treatment. The department is male-dominated. They are quite standoffish. They don't tell me the things I need to know. They are pleasant but underneath the knife is going in. I'm asked to do things at the last

minute, literally an hour before. Am I being set up to fail in front of the students? You can't do the job properly if you're not given information.

Also, they report feelings of intrusion.

They don't know how to react and respond to me. They are boys together and I don't fit in with that. As a woman, it's hard to penetrate that. I feel it but there's nothing concrete. There are so few women. The language in the university is male. I am made to feel that I am in men's territory. You are always aware of being a woman in this university.

In construction, women's visibility as minorities in the workplace has led to considerable resentment from their male colleagues when they managed to gain promotion.

There was real deep resentment at the fact I had got promoted to section engineer and that I was a woman. A lot of people thought that they deserved promotion rather than me and lots of nasty rumours went around about why I had got promoted when they hadn't ... It took a lot of effort to do my job. It made my life very difficult.

Threat to masculinity

Men's masculinity is closely related to and constructed through their paid work. Therefore, the question of whether notions of traditional masculinity are challenged or transformed for men when women enter their occupation is raised (Cockburn, 1985; Homans, 1987; Carter and Kirkup, 1990; Greed, 1991; Cockburn, 1991; Packer, 1996; Goode and Bagilhole, 1998a, 1998b). Williams (1989) argues that men are 'territorial' about 'their' occupations, and threatened by competent women, whose presence may result in a demystifying of their achievements, and a blurring of the boundaries between masculine and feminine identities. Men resent the intrusion of women, on the grounds that it suppresses normal conversation, and takes away the pleasure of working in an all-male environment. Also, they perceive women as unwanted competitors, whose presence will reduce the pay and status of their work. Thus men who work in male-dominated jobs seem particularly resistant to changes which improve gender equality (Evetts, 1994).

In construction, men certainly resent women entering their environment.

> We had been arguing about something to do with work, and no matter how hard I tried I could not get him to compromise. It makes you more determined to stick with it to show prats like that they are talking crap, because they are frightened, that's all it is, it's fright that their closed world may be changing.

Also, women workers threaten men's advantaged status in terms of jobs and wages that they maintain through segregation (Hartmann, 1976; Spencer and Podmore, 1987b; Reskin, 1988; Whittock, 2000). A woman priest gives an example of unease about and resistance to the numbers of women increasing:

> There is real anxiety about all the women teams running parishes. But there's no problem with all male teams! When a team ministry of eight appointed a third woman, there was a frisson of anxiety – 'the women are taking over'. A fourth woman was strongly resisted. When I pointed out that the women on the team saw no problem in the appointment of another woman colleague, I was told that the Team Rector (leader) thought it would be unwise to have another woman.

Sexual harassment

Many studies have explored the perpetuation of male domination through the way masculine sexuality is incorporated into organisations via sexual harassment (SH) (Kanter, 1977; Dzeich and Weiner, 1984; Hearn et al., 1989; Barkalow and Raab, 1990; Paludi, 1990; Paludi and Brickman, 1991; Yount, 1991; Itzin and Newman, 1995; Wajcman, 1996; DeKeserdy and Schwartz, 1998; ESIB, 1998; Hagman and Hearn, 1999). SH is a major issue, particularly for women who enter non-traditional forms of employment. They will often be more at risk of SH and more aggressive SH than their counterparts in traditional forms of female employment (Hadjifotiou, 1983; Ramazanoglu, 1987; Bagilhole and Woodward, 1995; Butler and Landells, 1995; Collier, 1995; Court and Moralee, 1995; Ledwith and Weaver, 1995; Clark et al., 1996; Collinson and Collinson, 1996; Willing, 1996; Dececchi et al., 1998).

SH is especially pervasive in male-dominated jobs, since it serves as a means for male workers to reassert dominance and control over women colleagues, who otherwise would be their equals (Gruber and Bjorn, 1982;

Westley, 1982; Pringle, 1989; Sheppard, 1989; Brewer, 1991; Yount, 1991; Brown, 1993; Lorber, 1994; Tallichet, 1995; Collinson and Collinson, 1996; Gruber, 1998). 'Emergent and potentially powerful women must be cut down to size by sexual means' (Cockburn, 1991, p. 141).

As a woman Civil Service manager explains: 'Unless you are extraordinarily ambitious, the sexism and sexual harassment soon puts you in your place.'

The Commission of the European Communities (1992, p. 2) defines SH as 'unwanted conduct of a sexual nature, or other conduct based on sex, affecting the dignity of women and men at work. This can include unwelcome physical, verbal or non-verbal conduct.' Herbert (1992, p. 30) gives a more detailed definition:

It can be: (i) Physical, ranging from suggestive looks to indecent assault or rape, (ii) Verbal, ranging from belittling or suggestive remarks and compromising invitations to aggressively foul language or unwanted demands for sex, or displays of sexually suggestive or degrading pictures in the work place ... The effect of such behaviour on the recipient is to create an intimidating, hostile, or offensive environment ... even if not intended.

Studies in the US and UK, reveal that from 42 per cent to as many as 88 per cent of women workers experience sexual harassment in the workplace at some time in their lives (Ragins and Scandura, 1995).

Virtually all the priests have experienced SH: 'I get mild sexual harassment from colleagues. It's minor, irritating, but very hurtful.'

Two of the women have experienced very serious incidents of violence from men in the public as a consequence of their occupation.

I've had problems with a stalker, and an incident with indecent exposure including going to magistrates court case and experiencing an abusive defence lawyer.

I was assaulted in the street by a fanatic.

Just over a quarter of the women academics answer yes when they are asked if they have experienced SH. This ranges across personal remarks, sexual touching and sexual advances.

I get comments about my clothes, particularly if I wear anything short. No one told me I was dressing inappropriately, but someone said so to a male colleague. They are not used to women being around in a variety of clothes. There was a lot of sexual innuendo at first, at staff meetings. A professor provoked some sexual innuendo at a meeting and he apologised to me afterwards. Male staff refer to attractive female students as a 'cracker'.

A senior member of the department is always very 'friendly' he puts his arm around you, his hand on your knee. I don't think he means anything by it but he doesn't do it to his male colleagues. I take evasive action, which is ridiculous.

I was harassed by a male member of staff who shared the same office. It was not physical, but there were comments about what we could do in the afternoon. He wanted to be one of the lads, but it didn't work. I never complained, because it would cause too much aggro. I shouted at him in the end, but he carried on sharing my office. Every time I looked at him, he was staring at me. This lasted for 12 months. He's still in the department.

Also, a very serious incident is reported, which could be categorised as sexual assault, and includes actions that involve physical force and require resistance.

At one Christmas party I was backed into a corner by a male colleague and kept there. He said, 'you're the most frightening female I've ever met'. Other male colleagues joined in saying things like 'I'm not surprised he's frightened of you'. It was a ludicrous situation.

These incidents occur predominantly with male staff, but also behaviour from some male students, especially in the male-dominated disciplines in engineering and science is difficult.

I stopped wearing short skirts following comments about my legs. I have to give as good as I get, sexual innuendo. I can handle it but some female staff find it more difficult.

I'd left some essays in the lecture theatre and had to go back to collect them. The students began whistling, shouting, sexual comments.

Importantly, a further substantial number of the women academics say they have not experienced any SH. However, they go on to describe incidents which can be classified as such, when they are asked questions about any comments, experiences or incidents that they feel are linked to being a woman academic, and about their relationship with male colleagues: 'There are a few members of staff who have a reputation for touching, but they reserve it for students and secretaries. I've made it clear that I won't stand for it. When I first arrived a couple pursued me but they soon cooled off.'

This discourse of personal control, independence and autonomy implies that the women could or should be responsible for men's behaviour, and shaped some women's definitions of what does and does not constitute SH. There is a reluctance to recognise themselves as victims of SH, which reflects their identity as professional women.

In construction, overt SH is found to be common.

> There were a few guys at my last job that used to get me down. They had these rude calendars and I had asked them twice if they would take them down from the office wall but they refused ... the language, it's horrendous, the crudeness is completely unnecessary. I have spoken to my line manager, I have said it to them in jest, you know what I mean, you do it in fun to start with and then if its offensive you start to say something. Swear words and that usually don't worry me, it's the crudeness about sexual things. I find that offensive but they still do it in front of me, and they seem to think that it's quite funny too.

> Last week I was using the photocopier and this guy came up behind me and undid my bra. Things like that really upset me because it shows a complete lack of respect for me and my feelings ... I used to think that if I made an effort with my male colleagues that they would respect me, but most of the time I just feel like a sexual object to them.

Again, there is a strong sense that the women feel they should be able to handle it.

> It was difficult on site because they used to bring their nudey calendars in and leave copies of *Penthouse* and *Club* on my desk. The way I used to handle it was to turn over the calendar on the first day of every month and say 'right boys what do you reckon?' It was all very 'cor blimey your tits are looking nice today' ... it's no good as a woman coming in thinking that you are going to

> change the world, it's never going to happen, you should accept the industry for what it is, and learn to cope with it.

> The rule is that you never step over people's heads if you have a problem ... You must always fight your own battles ... Last week I was talking to this guy and he kept looking at my boobs the whole time I was talking to him. He kept asking me 'what do you think, what do you think', but I didn't answer him, until in the end I said 'I don't think they speak you know, you would be better asking my face instead!'.

Despite the evidence from these studies, which shows that severe SH is experienced by many of these women, very few of the incidents are officially reported. The issue of SH is a prime example of the complex nature of power (Bagilhole and Woodward, 1995). Lukes (1974) proposes a third dimension of power, where systems prevent demands from becoming political issues or ever being made. This conception of power sheds light on the women who appear to be reluctant to label certain clearly defined experiences and incidents as SH. Either they feel that, as professional women, they should be able to cope and deal with the situation, or they use avoidance tactics for fear of retaliation. The academic woman, who is experiencing unwanted and repeated sexual advances from the colleague who shared her office, 'wrote a long paper about the difficulty of sharing offices in general, for a staff meeting'.

Collinson and Collinson (1996) find women's responses to SH (resistance, integration, indifference, distancing and denial) all prove to be self-defeating in the asymmetrical gendered power relations and fail to deal effectively with SH. Also, even when women do report and complain about SH very few are satisfied with the outcomes. The first example below comes from the Church of England and the second from the construction industry.

> I get occasional sexist and unpleasant comments from male clergy and their wives! I reported it to the Archdeacon – no action was taken!

> Things were getting very messy on site. This foreman had now been harassing me daily for months, so in the end I actually put in an official complaint to my senior engineer. He told me that he had spoken to him, and then told me to let it lie. It was like he got a slapped wrist and I got told to keep my mouth shut. I was told that,

if the contracts manager got to hear about it, that he would sack the person straight away, but that then no one would have anything to do with me again.

A common feature of women in non-traditional occupations is that they tend to keep a 'low profile' and are reluctant to admit that discrimination has affected them (Hawkins and Schultz, 1990; Stiver Lie and O'Leary, 1990). They experience tension between balancing resistance, on the one hand, with the need to protect professional interests on the other (Morley, 1994). Male cultures have the effect of silencing women, either because women silence themselves, or because when they attempt to articulate their thinking they are met with disbelief or non-understanding (Marshall, 1993; Maddock, 1999).

The following is an example of a woman in construction being silenced.

There is a guy on this site who thinks that women shouldn't be allowed in the industry, no way should I even be here. He says that I have done a good man out of a job ... I just stay out of his way, that's the only way to handle him ... women that confront that kind of behaviour only make a rod for their own back. I think that you just have to accept that as a woman in this industry you are going to have problems.

On the other hand, the few women who confront such behaviour have been found to attract additional criticism (Hemming, 1985). In male-dominated occupations, there is a 'dominance of "gender narratives" that ridicule radical and challenging women' (Maddock, 1999, p. 7).

Conclusion

This chapter examined the cultural environment of the four non-traditional occupations under study: academia, management, priest-hood, and construction engineering. Clearly, consistent themes and issues emerge that the women who enter these 'male territories' have to use energy to deal with. This leaves them less time than their male colleagues to concentrate on their careers. The overall culture is one that is hostile to women's presence and consists of both overt and covert resistance by men.

This begins with issues around the identified 'homosociability' of men who work in male-dominated occupations. They prefer to select men like themselves and use the dominance of the male career model to assist. Within the occupations, there are well-established, powerful men's networks that provide men with the necessary tools for their trade and exclude women. Men are thus provided with resources to do the job, including the necessary 'indeterminant' skills and experience, and role models and mentors.

In contrast, women are given the less useful jobs in terms of career enhancement, and tested out in difficult tasks and roles. Women's relationships with their male colleagues create a 'chilly climate' in which they find it hard to thrive. Women's entry can provoke emotional feelings of loss of masculinity and fear of loss of occupational prestige for the men. Some men try to regain their perceived loss of status by reasserting their authority through the insidious method of sexual harassment. Women in the studies have not found any effective solutions to this harassment, and do not appear to be assisted by the organisations involved. As professional women, they feel the need to cope themselves and to control the men's behaviour, or they use avoidance tactics for fear of predictable retaliation. Without greater numbers of women in these occupations, alongside effective and supportive equal opportunities strategies, these women will continue to underachieve.

8
Equal Opportunities Structures and Policies

There are subtle ways of favouring men.

An academic

This chapter uses women's experiences in non-traditional occupations to investigate the effects of equal opportunities (EO) policies and procedures within their occupations and specific organisations. The chapter is structured around three approaches to EO: first, the 'level playing field' approach, which seeks to treat women and men the same through formal bureaucratic procedures; second, the approach that treats women differently by providing support for their different needs, such as childcare; and third, the 'hearts and minds' approach, which attempts to go further than the previous two approaches to change the gendered culture of organisations.

Introduction

The predominant concept of EO in the UK is based upon liberal political philosophy. Therefore the anti-discrimination legislation that was passed in the 1970s is individualistic and reactive, rather than proactive and based on group justice (see Bagilhole, 1997 for a detailed analysis). This results in a model of EO, which assumes that inequalities between individuals and social categories can be corrected by increasing formal bureaucratic controls, thus limiting the discretion exercised by 'prejudiced individuals'. Jewson and Mason (1986a) expose the coexistence of at least two models of EO at either end of a continuum: the 'liberal' and the 'radical'. The liberal approach concentrates on fair procedures, whereas the radical emphasises positive action and the redistribution of jobs and resources in favour of those previously disadvantaged. In effect, organisations in the private sector generally use the liberal approach, and while some organisations in the public sector use elements of both approaches, they again predominantly favour the liberal approach (Jewson and Mason, 1986a; Cockburn, 1991; Bagilhole, 1993b; Breugel and Kean, 1995).

Liff and Cameron (1997) argue that EO policies conventionally have two elements. First there are measures to ensure that women are treated in the same way as men, for example, in relation to selection procedures or the provision of benefits. Second there are measures which treat women differently to address women's distinctive characteristics that disadvantage them in the workforce, for example, childcare provisions. A third approach can be added, which goes beyond either bureaucratic controls or individual remedies for women's extra responsibilities and seeks to change the gendered organisational culture by attempting to influence 'hearts and minds', for example, through EO awareness training.

This chapter explores women's experiences of EO policies in non-traditional occupations structured around these three approaches.

Women treated the same as men

The predominant liberal model of EO seeks to alleviate sex discrimination by advocating 'gender-neutral' policies or 'same treatment' (Rubin, 1997). Most existing organisational EO policies, in both the public and private sector, tend to rest on a belief in equality as 'sameness'. It is argued that women are able to be, and must be treated the same as men. This dominant model of EO is based on the assumption that inequalities arise from the interference of individual biases and prejudices in otherwise rational organisational processes. Thus, in this view, in the absence of such interference there can be 'fair' competition between individuals in organisations. This model suggests that inequalities can be corrected by the top-down introduction of bureaucratic controls of recruitment and promotion procedures. Formalising procedures is assumed to force managers to open up competition to atypical candidates, and to assess applicants on their individual qualifications.

These procedures certainly provide an appearance of fair practice. For example, formalised selection procedures can be viewed as neutral and fair for both women and men. It is assumed that women's disadvantage becomes a problem only when individual selectors ask individual women sex-specific questions or base their assessments of female candidates on their own gender-stereotyped assumptions. What is viewed as necessary to remedy this perceived problem is effectively to erase this subjective element of perception and judgement, thereby ensuring 'same treatment' of men and women. What this model of EO also assumes is that organisational processes and procedures exist in abstraction from the social relations and historical contexts in which they develop and are practised (see Chapter 6 for evidence that this is certainly not the case in the non-traditional occupations studied in this book).

This reliance on 'fair competition' has a limited effect on the majority of women as it ignores and refuses to address structural inequalities and the domestic economy. In this way, EO policies serve to individualise the problem and, in effect, to 'blame the victim'; that is, to attribute the absence of women in higher positions to their failure to take advantage of EO. If EO policies and 'fair' competition exist and women still remain relatively few in number at senior management levels, it is seen as a result of the women's own 'choice' or 'lack of ability'. McAuley (1987, p. 163) finds just this view in universities, where 'women are still unable to gain either appointments to or promotion within the institution, then men can suggest that women's failure is actually generated by their inability to meet the demands of the institution'. Thus, the existence of EO polices based on the 'same treatment' approach can themselves 'allow men to deny that inequality exists whilst simultaneously redefining the "good worker" as the one who gives most time to the organisation; time being a commodity women often lack' (Cockburn, 1991, p. 86).

Because the starting point for liberal EO measures is to allow women and men to compete equally for existing positions, the gendered nature of the positions and of assumptions permeating organisational cultures tend to be obscured. A 'sameness' model of equality superimposed on existing organisations has clearly not succeeded in bringing about a real transformation of organisational gender relations and the gendering of organisational power. Thus ignoring differences between women and men, such as the disproportionate responsibilities and duties in relation to the home, and arguing that in the workplace women are more like men than not, has failed to improve matters. Kessler-Harris (1985) suggests that by treating women workers more like men than as workers with different needs, women remain a disadvantaged group. Ruggie (1998) finds that in Sweden, because EO policies are gender neutral and based on the non-gender specific interests of the whole labour force, women's specific concerns become sidelined in a workplace environment dominated by men.

Feminist theorists point to the limitations of adopting an 'ideology of the same', because this is inevitably based on the values and norms of men. 'The representation of women workers as the same as men was, and still is, a denial of the different problems and needs women can have in workplaces, and the repudiation of their sometimes particular worker skills' (Fraser, 1999, p. 223).

Another consequence of this perspective is that there is no perceived need fundamentally to change organisational structures. For example, better selection techniques are introduced, but not new types of jobs or patterns of working. There is a belief in formal procedures as remedies to inequality. There is an assumption that all that is needed is that all jobs should be based on credentials and not on tacit skills and informally acquired expertise; that line managers should have EO objectives in respect of recruitment and selection and career development; and above all, that this is recorded and monitored in meticulous detail.

However, the same treatment approach has not made much impression on job segregation or pay differentials between women and men. Careful attention to the letter of the law does not deal with more deep-rooted aspects of gendered disadvantage, for example, the effect of a career break for women on the required continuous publishing record for academics.

In addition, studies of recruitment and career development show that the formal procedures, at best, receive compliance, but that informal mechanisms of selection persist. Research exposes the extent to which the legislation and its subsequent organisational policies are ignored in routine practices in a range of organisations. This demonstrates the extent to which direct, overt discrimination continues (Collinson et al., 1990; Bagilhole, 1993a, 1993b, 1994, 1996, 2001a, 2002a; Bagilhole and Stephens, 1999; Bagilhole and Goode, 2001; Dainty et al., 1999, 2000a, 2000b, 2001). Formal procedures are evaded by neglect or by design, and informal discretion can never be completely eliminated (Bagilhole, 1993b).

The following are comments that illustrate the way women recognise this discrimination occurs. The first one comes from a women academic, and the second from a Civil Service manager.

There is discrimination in appointing women in some departments. Certain departments are against appointing women. Some sections and departments regard women as inferior and treat them in that way in the processes of selection. They don't see women as equal contributors.

A friend of mine went to get her annual report from her supervisor. When she mentioned promotion he said, 'You must realise now that you are married, we understand you've got a lot on what with family responsibilities, etc'. That's all he needed to say, she knew what he meant.

Also, not only is it recognised that procedures can be ignored or circumvented, but the EO model of formalising procedures can be no guarantee of fairness unless the underlying gendered organisational culture is fundamentally changed (see Chapter 6). Otherwise managers can be antagonistic to the procedures and see them as an increased burden to be carried out as superficially as possible (Bagilhole, 1993b).

In recent years, there has been a growing debate regarding the effectiveness of formal EO measures within organisations (Jewson and Mason, 1986b; Webb and Liff, 1988; Bagilhole and Stephens, 1999). Collinson et al. (1990) suggest that, while the formalisation of – for example recruitment and selection procedures – provides the necessary organisational fix, enabling organisations to assert that they are 'EO employers', it leaves existing power structures and their supporting ideologies intact. Studies show how line managers continue to undermine formalised equality policies by acting counter to such policies in their everyday practices (Bagilhole and Stephens, 1999). As a result, processes of recruitment and selection continue to operate to the detriment of women and to reproduce the status quo. Crompton and Le Feuvre (1992, p. 115) sum this up as, 'a formal equality of access is not adequate to achieve a real equality of practice'.

Women treated differently from men

Concern with notions of women's differences from men recur periodically throughout the history of the modern women's movement (Bacchi, 1990). In its contemporary form it is characterised as a reaction to the 'equal rights', 'same treatment' EO agenda above, which classifies women as effectively the same as men, and as simply needing to overcome 'feminine socialisation' to compete in the labour market as free individuals.

The critics of 'equal rights' suggest that attention should be focused upon notions of 'equity' (valuing difference) rather than, as is presently the case, 'equality' (valuing sameness) (Cockburn, 1989, 1991; Phillips, 1992). Such an approach gives public recognition to the disadvantage accrued by women by the pretence that they can, or should, compete on the same terms as men in the labour market, while continuing to be identified with, and carrying primary responsibility for, the domestic sphere. In practice, organisations that are proactive on EO issues usually extend the same treatment model to incorporate difference initiatives (Liff and Wajcman, 1996).

However, there remains the danger that any arguments based on women's attributed differences from men, even if it is a realistic reflection of their added responsibilities, will be used to reassert their perceived essential inferiority and justifiable exclusion from certain public roles. The political dimension of constructions of women as essentially different is therefore ignored at some cost. As Liff and Wajcman (1993, p. 14) argue, within the workplace hierarchy 'there is no space for difference not to be constructed as inferior'. In this way, problems of gender discrimination and disadvantage are reconstructed into 'women's problems'. This in turn leads to EO policies and practices which help women comply with existing institutional requirements rather than changing them (Webb, 1997).

The Civil Service used this 'difference' approach to introduce a surfeit of EO policies:

> flexible working hours; special leave for domestic purposes; improved maternity provision; and a domestic-absence reinstatement scheme to encourage the return of women after a child-rearing break. Nursery provision was being developed experimentally at selected sites ... it was announced that anyone might request a reduction in their hours.
>
> (Cockburn, 1991, pp. 53–4)

However, such 'family-friendly' policies, because they are designed for and used almost exclusively by women, fail to challenge the uneven domestic division of labour. Also, there is a tendency for organisations to believe that, since they are doing women a 'favour', this should be reciprocated by extra work and other evidence of commitment. Lewis and Lewis (1996) demonstrate that in this way 'family-friendly' policies are constructed as perks granted by generous employers to support women in their childcare role within conventional families. Cockburn (1991) names them as 'mothers' privileges'.

Men, on the other hand, are viewed as free of domestic responsibilities and therefore able to work full time, continuous career patterns. Cockburn (1991, p. 12) argues that: 'The absence of any serious policy to extend such "privileges" to men, and men's unwillingness to make use of them when they exist, are identified as a significant form of resistance by men to women's progress in organisations.' She argues that these 'family-friendly' policies are a 'mixed blessing for women'. While enabling women to sustain careers of a kind, they also confirm them as the 'domestic sex'. Also, as Ledwith and Manfredi (2000) find, in universities such policies are overridden by the masculinist culture, leading to meetings scheduled late in the afternoons and the continuous culture of long hours. 'Thus in spite of the equality policies in place, managerial attitudes and practices did not necessarily recognise the need for balance between family and working life ... there remained an assumption that it was up to the women themselves ... to manage the boundaries and demands of their public and private lives themselves' (Ledwith and Manfredi, 2000, p. 22).

This is confirmed by women academics: 'There is a lack of recognition that people have families. No help for family responsibilities.'

Although only just starting on their road to establish equality, women priests are arguing for the need for policies to reconcile paid and unpaid work. Interestingly, this was not recognised when only men were priests, so again these developments can be viewed as for women.

Women priests are beginning to prod the establishment to see the need to introduce maternity leave, the need to look at the effects of a life in the ministry on marriage/family life, and the need to examine accepted patterns of development.

Some small changes are happening in policy. We're struggling towards better maternity/part-time working packages. Trying to be politically correct.

At the extreme, the construction industry is recognised and acknowledged as 'dire' in terms of lack of 'family-friendly' policies. Many women discuss the necessity for, but also the lack of viability of policy improvements that can help with work/family conflict. Most feel that they are unlikely to be supported: 'I looked through the phone book the other day and out of 167 execs there are three women. Because there aren't very many that have reached that level I don't think it would be accepted for them to have a career break.'

Even maternity leave entitlement is widely misunderstood, with many women unsure about their legal or organisational entitlement. Several women are concerned that using their entitlement may jeopardise their careers.

> One thing that worries me is their attitudes towards maternity benefits and career breaks and those sort of things. It's something I haven't really discussed with them because I feel that it would be inappropriate at this level, as I may jeopardise my career ... I was hoping that they would have communicated it to me rather than me having to ask as I don't want to be seen as the guinea pig.

> If I could find someone that would do a half job share with me then I would consider it, but I don't think it's something the company would ever consider. It's a shame because my position is ideal for this kind of role as I'm usually working on several projects and so I could handle some whilst she could handle others.

As mentioned above, the Civil Service does have policies that help with home responsibilities, and is therefore much more advanced in this approach than the other three professions, but there are still caveats and problems. There is resistance from some male managers. Cockburn (1991, p. 93) finds many managers in the Civil Service who feel maternity leave and flexibility are 'too generous' and 'had gone far enough'. Cunningham et al. (1999, p. 70) find 'most managers had at best a hazy perception of the role they are expected to play in maintaining and developing EO ... For the majority of managers EO was perceived to require only a fairly limited and reactive role, so that equality issues are seen as little more than a series of one-off problems, each of which could be handled in a fairly straightforward way.'

The Civil Service does have the facility of special leave when crises occur, such as accidents or illness in the family. However, less than a quarter of the Civil Service managers are familiar with the conditions for entitlement. Instead, mothers resort to 'diplomatic illnesses' or taking their annual leave if a crisis occurs.

> There is little help offered with home responsibilities, but it is possible to take annual leave, but difficult to get special leave.

> You have to take normal leave. You can take special leave if your annual leave runs out. There is an unwritten law that, if you have children, they let you take leave when you need it.

There appears to be a degree of flexibility and discretion in the decisions about special leave. Some women say that their manager makes them use up their annual leave first and then offers them unpaid leave, whereas other managers are more sympathetic and allow time off to fit in with crises: 'Flexibility all around helps. There are no definite provisions. It depends who you are working for and how sympathetic they are.'

Only one woman has used the facility of special leave: 'There is special leave for crises. I have had one week special leave when my son was mauled by a dog and another week when my father had open heart surgery as my mother is blind.'

The Civil Service also works a system of 'flexi-time'. Workers have to be in the office for a 'core time'. Outside of this time they can work flexi-hours with their manager's agreement. However the women managers do not feel able to use it, and perpetuate this by their expectations of their subordinates.

> Those in the higher grades in the Civil Service, particularly the men, are against it because they see it as being a concession for women with family responsibilities, which they are opposed to. I don't know any women managers who work flexi-hours. We are expected to work the hours to get the job done.

> I don't clock in or expect my assistant managers to. If I have to work weekends or evenings it's hard luck. I don't expect my assistant managers to work flexi-time.

This creates difficulties for women with family commitments and there is some resentment expressed about the length of the working week. Also, some women feel that a 'flexi-time' system had disadvantages, one of these being that they can be asked to work long hours, when the workload is heavy, without the ability to take time off to compensate.

Some of the women express a desire for part-time work instead of full-time work, now or in the future when their home responsibilities became heavier. Although it exists in principle, they acknowledge with regret that none was made available to them. It can be that in non-traditional occupations constructed with the view that they are predominantly, if not exclusively, for men, EO policies that intend to change the nature of working may encounter opposition. As Walters (1987, p. 26) shows, in the Civil Service: 'Normatively, part-time working is seen to run counter to the ethic of accessibility and the convention of "not clock-watching".' This ethos appears to remain: 'I would prefer part-time work. I asked but they said, "You're wasting your time and ours. There's no part time work available at this level".'

This lack of part-time work in the Civil Service forces some women with family responsibilities to leave. The following woman has two small children, with one under school age: 'Ideally I would like part-time work, job-sharing possibly. I would like to continue but part-time. Therefore, I feel I'll probably have to leave and I've already started applying for other work.'

Liff and Cameron (1997) argue that conventional 'family-friendly' EO measures have made a limited impact on women's position in the workforce. This is not simply the result of measures being inadequately implemented, as above. Instead, they argue that there is a more fundamental difficulty with this policy approach that focuses on women as having problems which need to be redressed, rather than on changing organisations. As a result women are seen as inadequate and men become resentful of the 'special treatment' that follows.

This quote from a woman priest confirms this: 'It is surprising how often women are spoken of in terms of being a problem.'

Liff and Cameron (1997) argue that this approach has not served women well because it fails to get to the root of gender equality. In particular, it focuses on allowing women to mould themselves to male working patterns rather than addressing the gendered nature of current organisational practices.

Changing the gendered organisational culture

It has been argued that the continuing concern and obsession with questions of whether women are the same as or different from men is 'entrapping and ultimately reductionist' (Bacchi, 1990, p. 261). This is because as Bacchi's (1990, p. 262) account makes clear: 'Seeing women as the same as men prevents us challenging the model against which women are being compared; seeing women as different prevents us changing it.' Thus, what is needed instead is to change the gendered culture of organisations, which is recognised as the hardest part of the organisation to change (Itzin and Newman, 1995). Influencing culture requires sensitivity to its impact on career development, and careful manipulation through recruitment, promotions, induction, codes of practice, mission statements and reward/appraisal systems. These are identified as mechanisms through which an organisation can lead its employees to conform to its philosophy (Brown, 1995).

If this need for fundamental change is accepted, then equality initiatives need to have a much broader approach and in particular to go beyond trying to manipulate behaviour to influence attitudes and values. 'There is growing recognition that successful equality measures will need to win hearts and minds rather than just achieve reluctant compliance. Without this one can expect, at best, to see managers following the letter but not the spirit of equality programmes' (Liff and Cameron, 1997, p. 44).

Masculine organisational culture, unless challenged and changed, determines the very shape, as well as the operation, of EO policies. The effectiveness of EO policies and practices can thus be undermined when 'merit' and 'ability' are defined in terms of total commitment to the organisation as is the case in many non-traditional occupations (Buswell and Jenkins, 1994). Certainly in academia and the Civil Service, meritocracy is held up as the founding principle that governs job assignment and career progress. This means that a well-rehearsed argument against EO measures that positively favour women is their potential threat to this merit principle. Even though the concept of merit itself has been exposed as gender biased and based on processes and measurements that favour men (see Bagilhole and Goode, 2001).

However, an example of a proactive success story in the early 1990s is the NHS, which made an extensive investment in the promotion of women into senior management positions. Mainly through their Women's Unit, the NHS supported training, career development, mentoring, and work shadowing for women, as well as setting national equality targets for managers (Bagilhole and Stephens, 1999). By 1994, the number of women in senior positions rose to 40 per cent. However, it would appear that while 'minds' were influenced, 'hearts' remained less affected. Cultural changes are not as positive as the figures would suggest. Patronage is still found to exist for certain positions and decision-making bodies are still very male by nature and composition (Maddock and Parkin, 1994).

Wajcman (1996) studied companies that are part of the Opportunity 2000 campaign, which can be expected to be at the forefront and cutting edge of EO policies. Opportunity 2000 is a government supported campaign to increase the quantity and quality of women's position in the workforce. However, when looking at women managers in these companies, she finds that 'after some years of the implementation of equal opportunity policies there is increasing recognition of the informal barriers that inadvertently maintain and reproduce a world where there are so few senior women managers' (Wajcman, 1996, p. 259). In conclusion, she points out that while these companies proclaim a serious commitment to EO at the very highest levels of decision-making, nearly three-quarters of the women managers believe that a 'glass ceiling' exists for them, and almost a third of the men agree. Women perceive the prejudice of colleagues and the 'cliquiness' of senior management as an obstacle to their progress. 'What emerges is the salience of informal gendered cultural practices, which continue to operate despite considerable changes in the formal norms of these companies' (p. 270).

Even in the Civil Service, with its more advanced EO policies than the other three professions studied in this book, two-thirds of the women feel there is discrimination against them. In contrast, it is felt that men are pushed and encouraged to get promotion sometimes more than their abilities would demand, again exposing the impact of prejudice and male 'homosociability' (see Chapter 6 for a full analysis).

> Men of middling ability are pushed. Women have to have something special and really push. The discrimination is very insidious. Men are expected to be ambitious unless they state otherwise. It is regarded as more of a right for men to get promotion.

> When a young man enters the Civil Service he is encouraged. He's told 'You are a young man and you've got your career to think about'. This doesn't happen to young women. A lot of women in the Civil Service have got a lot of talent, but management is very worried and cautious about giving women a chance.

The academics also perceive discrimination. Three-quarters of the women feel that there is discrimination against women in their university. This ranges from direct discrimination in recruitment and selection, to what can be categorised as indirect discrimination in areas such as representation on committees, difficulties with family commitments, lack of support for gender research, workload balance and time pressure.

Some of the discrimination is described as subtle, and the women are not sure whether it is intentional or deliberate, but it is present and has an effect. There seems to be an undervaluing and stereotyping of women as part of the male organisation. Subtle behaviour is both more prevalent and more problematic than overtly discriminatory behaviour. Often inadvertent, sometimes well intentioned, it can seem so 'normal' as to be virtually invisible, yet creates an environment that wastes women's resources, takes time and energy to ignore or deal with, undermines self-esteem, and damages professional morale. It leaves women professionally and socially isolated, and makes it difficult for them to keep informed about professional matters and promote their views.

> There's an in-group of men who all know each other. A lot of discussion goes on in unplanned meetings where decisions are made, and if you're not in that you're not part of the decision making.

> There is no understanding of the way women are put down. Women say things in committees and meetings and they are ignored until a man says them. These are male structures and women are less easy in them. There is an ethos of a male organisation and any women in it feel enormously threatened.

> It's not ill intentioned. It's ignorance and blindness, not deliberate. Men who've never thought about it, and don't recognise it unless it's pointed out to them.

> Whether it's deliberate or not, most people making decisions see women as good at some things and not appropriate for other things. It's so subtle, they think that they're being objective but they're not. Women are filtered out. We need to make explicit what we've always felt to be implicit.

In fact, the concept and role of EO in the university is treated with caution by some of the women. Some of them find themselves in an 'equalities double-bind' whereby promotion of more women is seen in some quarters as being undermined by its association with EO initiatives. Patronising comments are made as part of what the women identify as a 'backlash'. This can be seen as a paradox of EO policies and how they interact with gendered organisational cultures. In this way EO policies may be viewed by women as not always working in their favour (see Chapter 6 where women's non-reporting of sexual harassment incidents demonstrates this).

Given a traditional ideology of paid work, men's resistance to EO policies would appear to be rational behaviour. EO policies, if they work at all, are opening up men in organisations to competition from women. As Cockburn (1991, p. 216) finds in her study of the Civil Service, men are thus 'engaged in a damage-limitation exercise, holding EO to its shortest possible agenda'. Some men can respond in a very emotional and threatened way when confronted by talented challenging women whom they perceive as supported by EO polices (see Chapter 6 for the hostile reactions towards some women). As Cockburn (1991, p. 47) shows, men 'often respond as though the end of the world were at hand'.

However, most of this extreme overt hostility can be seen in the previous chapter to come from the more 'macho' culture of the construction industry, although it should be acknowledged that some of the Civil Service managers, academics and priests have also experienced aggressive reactions by men to their presence. In the more sedate and apparently rational cultures of the Civil Service, academia and the priesthood resistance appears more subtle, but can be just as damaging to women's chances of success.

Nearly two-thirds of the women academics report that they had personally experienced resistance from men, such as not being included in networks or collaborative research, which would have been good for their careers, and being generally excluded.

> My work on gender is trivialised and dismissed. I think I offend male staff because I'm not as obsequious as they think a woman ought to be. I often make a point and then it's ignored, then a male colleague takes it up and it becomes his point.

> They don't want to use you for collaborative research because you're not part of the network and they feel they can't profit from you. It's subtle, what you get asked to do and what you don't get asked to do. Women's time is regarded as less important.

To ease the introduction of women priests, the Church of England set up a role of adviser on women's ministry in each diocese. All of the women priests reported here have taken on this role. They give a long description of the complex and varied, but often limited duties.

> Attending Bishop's Staff meetings, advising the Bishop on any issues which affect women (only happened once!), offering pastoral care and support to women clergy, and being there as a Senior Woman.

A listening/pastoral role, welcoming new women to the diocese. A watching brief on equal opportunities and gender issues. But no time allocated to complete this role and an annual budget of £500.

Importantly, it is up to each individual bishop how powerful the post is, and thereby we can interpret some of their reactions as passive resistance to women by failing to utilise these posts fully, and in some cases watering them down in subtle ways to make them ineffective. Some bishops do not appoint an adviser and some give them responsibility for men as well.

Some object to the role – as sexist against men.

Our diocese considers that women's ministry is no longer to be distinguished from men's ministry. I am the "Woman Adviser in Ministry", who acts as the sole female voice on Bishop's Staff and Council, and in all areas of decision-making. I also carry a pastoral brief for the men as well as the women, and am involved in clergy appraisal and deployment.

I am not consulted or informed about appointments or new arrivals in the diocese. The hierarchy only refer to me if there is trouble. The Diocese does not take the role seriously in terms of involving me.

Thus it would appear that despite, and sometimes because of, EO policies women are being actively and passively resisted by men.

Conclusion

This chapter exposed women's experiences of EO policies in the four non-traditional occupations under study in this book. Their experiences have been analysed within the structure of three potentially complementary but also ideologically different approaches to EO. These approaches move from: a 'level playing field' approach, which seeks to deliver the same treatment to women and men with formal bureaucratic procedures; through an approach that having recognised and acknowledged women's extra burden of unpaid work that they carry to the workplace, attempts to relieve this burden in ways that make women more able to fit into existing work patterns. The final approach can be seen as far more challenging to the status quo. It recognises the gendered nature of organisational culture, views it as damaging to EO initiatives, and therefore seeks to change it. This has been shown to be one of the most difficult approaches to EO, but is also acknowledged as essential.

As the chapter demonstrated, organisations often use different elements of the three approaches, but predominantly the emphasis has been on the 'same treatment' approach. This is certainly the case in the construction industry, academia and the Church of England. In the construction industry 'family-friendly' EO policies are non-existent. Academia fundamentally retains a culture with a definition of 'meritocracy' that encourages a 'level playing field' approach, and the Church of England is only just beginning to encounter issues that are, as usual, being defined as 'women's problems'. In contrast, the Civil Service has introduced a whole tranche of 'family-friendly' policies, although it seems to have attempted to do little to change the culture of the organisation. Thus, these policies are still predominantly perceived as for women and to define them as inferior workers. Importantly the higher the women travel up the hierarchy the harder they find it to avail themselves of these policies, thus reinforcing the 'glass ceiling' phenomenon.

Finally, the experiences of these women in non-traditional occupations has illuminated the resistance to EO policies from men. Some of this resistance is active and extremely aggressive, some is more passive and subtle. All of it works successfully to limit women's success within the existing structures and cultures of non-traditional occupations.

9
Men Were There First – Becoming One of Them!

They look for carbon copies of themselves.

A Civil Service manager

This chapter examines the proposition that women are being changed by the roles they feel obliged to take on in non-traditional occupations. It explores the impacts on women of hierarchies and the established and traditional ways of being a manager, academic, construction professional or priest laid down by men. Men were there first, and they have set down a male model for the occupation and profession. Therefore, some women, to achieve success on male terms, are conforming and changing, and becoming 'honorary men', and/or 'queen bees'.

Informal socialisation

Dunnill (1956, p. 47) gives a stark description of the informal nature of the process of socialisation into a profession:

The Civil Service is one of those callings ... that frequently leave their mark upon a man [sic] ... Training must obviously be linked with the nature of the work, the way it is organised and the methods by which it is done ... largely instinctive rather than rational, piecemeal rather than planned ... a haphazard and fortuitous business of picking up tips, learning wrinkles, guessing at the motives and reactions of one's superiors, relying on their personal goodwill and generally floundering about in the deep end until one has somehow taught oneself to swim.

Illustrative of this process are the number of books that try to teach women who enter non-traditional occupations how to fit, how to learn the rules of the game and how to overcome the numerous obstacles to succeeding. This kind of approach involves the risk of constructing women as a remedial group, with the emphasis on them getting into 'better shape' with regard to the prevailing organisational culture. Marshall (1984) argues that women in these male-gendered organisations are like immigrants moving in a male country. Also, Cockburn (1991, p. 13) warns that: 'The dominant group sets assimilation as the price of acceptance. You can't be equal and different. In the past the only women who have been able to succeed have been those without children, often unmarried ... The environment they have joined, which is that of men of power, has threatened to repel them if they do not adopt its culture.'

When looking at the lack of success of women in science, Acker (1983) argues that because men rule, their ideas are the 'ruling ideas'. This produces a valid hegemony, which has a detrimental effect on women's careers. 'We all ask why girls lack the science orientation of boys or why women fail to apply for promotion like men, without questioning why science alienates girls or how career structures exclude women.'

Being both a woman and a professional can be problematic for women's identity. Mumby and Stohl (1991) find that workplace discourse about and by women both reflects and structures their identity. Both Holmer-Nadesan (1996) and Katila and Merilainen (1999) elaborate on the essential constructive feature of discourse for identity. The concept of 'woman' cannot be fixed, but depends upon its appropriation in each act of communication or articulation. Some discourses are, however, privileged over others.

According to Holmer-Nadesan (1996), in academia patriarchy is one such discourse (see Chapter 2 for a definition of and discussion on patriarchy). Patriarchy organises material and linguistic practices around a primary signifier, which might be expressed as 'male authority'. Scientific discourse also generally manifests itself as a patriarchal dominant discourse. A set of masculine qualities, such as reason and public presentation has become synonymous with scientific enterprise. Hence, women are discursively characterised, as 'lacking' in relation to the characteristics required for the professional academic identity. Packer (1996, p. 142) finds that women scientists feel that their own gender identity puts them into conflict with this symbolism or discourse. Also, as Holmer-Nadeson (1996, pp. 165–6) points out, 'adopting the language of the dominant discourse to gain legitimacy might also involve the risk of losing the language and identity of the outsider'.

McIlwee and Robinson (1992) study the adjustments women have to make upon entering a traditionally male-dominated workplace. They conclude that this transition is a difficult one for women due to the preference given to what are seen as traditional masculine strengths. In a similar way, Witz (1992) describes medical professionalisation as one of social closure to women. Likewise Walby (1986) argues that the early origins of engineering involved organised men forming a social closure to women.

Dryburgh (1999) examines the educational phase as an early part of the socialisation process into the professional culture of engineering. Professionalism is seen to involve conforming to a particular set of norms and values, internalising the professional identity and showing solidarity. The professional culture of engineering is a very masculine one and therefore women have to work hard to conform. In this process, women appear to suppress their feminine qualities and to 'become one of the guys' (Hacker, 1989). Women are found by Dryburgh to use 'impression management' to convey an image of being united professionally with their male peers. The professionalisation process in engineering is found to operate at two levels, work and play. The work-hard culture consists of managing the heavy workload, and showing solidarity and confidence. Women are required 'to demonstrate confidence in the face of strenuous challenges, anxiety and self-doubt' (Dryburgh, 1999, p. 669). The play-hard culture has altered in recent years from images of pornography and masculine virility to one of partying and drinking, although still associated with the masculine. She finds that women have conformed to this image.

Evetts (1993) agrees that in the area of traditional engineering women have to become 'men', and in doing so the women reinforce the masculine culture already present. Also, Greed (2000, p. 183) finds in the construction industry that 'some women are more acceptable to the construction industry than others ... it should never be assumed that any woman professional is going to hold substantially different or more enlightened views from her male counterparts. Those who "fit in" are the most likely to gain seniority.' As Cockburn (1991, p. 164) starkly expresses this argument: 'If you want to join men as equals in the public sphere you must leave behind womanly things, you must be indistinguishable from a man, you must, in short, assimilate.' This is illustrated by the following comments from a woman academic and a priest:

> A certain way that academics behave is defined by men because they were there first.

> We are encouraged to conform, and to tolerate things we would never have countenanced when we had nothing to lose. There is subtle pressure to conform to inherited, traditional modes of being in relationship to authority, structures, etc.

Managerial roles are seen as particularly susceptible to the need for women to conform to conventionally masculine ways of filling the role. Fagenson and Jackson (1993, p. 315) point to research which shows that 'the more "masculine" characteristics possessed by women, the more likely the women are to be perceived as successful managers and located in powerful corporate positions'. Legge (1987, p. 56) argues 'that unless women behave very similarly to men they will not be considered suitable as managers'. As Cheng (1996) shows, women who are successful as managers are said to perform hegemonic masculinity (see Chapter 2 for a definition of and discussion on hegemonic masculinity). Evetts (2000) finds that beliefs about good management are perceived to be in conflict with women's other roles and responsibilities. Also, Packer (1996) finds that in laboratory work, managers viewed as having career potential can be said to be male gendered in terms of style of work, which is entrepreneurial and assertive.

Again Dunnill (1956, p. 108) illustrates women's past acceptance of male characteristics in the Civil Service: 'The good female senior executive or higher executive is an executive first and a woman ... afterwards. She has all the strength and doggedness which we have seen to be typical of the executives, and her touch is not noticeably lighter than that of her male colleagues.'

It would appear that the position has not changed very much. Certainly, women Civil Service managers recognise the success potential of showing conventionally male qualities and see this as a bias against some women.

> Managers look for male qualities and therefore give men the promotion as opposed to women.

> I'm not seen as an outward going person controlling staff. I've been told to do this. Once they get an idea it's hard to shift them from it. They seem to think you have to have a dominating personality, but

I think you have to get on with staff. There are different ways of doing things.

In construction male managers were seen to be putting pressure on women to show 'male' traits.

I think that managers assess people in terms of how they see successful managerial style, which in reality will mean who gets closest to their own style. It is a concern for women I think, because male managers carrying out the assessments may overlook the particular skills that women bring to the job.

Indeed, as Grosz (1986) posits, it means women become 'deviant or duplicate men'. Women academics demonstrate this where many talk about having to become an 'honorary man'.

Successful women academics have to demonstrate that they are more committed to the task in hand, and better. If you are accepted as a successful academic then you become an honorary man.

I was the first woman on the committee. At my first meeting I was told that I was being made 'an honorary gentleman', and that they needed a 'lady' for that committee, and weren't they being 'broad-minded'. Once you get on with it, you're judged in terms of the work that you do, but there is still a tendency to expect you to do women's things. I've had to establish myself as equivalent to a man.

Ways of becoming one of the 'boys': masquerading as men

To succeed in organisations people may have to conform to a model of success, which often includes accepting the 'uniform' of the occupation. As an illustration, Packer (1996) finds that the ambitious men scientists in laboratory work dress in similar ways to the male managers. In the past, continued resistance to recruiting women into better paid or more adventurous men's jobs such as the military led some women literally to masquerade as men (Wheelwright, 1989). In more recent times, there are less extreme cases of women using gender neutral curricula vitae to at least gain an interview in occupations reluctant to accept women (Devor, 1989).

Connell (1993, p. 80) believes that there is an obsession with the sex typing of clothes. He argues that in practice, such distinguishing marks of gender do not reflect natural differences, but weave 'a structure of symbol and interpretation around them, which can distort and exaggerate them'. One way of women avoiding this exaggeration of difference, particularly in manual work is literally to wear men's clothes. Yount (1991) finds that women miners in the USA recognised the need to 'look the part'. They wear men's clothes, which disguise any notion of a feminine form. Whittock (2000) also finds women in non-traditional manual work who wear lots of 'manly' clothes, big coats, boots and hats to disguise their womanly figures.

The following construction professional and priest demonstrate the symbolic nature of the 'tools of the trade', and in looking the part.

> Once you've walked around with your theodolite strung over your shoulder and climbed up a few ladders, you become part of the site and it became easier to get accepted by the men.

> Men priests wear dog collars so, so do we. But sometimes we do adapt them a bit to make a point.

These adaptations include wearing different coloured collars and in some cases patterned ones.

Even in non-traditional office-based occupations dress is an important symbolic factor. Rubin (1997) finds that women are seeking to avoid marking themselves as different in their self-presentation. Kanter's (1977) study of saleswomen in the corporation reveals some women who attempted to minimise their visibility, particularly their sexual attributes, since these were likely to eclipse their technical ability. One way of doing this is to adopt mannish dress. Maddock (1999) also finds that dress presents a particular problem for women managers who tend towards conservatism to avoid visibility. 'Women managers do not want to be perceived as sexual beings and attempt to desexualise themselves ... they joined the professional gang and wore appropriate clothes' (p. 102).

One woman academic describes the 'uniform' adopted by many women academics so as to be accepted, and not to stand out as 'different' academics: 'Women academics are beige, beige hair, beige make-up, beige clothes and beige shoes.'

Women cannot completely successfully pass as men, so they may have to find other ways to show that they are 'one of the boys'. In the early 1970s, Cecily Cannan Selby became the first woman to sit on the board of a top American company. She recalled that one of the first meetings she attended was a dinner meeting, and the atmosphere was rather tense. After the meal, one of the men offers her a cigar. She recalls: 'When I accepted, I could feel them all relax' (*Los Angeles Times*, 1995 quoted in Zweigenhaft and Damhoff, 1998).

Marshall (1984) agrees with this illustration that women deliberately adopt certain behaviours to blend in. However, Cockburn (1991, p. 69) argues there might be more subtlety to this process. It may also be the case that men select women who already demonstrate 'masculine virtues'.

An academic reinforces this idea: 'Because there are so few women, they will only select "male" females. You have to adopt that model to get on.'

One type of behaviour often cited as required by women to fit in to non-traditional occupations is aggression. In academia, McAuley (1987, p. 20) shows that the accepted mode of behaviour is to be 'forthright' in social interaction. She shows that indeed, some women learn to become as abrasive as their male colleagues. In both Reimer's (1979) account of construction and Yount's (1991) account of mining, it is certainly the 'tomboys' who are the most likely to be accepted by male colleagues. This is due to the fact that they sustain a tough and assertive demeanour. Similarly, Maddock (1999, p. 201) argues that women are not visible or recognised until they conform to male behaviours. 'Many women said that they had tried to make themselves more accepted by being more aggressive, pushy and "cooler" at work ... Being passionate about anything ... continues to be considered unusual and strange.' Interestingly, she also argues that this is even more pronounced in America where women are more inclined to model themselves on men than women in Europe. She argues this is because male role models in American companies are more exaggerated than in Europe and that 'pushy' women are more accepted.

The vast majority of women priests feel that they are being changed by the establishment.

Trying to reconcile being a woman with being 'in' may make us appear (or actually be) more militant and aggressive.

I think there is evidence of roles shaping people. Roles have not been redefined so women are changing as they take up more and more senior roles. Ministry can be brutalising and our ideals are real but fragile. The institution is tough and old and reluctant to change. Why should it, from its perspective?

Aggression is a way of life for the construction professionals.

> If someone is giving me hammer and tongs, then I will give them hammer and tongs back. I will fight my corner and prove my point … Everybody asks me what it's like being a woman on site but I can honestly say that you become immune to it in the end. I've learned to act like a man to make myself heard.

> There is a need to be aggressive, unfortunate, but part of the job. It's no good trying to talk your way out of situations, you need to be in there, in with both feet, if you know what I mean.

The women Civil Service managers argue that to gain promotion you have to show yourself as a forceful character. You have to be 'aggressive', 'pushy' and 'dominating'. You have to 'stand on your own two feet' and 'be decisive': 'I think you have to push yourself and you have to keep making it obvious that you want promotion.'

The women academics agree.

> Promotion and career development is made as difficult as possible. There are disadvantages for women going for promotion. Because of managerialism you need a tough corporate persona.

> You have to divorce yourself from one's femininity in order to be taken seriously as an academic. You have to be harder, more professional because of all the preconceptions about your ability which you have to overcome before people actually see you.

Kanter (1977) argues that another way that women in the minority in non-traditional occupations demonstrate loyalty to the 'dominant group' is by allowing themselves and their category to provide a source of humour for the group, by colluding with dominants through shared laughter. Yount (1991) finds women miners inclined to maintain a high threshold for tolerance of sexual harassment or a 'thick skin'. Invariably, women interviewed by Whittock (2000) agree that this 'thick skin', coupled with a sense of humour and acting as 'one of the boys', is a necessary prerequisite for working in non-traditional occupations. Legge (1987, p. 55) argues that women must be prepared to 'condone conversation derogatory of their gender, which in turn classifies them as "one of the chaps", not a "real" woman at all'. As Kanter (1977, p. 979) starkly observes 'for token women, the price of being "one of the boys" is a willingness to turn against the "girls"'.

This is illustrated by a woman academic.

> I'm one of the lads. They don't see me as a woman but as a colleague. I deliberately make sure that they can say anything in front of me. I don't find it offensive – even talk of female students. In the pub they make sexist jokes, jokes about sex, comments about students. One woman researcher gets very upset – she purses her lips – but this only makes for difficult relationships.

Becraft (1989) in his study of the American military concludes that women in these male jobs become just like the men. He argues that they assume masculine attitudes toward everything, such as driving fast cars, competing at sports, and devoting themselves totally to their careers. Women priests feel that the system is effectively putting pressure on them to conform and not challenge devotion to career and the accompanying acceptance of long hours.

> We're more inclined to toe the line and get on with the job. We now have jobs to lose so we are less likely to agitate. We work ridiculously long hours because our male role models often don't even take days off. We are becoming part of the system.

> I think we are less changed by the establishment than many men – but a traditional way of working has taken me over, with the result that family and friendships are low on priority of time.

Double bind

Having to perform like men, and present male behaviours and practice at work, can present a complex and complicated process for women in non-traditional occupations. To be professional is often seen as to be male, so women are in a double bind. They cannot be women and professionals, but neither can they be men. Savage and Witz (1992, p. 53) argue that these gender processes pose numerous paradoxes for women in professions: 'At the same time, they must behave like men and yet be women.'

Jamieson (1995) shows that women are in a no win situation. If women act like men, they challenge men's 'natural' right to positions of power. However, if they act like women, they are seen as not belonging to an occupation where they have to take charge, or in other words act like a man. Legge (1987, p. 55) also argues that 'copying male patterns of behaviour, gaining the skills and knowledge to pass as honorary men enmeshes women more firmly in the double-bind'. Maddock (1999, p. 66) sees this as a 'catch 22' for women: 'They cannot join if they are a woman and once they start to behave like a man, they cannot be a "proper woman".' Martin (1980, pp. 93–4) illustrates this bind for policewomen on patrol: 'The more a female partner acts like a police officer, the less she behaves like a woman. On the other hand, the more she behaves like a woman, the less protection she provides, the less adequate she is as a partner – although such behaviour preserves the man's sense of masculinity.'

Kimmel (2000, p. 504) finds women entering the military faced with the same dilemma:

> In a sense, the phrase 'woman cadet' is an oxymoron – one can not be both a woman and a cadet at the same time. Thus, women were trapped in a paradox: to the extent that they are successful cadets, women cannot be successful women; to the extent that they are successful women, they cannot be successful cadets. Either women are unsuccessful cadets or unsuccessful women; they cannot be both, and either way they lose.

Management and leadership are again particularly illustrative of this problem. Authority is often defined as a masculine trait and therefore questioned in women. As Lorber (1994) argues, a woman leader is expected to be empathetic, considerate of other's feelings and attuned to the personal. If she is not she is likely to be called 'abrasive'. On the other hand a more conciliatory style may be criticised by men and women colleagues as insufficiently authoritative.

Civil Service managers also show that even when women do adopt male characteristics, they still have problems.

> Women are fighting a lot of prejudice and unfortunately people don't realise they've got it. You become labelled in the Civil Service if you're female. If you're efficient you're called officious. If you're organised you're called bossy. The labelling process goes on and doesn't seem to apply to men. Men are considered strong and to have character when they're managing. A lot of the qualities required are not classically feminine. A lot of people say to me 'I wouldn't like to be your husband', but I never say that about their wives.

However, some women have been successful in this complex game. Wilson (1995) shows that women who have reached the higher echelons of management have used 'gender management strategies ... They learn how to redefine and manage their "femaleness".' Rubin (1997) also demonstrates how women in male-dominated occupations 'manage gender' at work in order to fit into existing organisational structures and cultures. The most used strategy appears to be one of attempting to blend in with an existing organisational culture, trying very hard to be feminine enough, while simultaneously being business-like, and exhibiting stereotypically male characteristics such as rationality and instrumentality. Women find they must behave like men to succeed, but not be men, and behave unlike women and yet be women (Witz and Savage, 1992).

Maddock (1999, p. 101) argues that women have to 'control other people's perceptions of them as women; they have to measure reactions and ascertain whether they were being too aggressive, or too feminine'. However, as McAuley (1987, p. 35) argues, for some women 'this process of re-socialisation brings with it a sense of separation from valued aspects of an earlier self ... some felt that, in developing themselves into (relatively) powerful professional women, they had lost touch with the positive aspects of their identity gained from earlier socialisation'.

Women academics find themselves in this classic double bind. Academia is perceived as male and most of the women feel that there is a problem with the concept of a woman academic. Many of them feel that this is a bad thing for the profession and denies female qualities and potential:

> Because of the male perception of what an academic is, a male role model, women are put into a different role model, and men find it difficult when the two come together. If you're a woman academic you are seen as masculine. You don't fit, it's against all the rules.

> I've been told by many people that I'm not a normal woman. An academic is either male or neutral. I don't know what a woman academic is. Women are only playing at being academics, not a real academic.

> You've got to get over that hurdle of male perception. It's very difficult, because you can't be too feminist, women's lib, aggressive. You can't display typically male characteristics. You have to be more

intelligent, special without being threatening. There isn't a clear path, an acceptable way of behaving and performing.

There is also a second twist to the double bind, or may be a triple bind involved for women in non-traditional occupations. A woman must be a professional first and a woman second (if at all) at work, but also often a woman outside. One of the strategies that Kimmel (2000, p. 506) identifies in his study of women military cadets is 'asserting traditional femininity in social situations and down playing it in professional situations'. Maddock (1999) also identifies similar strategies adopted by many successful women, such as keeping public and personal roles totally separate. These women believe that 'masculine behaviours are necessary in business and that more feminine responses such as intuition, co-operation and emotional openness are thought to be a disadvantage in public life' (p. 45).

This struggle to keep home life and professional life separate is illustrated by this woman academic: 'When I come into the office I have to behave like a man and then become a woman when I get home.'

The women Civil Service managers have a particular problem when dealing with their role at home. It is often seen as being in conflict with the type of characteristics they have to display at work. Many women mention having to make a conscious effort to become a different person at home when with their husbands.

At work I'm playing a role. I'm paid to adopt a certain stance. I'm more decisive at work. I have a lot of authority and responsibility, which I'm happy to cope with. But I'm happy in my private life not to take the lead. I'm less dominant at home.

I'm always bossy and ordering people around at work. I'm not like that at home. At work the last decisions have to be mine. I try not to be the same at home.

At work I have to be hard. I have to put up a front at work. I'm a manager in charge, whereas I can't be a manager at home. I have to consciously try not to be. I have to catch myself from treating my husband like I treat my staff at work. At work I make decisions and organise things. In the home I have to pull back. I have to make decisions at work and not at home.

A few women voice doubts that they are actually successful in suppressing their work characteristics at home. This leads to conflict and stress in their home relationships.

> I try not to be so bossy and organising at home, but I possibly don't succeed. I'm less reasonable at home. I give people less benefit of the doubt and I'm less sensitive to their needs. If I've had a bad day at work I go home empty-headed. The job gets the best bit of me.

> At work, I'm more dictatorial dealing with staff. Often I carry it on at home. My husband tells me this. I'm precise and pernickety and this is carried over into my home life. But usually I'm more soft at home.

The creation of 'queen bees'

The change that women experience in themselves in non-traditional occupations is not always perceived as negative. In fact, many women Civil Service managers feel that their career has socialised them into becoming more ambitious. Also, the promotion that they have achieved has enhanced and reinforced their confidence.

> I didn't realise such opportunities and variety of work existed. My eyes have been opened and I have been shown.

> I feel more capable now. This started when I got promotion.

> Before I came into the Civil Service, I wouldn't have seen myself holding such a responsible position. But my road's not been difficult to promotion so this may have affected my views.

However, Rubin (1997, p. 30) finds that women are not inclined to express interests and concerns which diverged from existing occupational norms in order to avoid 'bringing gender into what is otherwise viewed (incorrectly) as a gender-neutral environment'. This has implications for the support or lack of it that women give to each other in non-traditional occupations. It is certainly clear that there are many women who do not want, or do not feel able to associate with other women or to be seen to be concerned about 'women's issues'. For example, many of the women academics do not want to be associated with women's studies or seen as a 'women's woman': 'To become an academic, I've had to take on a man's model. I've avoided women's groups and not wanted to be identified as a women's studies person or feminist.'

Also most of the Civil Service managers insist that there is no difference between them and their male colleagues. There is a great deal of hostility to any consideration of women getting special treatment, because of their responsibilities in the family. Many insist that women do not have any particular problems at work.

> The problems women face at work are irrelevant. Women shouldn't be pandered to, women are here and they should fight for their work.

> Promotion is there for the having if you display the right qualities.

There has been a considerable amount written about successful women and their failure to support other women. These are seen as token women who have to become male to succeed using male criteria. Staines et al. (1974) call such women 'queen bees'. They are seen as strongly individualistic and tend to deny the existence of discrimination against women. Sutherland (1985) finds a small group in her sample of women academics that go further and feel that married women with family responsibilities who put additional burdens on colleagues should be discriminated against. Maternity leave is seen as positive discrimination. They feel that women with children should stay at home to look after them, and that to appoint a young woman is taking the risk that she may become pregnant. 'For those in senior or isolated positions the role of "honorary man" is easily accessible and has a certain piquancy' (Sutherland, 1985, p. 29).

Strikingly, over half the women Civil Service managers feel that women themselves are to blame for their lack of achievement. They are only too happy to blame women for their lack of achievement.

> In the higher grades of the Civil Service they're mostly men. A lot of the fault lies with the women. They don't want to better themselves. A lot get married and don't bother working again. A lot of women are their own worst enemies.

> It's women's fault they don't expect to be treated equally to men. Some want the best of both worlds. A lot of women take responsibility for the whole of the running of the household. This is bound to have an effect on their career and how they're viewed by their managers. Strong women get on.

Women do not necessarily have to be 'queen bees' in the hierarchy of non-traditional occupations to act as one of the 'swarm' and attack other women. Site secretaries in the construction industry are a key figure in project teams, and usually women. However, they are often seen as resentful of their female managers. Many examples are given where they have tried to undermine women managers by embarrassing them in front of their peers or refusing to perform administrative tasks for them.

> This secretary used to stab me in the back at every available opportunity. She was always telling the blokes things about me and making things up about me having affairs with people left right and centre. I tried everything with that woman, but in the end I just gave up because she had it in for me.

Kanter (1977) argues that women as minorities in non-traditional occupations fear the success of other women, which might challenge their power. However, this explanation can be challenged. The behaviour of so-called 'queen bees' may have been misinterpreted. An explanation for not supporting other women may be that powerful women rarely see themselves as powerful. Delamont's (1989) idea of 'dominant and muted groups' might help us here. The explanation of the observed conservative behaviour of muted groups is that, having expended much energy conforming to the dominant model, they cling to this accommodation and fear a fresh start. Women in non-traditional occupations have often had to rid themselves of all female characteristics, feelings and interests in order to survive. Therefore, it might come as no surprise that, in contrast to male colleagues, they do not appear to favour members of the same sex. They find themselves in a situation of conflict well known in research on minorities. They behave in accordance with their minority status. They are determined to succeed on the basis of their own merits, with no hint of patronage and expect other women to do the same.

Importantly, the potential support that women can give other women may also be inhibited and controlled by men. The following comment highlights the restrictions placed on women associating with other women in the construction industry.

> I did work with another woman on a project, an assistant construction manager. We got to know each other quite well, but in the end the men on site began to resent our friendship. I don't know why it worked out like that but we both agreed to keep a low profile in terms of doing things together, which is a shame because I really liked her.

Therefore, Maddock (1999) describes women as being 'in a cleft stick'. They may want to reject masculinity, keep hold of women's values, and support each other, but this is not where the possibility of success lies within non-traditional occupations. Daring to be different can be dangerous. As Phillips (1987, p. 19) argues, once women 'admit the mildest degree of sexual difference, they open up a gap through which the currents of reaction will flow'.

Conclusion

So it would seem that the way to be an academic, an engineer, a manager or a priest is the way that men do it; the way that they have defined and encapsulated it. We are left with the impression of an 'in-group' versus an 'out-group' situation. Women can accept isolation, or they can attempt to become insiders. Many women try to infiltrate the dominant culture by getting closer to the men. Women in a minority do not want to draw unnecessary attention to themselves. They wish to deny their experiences as 'outsiders'. There is an understandable fear of being identified as a member of the 'other sex', and being pushed into an outsider role. Also, the fewer women there are, the more likely they are to become part of the 'prevailing male ethos', to reinforce its values and preoccupations, and be unwilling to raise the interests of the minority.

Therefore, it would appear that, although women are penetrating traditionally male areas of work, for many it is on male terms and therefore does not provide much hope of this masculine culture being challenged and changed. However, a few women did feel that the picture is more mixed in non-traditional occupations, with some women becoming empowered, while others were conforming to a male-dominated and male-constructed establishment. The following comment from a woman priest illustrates this position: 'Some are less willing to speak out. Some have been tamed. Some have become honorary men, whilst some are more aware of gender issues, and some have been empowered and grown in confidence.'

Therefore, the next chapter examines the influence of the women who have become empowered and may be changing both the accepted ways of doing things and the occupations themselves.

10
Titles Don't Always Count

I think we sometimes get the 'women's problems' cases and more pastoral work, while the men think they're doing the 'important' work of decision-making!

A priest

Generally women hold different posts to men in non-traditional occupations. They do different types of work in different proportions to men, and take on different roles even within the same occupation. An example of this among women academics and priests is performing more pastoral and caring work. This can be either self-imposed, and/or enforced or reinforced by the expectations of colleagues, managers, clients and customers. The key question then is whether women, by taking on different roles and different ways of doing the job, change the way the occupation is organised and practised?

To attempt to answer this question, this chapter examines evidence on whether women actually do their jobs differently from men, whether they bring different perspectives, values or skills to the job, and finally whether this has any potential to change the occupation and the accepted way of doing things. Examples of this might include making occupations less hierarchical, more inclusive, non-threatening and collaborative.

Women do different work

The concept of the 'gendered organisation' is well-established (J. Acker 1989, 1990). In one study, J. Acker (1994) discusses the existence of 'gender regimes', that is, the internal structures, processes and beliefs that allocate women and men to different tasks and positions within an occupation. As scholars explore the trend of women moving into male occupations, they identify certain patterns to the gender regimes. Reskin and Roos (1990) find that women may have gained particular occupational titles, but where they work in the hierarchy of formerly predominantly male fields may be different from men, or they may perform different tasks. For example, women might be limited in their areas of speciality or task. 'In short, despite reduction in women's under-representation in, or an end to their near-exclusion from, the occupations we studied, sex-based job differentiation has remained robust' (Reskin and Roos, 1990, p. 306).

So segregation occurs within, as well as across occupations. Even nominally desegregated occupations remain internally segregated, for the same reasons that the labour force as a whole does so. White men's advantaged position ensures them the most desirable and most highly rewarded jobs.

Different roles and tasks

Kanter (1977) argues that women might be inducted into stereotypical roles in male-dominated occupations, which preserve the familiar form of women's tasks. She identifies four typically female roles:

> *mother/daughter* – in whom men confide, or who does such tasks as caring for male colleagues; *seductress* – rewarded for her femaleness and assured of the group's attention; *pet* – 'a cute amusing little thing' who is expected to cheer male displays from the sidelines, but not to enter into them; *iron maiden* – a contemporary variation into which strong women are placed. Usually assigned to competent, forthright women.
>
> (Kanter, 1977, p. 983)

Also, adopting any of the above roles invariably limits women's advancement opportunities. More recently, Delamont (1989), using the analogy of C.S. Lewis's *The Lion, the Witch and the Wardrobe*, describes the dilemma facing the contemporary woman academic. 'She can be a literary and scholarly lion in her own right, or concentrate on being a bewitching seductress who maintains her academic position by consorting with famous men, or she can be a good housewife who stays in the wardrobe, close to home' (p. 129).

Women are sometimes actively recruited to do different kinds of work to men in non-traditional occupations. King (1994) finds women scientists are recruited to do the detailed laboratory work and to develop careers as research assistants, rather than taking part in policy decisions and building scientific reputations. Evetts (1996) also shows that the work women have done in their scientific and engineering careers has enabled men to progress into managerial careers while they have done the backstage work.

Even if women do not conform to stereotyped roles in non-traditional occupations, often the work they do or the way they do it can inhibit their promotion opportunities. Packer (1996) finds that women in a scientific laboratory spend more time with the high-tech equipment and show high levels of technical competence. However, the men spend more time on administration, 'the type of work that denoted a position of responsibility and prepared them for management' (p. 138). Benschop et al. (2001) also find this in the banking sector in the Netherlands. For example, although both women and men are engaged in the job of awarding loans to clients, in day-to-day practice the male employees interpret their tasks broadly and take initiatives to expand them to a higher level, but the women do not.

The women managers in the Civil Service experience men getting different jobs to make them fit promotion.

> Men get the jobs, which are important for promotion. They try to give most of the men at least a chance at them. This isn't true of the women.

> There's a problem for women getting some jobs. But you need the experience for promotion.

In construction, women believe that they need to spend a period of time demonstrating their ability on lower grade tasks because men do not accept their commitment or abilities unless they do so. They spend longer demonstrating their ability than their male colleagues.

> On site you have to prove yourself not only at the beginning of each project, but with every new sub-contractor that works on the job. It was really frustrating because there was a definite element of 'does she know what she's talking about?' As a woman you have to constantly prove that you're twice as good as everybody else. You have to earn the respect that a male gets automatically.

Women priests undertook less committee work, particularly dealing with finance. Unfortunately, this means they took less of a role in decision-making: 'I suspect that women are still shouldering a disproportionate pastoral burden, but leaving finance and buildings to the men.'

The majority of the women academics do carry out committee work within their own departments: 'I've got far too many. I'm put on a lot of committees. Everything comes to me. The HOD thinks it's important to have women on committees and he knows I'll do the work.'

However, very few are members of decision-making bodies within the establishment of the university. Women still form a very small minority voice on important committees. The hierarchical organisation of these committees works against the participation of women staff who are concentrated in the lower grades: 'The structure says that you don't get major chairs of committees unless you're a professor. So it's a waste of time, you're not taken seriously unless you're a professor. They don't see you.'

One role or area of work that women often find themselves occupying more than their male colleagues is caring or pastoral duties. Lunneborg (1990, p. 18) argues that 'women are often manipulated to be nurturant, when we should be assertive, independent, and selfish. We are so well socialised to be nurturant, and men are so well socialised to the fact that they don't have to be, that we sometimes fall into "the compassion trap".' Cockburn (1991) also argues that women do more emotional labour than men. Employers and male colleagues make use of women's feelings and emotions. Hochschild (1983, p. 163) points out that 'for each gender a different portion of the managed heart is enlisted for commercial use'.

Just over half of the priests feel that women were doing different proportions of certain work in comparison to their male colleagues. Women priests are seen as carrying out more pastoral duties, particularly those connected to children.

> Women do more pastoral, listening, people things, certainly as far as my experience with male colleagues goes. 'She's good with children' is my most hated quote.

> They head up pastoral care work in parishes and the diocese. Sometimes they are made to, as this is seen as working to their perceived distinctive gifts.

The type of work that women are more often directed towards is often viewed as a soft option, but this is not accepted by the women themselves: 'Some say that women priests should take on the softer pastoral type of ministry, say in hospitals and hospices. I would challenge anyone who thought of hospice ministry as a soft option.'

It is important to note that doing pastoral work does not equip women for promotion. Being 'good campus citizens', women academics have higher teaching and pastoral care loads than men. However, the academic reward system is biased toward research and publications. The tendency for women academics to emphasise their teaching rather than research has been noted in several studies. Men retreat into research and this is seen as legitimate, whereas women take on the role of nurturing students.

The majority of women academics have different roles to their male colleagues on equivalent grades. This is mostly to do with more pastoral duties, either self-imposed, student initiated or colleague driven. This often gives them a problem with time management and is felt to be damaging to their careers because these duties are not recognised or rewarded by the university.

> The role is not different, but the enactment of the role is. I'm given the pastoral side. I take more personal responsibility for students. This is difficult in the present climate because there's little recognition for this. Men will wash their hands of the problem student and they end up at the door of women staff. This has a serious impact on my work.

> We are the ones who are concerned about the students. Women have the capacity to respond emotionally to a wide range of people on a variety of levels. We can juggle a lot of plates. I have more contact with the female students in general. It's what makes the job worthwhile.

Male colleagues are seen to manage to get more time for their research.

> Men are a bit more single-minded. If they perceive research as important to their career they are more prepared to sacrifice other parts of their work. Students are sent to me by the male staff without asking me beforehand – buck passing. I can refuse but it makes me feel awkward to say no.

> Women do all the teaching and caring for students, whilst the men do the research. One of my male colleagues sticks a note on his door

telling students when they can see him – a couple of hours a week. In other words, his door is never open to students. Because women care more, they get overloaded with day-to-day administration and students. So they can't do research and publishing, which is necessary for promotion. There's a need for what women do well to be equally valued within academia.

Different specialisms

The professional marginalisation of women is encouraged by male prejudice and stereotypical views, such as the 'fact' that they are emotional, unstable and not decisive enough (Spencer and Podmore, 1987b; Rees, 1992; Maddock and Parkin, 1994). For example, Spencer and Podmore (1987b) find women in the legal profession channelled – and indeed channelling themselves – into lower-status and less 'visible' work, such as conveyancing and matrimonial work, which is deemed appropriate for them. 'Company and commercial law is high-status, high-prestige work, highly "visible" and amply remunerated. Not surprisingly, few women work in this field' (Spencer and Podmore, 1987b, p. 118). Maddock and Parkin (1994) show that women medical students are encouraged into community health and primary care and discouraged from surgery. Also, when women are employed as managers they specialise in personnel, public relations and training. These are the 'caring', support or marginal services with social or welfare functions (Cockburn, 1991; Maddock, 1999).

The concentration of women clergy in more marginal, interim positions, and specialised ministries, carrying on the religious support work in less well paid jobs, with less prospect of promotion has been documented in America (Nesbitt, 1997; Zikmund et al., 1998). The majority of the women priests state that women are in different posts to their male colleagues. They are proportionately more in sector posts outside parishes, for example, in hospitals or universities, in less senior positions, less in charge, and in more 'difficult' parishes.

Women tend to do more sector ministry jobs and get the more difficult parishes. Many more women proportionately have taken sector posts in training and chaplaincy.

I think care needs to be taken to distinguish between 'priest' and 'vicar/incumbent'. As the legislation goes, many women are priests without being 'in charge' as a vicar/incumbent. Most of the cutting edge comes when you're 'in charge' rather than just being a priest.

In my own Diocese, the only opportunity for women to be in charge of parishes has been in difficult/run-down parishes. I think women may be working in parishes, which are difficult to fill, parishes the men don't want.

Also, women priests are less likely to follow a career ladder, and more likely to move horizontally to different jobs. They are seen as working more quietly, but perhaps taking on the tougher jobs.

Women have to move more laterally rather than hierarchically upwards.

Women do quiet work in the background. They are more prepared to take the tougher jobs.

In construction, organisations prescribe gender roles, in that they tend to allocate female staff to office-based support positions, and men to site-based positions. Site-based roles are acknowledged to offer greater scope for gaining responsibility and rapid promotion in the early career stages. Moreover, most women resent the isolating, rigid and oppressive nature of the office environment. They prefer the flexibility of site-based positions. The actual career paths that these graduate women follow are often made by their company and do not necessarily match the vocational content of their degree courses.

When I joined I was a bit confused. I didn't know whether to go for quantity surveying or construction management because I had done construction studies, but they pushed me towards surveying. It wasn't until afterwards that I realised that a lot of people feel that if women want to get on in the construction industry they are better off to go into the surveying side, because they will never be listened to if they go into construction management.

Do women bring different perspectives, values and skills?

Initially, to combat the biases and prejudices that women are less effective than men in professional and managerial positions, they were concerned to demonstrate that there is no difference in their leadership styles and task performance from men (Evetts, 2000). However, in the 1980s, feminists began to pursue a different strategy, which emphasises gender differences and gives significance to female attributes.

Many have noted that women and men differ in their approaches to managing people. A specifically female work culture is seen as emphasising collegiality (rather than hierarchy), and communication, cooperation, caring and sensitivity in relationships (rather than authority) (Marshall, 1984; Grant, 1988; Bass and Avolio, 1993). Lipmen-Blumen (1992) talks of women's 'connective leadership', and Fagenson (1993, p. 15) suggests that women managers have a ' democratic "web" rather than a hierarchical style of leadership'. Also, women managers are judged to have more satisfied subordinates and to be more likely to generate extra effort from them (Bass and Avolio, 1993; Fagenson, 1993). It is claimed that women were more likely to be 'transformational' leaders focusing on change as well as career development (Rosener, 1990; Alimo-Metcalfe, 1995; Maddock, 1999). As Maddock (1999, p. 57) argues, 'those most oppressed by gender cultures are most conscious of the need to transform value, work patterns and cultures'.

Unfortunately, women's preference for relational processes and organisational development is rarely valued or formally acknowledged within recruitment, appraisal and performance measurement. Instead women managers are selected and appraised against male characteristics. 'Men and women continue to be rewarded for being decisive, competitive and playing-by-the-rules' (Maddock, 1999, p. 43). So managers continue to conform to traditional practices and reinforce male behavioural responses. In fact, women, feeling more challenged in a managerial role than their male peers, may emphasise this behaviour even more than men.

The women managers in the Civil Service were asked for their own experiences of working for male and female managers. The majority acknowledged a difference and felt that women were harder to work for than men. A different relationship is experienced and a sexual factor enters into the equation for some women dealing with a male manager.

> I prefer to work for a fellow. Women can be bitchy. It's easier to work for a man. You can negotiate with him more easily. You know what I mean. I've had better deals from men. You can twist them around your little finger.

> Women use ploys if men are above them. Men's ego is a source of manipulation. Women are harder than men and a little more astute. It's not so easy to pull the wool over a female manager's eyes. A sweet smile doesn't go very far.

In recent years the problems associated with thinking about working women as being either different from or the same as men have been highlighted. Both positions are shown to disadvantage women and define them as inferior workers (Fraser, 1999). Furthermore, assuming a collective identity for 'women' essentialises them and hides their diversity (Cockburn, 1991; Billing and Alvesson, 2000). In fact, most comparative studies of male and female managers conclude that there are modest if any differences (Marshall, 1984; White, 1995; Billing and Alvesson, 2000). The general conclusion is that women and men in managerial positions have similar aspirations, values and other personality traits as well as job-related skills and behaviours, and accept the 'male' norms in organisations.

However, there are still hopes and beliefs in women's transformative ability in non-traditional occupations. It is predicted that the increasing involvement of women in science and engineering will change the organisation of scientific labour, and the nature of scientific knowledge (Arditti, 1979; Janeway, 1982; Josefowitz, 1983; Florman, 1984; Byanyima, 1994; Rose, 1994). Also, Cockburn (1991, p. 71) argues that some women are 'speaking for a different way of doing things'.

As an example, in construction some women manage less aggressively and are more willing to listen than their male colleagues.

> If I was a man sitting there they would start ranting and raving at you but as a woman they don't appear to be so stubborn ... as a woman I find that I can gain respect by being civil to them and trying to see things from their point of view and I think they respect that I don't have this big macho front to keep up.

The majority of women feel that adopting a 'male' managerial approach is counterproductive.

> I've seen women go in really aggressive. 'I'm as good as the men', it just doesn't work at all. It just gets people's backs up. They think, 'what are you trying to prove'. And at the same time, if you go in all tetchy and upset when someone shouts because they have done something wrong, it's the same reaction. It's all about how you deal with people, getting the right balance, knowing how to handle people. I used to work with a woman that used to shout and scream until she was blue in the face asking them to do something and they just refused to do it.

Charlton (1997, p. 604) finds women clergy 'consistently expressed the opinion that their experience, and the experience of their parishioners, is profoundly affected by their gender'. The majority of women priests feel they are different to their male colleagues, although many raise caveats and reservations to this assertion.

> My experience is that there can be huge variety of gifts, opinions and personalities within a group of women priests. Indeed, as much variety as between male and female priests. But at the present time, women do come with a common perspective of being somewhat outsiders, and of having limited access to hierarchy. I am resistant to saying that there are stereotypical differences or similarities between men and women.

Where it is felt there is a difference, this is identified as women bringing different experiences and gifts to the priesthood.

> In the ways women are different to men, bringing their own gifts, completing the whole. I was told by my parishioners that I was more amongst them than men priests had been.

> We bring the perspective of the outsider, the lack of certainty about our identity, and the skills that have been strongly developed in us through our history. We are often organic in approach and have different cognitive skills to the men.

Important ways that women are seen to be different is that they are more inclusive of the laity, particularly other women, more open and collaborative.

> Women priests tend to be more 'of the people' my congregation tells me, and they understand my sermons. They haven't understood the last five male priests, but that may just be my character. Women priests also sound different. Generally they are more collaborative.

> I find this question really difficult to answer, but members of my congregation tell me that sermons by women often seem to relate more to life and experience – perhaps we find it easier to make sense of those connections – for example, the constant interaction between sacred and secular, because that's the way woman live – less in compartments.

We relate to people, especially women through experience, heart rather than head, preach from a perspective not heard before, patient. We are prepared to engage with their emotions, be vulnerable. We release the feminine side of men.

Women's power to change occupations

Perhaps the most important thing to acknowledge initially is that one cannot assume that all or even most women want to transform or change the non-traditional occupation they have entered. Cockburn (1991) argues that many women she comes across are as conventional in their view of hierarchy, bureaucracy and management as most of the men that they have joined. Carter and Kirkup (1990) find that none of the women engineers in their study have entered engineering because they wanted to transform the profession by their presence.

Kanter (1977) predicts that as the number of women increase to a 'critical mass', they will sponsor others for leadership positions. When they become almost half the group, they will become a recognised sub-group, with alternative views and work practices, and their own inner circles. However, Zimmer (1988) argues that it is not the number of women in an occupation that is relevant, but their status, prestige and power, or indeed lack of them, that can make a change. Evans (1995), in her study of academia, agrees that merely increasing the number of women would not necessarily shift the nature of an occupation. As Delamont (1989, p. 131) so vividly puts it: 'Underdogs cannot change the rules.'

In fact, researchers find that women working in strongly male occupations are more likely to deny difference between the genders (Ledwith and Colgan, 1996). Indeed, women academics are seen to act in an ambivalent way, perhaps symptomatic of minorities. They respond to women students, but also show strong commitment to the male model of their profession and do not want to be suspected of 'exaggerated' identification with women (Bagilhole, 1993b, Ledwith and Manfredi, 2000).

Certainly more women are entering non-traditional occupations than ever before, but the key question remains. In addition to shifting the gender balance, do increasing numbers of women signal a more fundamental change in the way in which non-traditional occupations are organised and practised?

A growing body of research suggests such change is occurring. Whittock (2000) emphasises that women as capable agents do have the potential for transforming existing gender relations within employment systems. Williams (1999) studied women's rapid entry into medicine in Canada, a historically male-dominated occupation. His results reveal that men, and the profession as a whole, are changing. Male physicians are moving away from traditional patterns and norms, in part at least, because women have broken new ground, established alternatives to traditional male role models' continuous full-time working and, in doing so, expanded the possibilities for both sexes. Lunneborg (1990) also argues that women in non-traditional, male-dominated jobs, not only do their jobs differently from their male colleagues, but that they eventually change men's ways of working. Pascall et al. (2000, p. 66) find that women in banking, 'even when wrestling with the difficult area of trying to combine paid work and family responsibility actually made a change through this very activity'.

Women's marginality may not simply be a symptom of oppression, it can also be a site that can be chosen as a launching pad for women as agents of change. Martin (1996, p. 206) argues that feminism has the potential for changing work organisations, when it 'is framed as a project that seeks to value women equally with men'. Also, Cockburn (1991, p. 73) argues that for change to occur: 'Having more women in management, even women "doing things in womanly ways" is not the same thing as having feminists in control.' In academia feminists have transformed many disciplines 'by exposing the gendered basis of knowledge and providing intellectual space for women's ideas' (Morley, 1996, p. 118). However, so far, such projects of transformation are in relatively isolated pockets, in particular institutions, where small groups of senior women are engaged in attempts to create different organisational patterns (Goode and Bagilhole, 1998a; Pritchard, 1996).

The phenomenon of women priests doing different jobs may be interpreted as a consequence of discriminatory factors pushing women out into the secondary labour market of priesthood. However, another interpretation for women clergy's position involves the possibility of the influence of their own agency. Women may be proactively creating new ministries that they find spiritually more rewarding, even if they offer less financial reward (Zikmund et al., 1998).

In the UK, women priests are relatively older than their male colleagues because of their long fight for ordination, and they have many years experience of different occupations. Also, they have been highly politicised by the bitter struggle and identified themselves as feminists interested in the transformation of the Church they have joined. They all feel that being a feminist affects their work.

> Profoundly. I'm more conscious of responsibility in challenging pre-vailing attitudes and cultures, which disempower women (and some men). I try hard to treat men and women with equal respect and affirmation. I do everything I can to progress the interests of women in the church. I affirm women as valued in the eyes of God, in preaching and speaking, not to make a point, but when it comes naturally. I encourage women to value themselves, and stick up for themselves. I hope I am a good role model for youngsters – I worry that we women are expected to be super women!

> I try to encourage women to be more active and take more responsibil-ity in the church. Lay women often tell me – as do lay men – they felt liberated by women's ordination. This is wonderful and intriguing! Equal opportunity equals a healthy society!

They also all feel that they are making a change in the Church, some-times from just being there: 'A parishioner's child was not able to come to church because he was ill. When his mother got home, he asked if Sue [the vicar] had taken the service. She said no, Jonathan, a visiting priest. He said, "Can men be priests too?".'

The majority are quite optimistic about the changes they are making, which they feel are advantageous to the Church, and their male colleagues. These changes include examining the nature of priesthood, use of language and symbolism, being more collaborative and less hier-archical, challenging male values, increasing colleagues' understanding of women, and exposing the need for pastoral care of priests and more family-friendly working conditions.

> We are encouraging the church to face gender issues – just by being there, but also by raising awareness. Encouraging it to re-examine the nature of the priesthood – traditional models and stereotypes. Looking at language and liturgy – symbolism. We are raising the awareness of discrimination and minority groups, the need for pastoral care of clergy, and challenging models of priesthood.

> By being there, by coping and changing parishes creatively we are earning the right to be considered as good as or better than our male peers! By different views of authority in most but not all ordained

women. We are challenging certain male values and aspects of male, clubby culture. Challenging issues of justice, management of people, equal opportunities, and raising awareness.

Breaking down hierarchical models – providing patterns for working in teams. Making it easier to be open about vulnerability – encouraging openness. More fun. Sharing – more collaborative ministry. Many are less competitive. Fewer power games. More enabling ministry taking place.

However, some of the women feel it is important to point out that any changes are slow and gradual.

If there is change, it is very gradual, and simply by being there and challenging assumptions. As more women assume posts of responsibility, they will be able to affect change. Small movements towards openness and collaboration, due to women's influence. Little noticeable at establishment level.

However, importantly it has to be added that some women priests are less optimistic about the potential for sustaining this momentum for change, especially with many younger women priests now entering the Church straight from college who have not been politicised in the same way. As one women puts it, they do not want to hear about the 'war stories'.

Younger women priests coming in didn't have to fight the same battles. They tell us they are fed up with hearing 'war stories' from us.

I have to say I am disheartened by the numbers of younger women priests who simply want to 'keep their heads down' and get on with their job.

Conclusion

This chapter initially demonstrated the phenomenon of the internal segregation of occupations. Although women are entering non-traditional occupations in greater numbers than ever before, they appear to be doing different work to their male colleagues. They find themselves performing different roles, taking on different tasks or a different proportion of certain tasks and roles, and being encouraged into certain specialisms. Importantly, the different tasks they have been specifically recruited for, or that they find themselves performing once in their chosen occupation, mean that they are less fitted for promotion. Also, a major different role that they are performing disproportionately to their male colleagues, is pastoral and caring responsibilities. Again, it is important to note that, despite the essential nature of these activities, they are not rewarded in the same way as typical male activities. Women are marginalised in these non-traditional occupations by being channelled or feeling they should channel themselves into what are seen as appropriate specialisms for women. These tend to include social and welfare functions and support work; the marginal services.

There is, however, evidence to demonstrate that some women do their jobs differently from men and may be bringing different skills to the job. In some cases, particularly within the group of priests in the study, this appears to have the potential to change their occupation and the accepted ways of being a priest.

11
Challenging Gender Boundaries: Common Themes and Issues for Women in Non-Traditional Occupations

> A priest is a priest. Does gender change being a priest? Or does being a priest change gender?
>
> A priest

> Women academics have to say over and over again that we have a right to be where we are. It's a constant defence of ourselves.
>
> An academic

General persistence of occupational segregation

Chapter 1 shows that women's general position in the labour market remains pervasively segregated from men's. Even with the introduction of sex equality legislation women have not moved in any great numbers into many areas of employment, which have traditionally been associated with men. Rather, mostly they have consolidated their position within a narrow range of stereotypical female occupations, which are generally low paid.

The pattern of a small number of professional women entering some traditionally male occupations can be interpreted as slow horizontal desegregation. However, to confirm this there is a need for studies of the position of women in various occupations at the organisational level, to try to reveal the tacit or unspoken strategies that either create and recreate segregation or reduce it.

This meso level approach is adopted in the later chapters of this book, which recount qualitative empirical studies undertaken by the author into women's experiences in four male-dominated occupations: Civil Service management, academia, construction engineering and priesthood in the Church of England. Chapters 4 to 10 draw together the common themes and issues that emerge from the analysis of these studies, with the objective of coming to a clearer understanding of both the consequences for the women themselves of entering these relatively uncharted terrains, and also for the occupations.

Chapter 2 looks at organisational level analysis, which has become an important development in labour market theory in trying to understand the persistence of occupational sex segregation. Both formal and informal interdependent processes within organisations can be seen to militate against equality for women. The reality is that women still have the prime responsibility for childcare and home management. Also, there is evidence of exclusionary and segregating practices by both employers and male workers within internal labour markets.

Having examined where change needed to occur to affect a desegregation of occupations, potential levers for change are identified. Firstly, rather negative levers like economic difficulties for organisations are analysed. These economic levers can change the remuneration and conditions of an occupation, whereby men desert it leaving opportunities for women. Then the more positive lever of a critical mass of women is investigated. These ideas around a critical mass include an examination of some rather crude numerical solutions and other more sophisticated ideas of achieving a threshold of acceptability and normality. Also, role models and mentorship, that have been advocated to change segregation patterns, are examined, and finally attention is drawn to the women's own agency in potentially affecting change.

Occupations and jobs are internationally designated as either suitable for women or for men by processes that include gendered concepts, discourses, language and symbolism. Thus leadership, managerial positions and technical occupations are seen as suitable for men, in contrast to caring and emotional work, which is designated almost exclusively for women. Theoretical perspectives utilised to explain this are examined in Chapter 3. They are found to fall basically into two camps; either citing differences in labour supply from women and men, or different labour market demand for women and men. The first perspective looks at possible innate or learned differences in women's and men's skills and abilities. The second investigates the processes of exclusion and inclusion of workers of a certain sex through the power of employers and male workers.

Despite women's increased participation in paid employment, Chapters 1 to 3 show the considerable inequalities that remain in the employment system. However, as noted above, a minority of women have succeeded in carving inroads into some areas of non-traditional employment. Therefore, Chapters 4 to 11 use qualitative research undertaken by the author to compare and contrast women's experiences and perceptions of working in four non-traditional occupations around common themes indicated by previous work in this area.

These women are the survivors, despite processes that have conspired and militated against them. They have been successful in occupations that are still overwhelmingly male-dominated. Through them, we can begin to understand some of the processes that contribute to women's inequality. From their evidence, there may not emerge a clear-cut solution to the problem of improving access and success for women, but the processes involved begin to be illuminated.

Women's unpaid work

Chapter 4 sets out the historical and contemporary position of women in each of these four occupations. Then Chapter 5 begins to explore their experiences by looking firstly at their outside work situation; the relationship for women between unpaid and paid work. There certainly seems to be a spillover from one domain to the other, but for women the real and assumed impact of unpaid work on paid work has been shown in many studies to be greater than the other way around.

Assumptions are made about women's 'domesticity' and how this constrains their performance at work. There is an assumption here of women's homogeneity, and the primacy they will all give to family responsibilities on the part of employers. The mirror image to this is the assumed primacy men will give to their paid work, and thus their families and family responsibilities remain invisible.

Some organisations, including the Civil Service, have introduced family-friendly policies focused on helping women combine their unpaid and paid work. Therefore, despite being well intentioned, they have served to reinforce traditional gender relations. Also, the relative discretion that managers have in implementing these policies discourages women from utilising them, when they discern disapproving managers, both men and women.

There is a very real effect on women of taking on disproportionate unpaid work. Although paid work affects home and home affects paid work, this two-way process is not gender neutral. Women's unpaid work impinges on their paid work, limiting their chances, whereas men's paid work impinges on their desire or ability to take on more unpaid work. Thus most of the women in the studies acknowledge their partner's support for their careers is ambivalent and often conditional on them maintaining responsibility for the lion's share of the domestic division of labour. They also acknowledge doubts, contradictions and ambivalence in their own relatively uncharted role as professionals with home responsibilities.

Importantly, women's perception of being required to 'choose' between paid work or a family has led to demographic changes. The Civil Service managers, academics and engineers have all 'economised' on domestic demands. They have relatively few partners and children compared to other groups of women and their male colleagues. The exception to this pattern is the women clergy, but they had often formed their families before they had won the struggle to be ordained, and acknowledge this as a reason for their relatively bigger families.

In contrast, the effect of paid work on the unpaid work of women with family responsibilities is limited. Some of the women's partners have increased their contribution to unpaid work, but it is important to note that sometimes this is done begrudgingly. Also, women still retain, on the whole, the responsibility for getting unpaid work done. One major way that these professional women have eased their burden of unpaid work is by paying other women to do it for them, and here again we see them having to take the responsibility for organising this, and often paying for it too.

Internal labour markets

Subsequent chapters investigate women's experiences and perceptions of the internal labour markets of the organisations they work in. Chapter 6 presents evidence of structural disadvantage for women, some of which appears to be intentional and some that constitutes indirect discrimination. These discriminatory institutional structures follow women through from recruitment processes, both informal and formal, through career development, selection and promotion procedures, and finally into their day-to-day working conditions. The conditions and demands of these occupations tend to be structurally gender biased.

Chapter 7 examines the cultural environment of the four non-traditional occupations under study. The overall culture in each occupation is found to be hostile to women's presence and consists of both overt and covert resistance by men. Clearly, the women who enter these 'male territories' have to use up energy dealing with this resistance and this leaves them with less time than their male colleagues to concentrate on their careers.

The concept of the 'homosociability' of men who work in male-dominated occupations identified in many studies (see Bagilhole, 1993a) means that they prefer to select men like themselves and that they use the dominance of the male career model to assist with this. Thus, those involved in recruitment need scrutinising for prejudice. At present, recruitment and selection is done by men, mostly in their own image. Changes need to be made to this process to give women a fair chance, for example, formalisation of the recruitment process, and the inclusion of women members on recruitment panels where possible.

Even if able to enter these occupations, women then suffer from a lack of role models and informal support systems, which play a major role in enhancing reputations and status, and inducting men into the reward system. There are well-established powerful men's networks that, at the same time, provide men with the necessary tools for their trade, and exclude women. It is these processes of exclusion that the women in their small minority endure within their professional life. The everyday roles of women are different from their male colleagues in ways that work to their disadvantage.

On top of this women believe they are being discriminated against, and can give examples of these experiences. Women are allocated jobs that give them less chances of gaining the necessary experience for promotion, and are also assigned stressful and difficult tasks and roles such as disciplining staff. This has the effect of impairing their professional performances. They may be convinced by this process that they are not 'proper professionals'. Hence, the strong feeling among them that women need encouragement and support in a male-dominated hostile climate.

Women's entry into male-dominated occupations can provoke emotional feelings of loss of masculinity and fear of loss of occupational prestige for the men. As Maddock (1999, p. 68) argues, 'women entering uncharted workplaces are a challenge merely because of their sex, and risk ridicule [from men] as one way of punishing them'. Women perceive some men, in the studies described in Chapters 4 to 10, trying to regain their perceived loss of status by reasserting their authority through the insidious method of sexual harassment. Women have not found any effective solutions to this harassment, and do not appear to be assisted with this by the organisations involved.

Chapter 8 exposes women's experiences of equal opportunities policies. Their experiences are analysed within the framework of three potentially complementary, but also ideologically different, approaches to equal opportunities. These approaches move from a 'level playing field' approach, which seeks to deliver the same treatment to women and men, through an approach that recognises and attempts to relieve women's extra burden of unpaid work that they carry to the workplace. The final approach recognises the gendered nature of organisational culture, and views it as damaging to equal opportunities initiatives that seek to change it.

Organisations often use different elements of these three approaches, but predominantly the emphasis in the organisations studied has been on the 'same treatment' approach. This is certainly the case in the construction industry where 'family-friendly' equal opportunities policies are nonexistent. Academia fundamentally retains a culture with a definition of 'meritocracy' which encourages a 'level playing field' approach, and the Church of England is only just beginning to encounter issues that are, as previously in other organisations, being defined as 'women's problems'. In contrast, the Civil Service has introduced a whole tranche of 'family-friendly' policies 'for women', although they seem to have attempted to do little to change the culture of the organisation. Also, importantly, the higher the wome i travel up the hierarchy the harder they find it to avail themselves of the policies, thus reinforcing the 'glass ceiling' phenomenon. Finally, the resistance to equal opportunities policies from men is exposed, both active and extremely aggressive resistance and resistance that is more passive and subtle.

Chapter 9 examines the premise that being an academic, an engineer, a manager or a priest is 'like men do it' and how they define and encapsulate it. In fact, many of the women in Civil Service management, academia and construction engineering have taken on a male model of their profession and made the choice to forgo a conventional family life for their career. The occupations do not appear to accept married women with children, although there are many highly successful men in the same situation. Also, the women priests in the study are beginning to experience difficulties combining their family responsibilities with their demanding jobs.

We are left with the impression of an 'in-group' versus an 'out-group' situation. Women can accept isolation, or they can attempt to become insiders. The smaller the number of women there are, the more likely they are to become part of the 'prevailing male ethos', and to reinforce its values and preoccupations, and be unwilling to raise the interests of the minority.

Therefore, these studies appear to show that, although women are penetrating traditionally male areas of work, it is on male terms and therefore does not provide much hope of this masculine culture being challenged and changed. However, a few women feel that the picture is more mixed. While some women are conforming to a male-dominated and male-constructed establishment, others are becoming empowered. Therefore, Chapter 10 examines women's attempts at challenge.

Women appear to be doing different work to their male colleagues; performing different roles, taking on different tasks or a different proportion of certain tasks and roles, and being encouraged into certain specialisms. A major role that they are performing disproportionately to their male colleagues is pastoral and caring responsibilities. However, despite the essential nature of these activities for organisations, they are not rewarded in the same way as typical male activities. So we see women marginalised in these non-traditional occupations by being channelled, or feeling they should channel themselves, into what are seen as appropriate specialisms for women.

There is a continuing debate as to whether women bring different perspectives, values or skills to non-traditional occupations. The early claims from feminists, to attempt to avoid prejudice, were that women were the 'same' as men. Then recognition began to be given to women's difference and, it is claimed, better ways of performing, particularly regarding the management of people. However, both women and men still have to demonstrate 'male' characteristics to succeed. In fact, sometimes women have to be more 'male' than their male colleagues.

Despite many studies, especially of managers, showing negligible differences between women and men, there still remains hope for a belief in women's transformative potential in non-traditional occupations. Some women are doing things differently, bringing different skills and abilities to their work. However, the crucial question then, is does this lead to change in the occupation and their male colleagues?

Importantly, here it has to be acknowledged that not all or even most women want to change the occupation they have entered. Also, crucially, not many can. It is highly unlikely that all women engaged in non-traditional occupations consider their activity as a 'social struggle', nor is it probable that most are intentionally seeking to change the existing gender order, although, possibly, some might be. Rather, if such a transition is occurring it may be as an unintended consequence of their practice.

On a positive note, there is some evidence of possibly small pockets of movement, where women are changing occupations, and creating new spaces for themselves and their male colleagues to occupy. A potentially important example of this feminist potential of transformative change comes from the women priests in the study reported in this book. They are a unique group having been very politicised by their long and bitter fight for ordination. They do appear to be actively seeking and creating new ministries, and they all feel they are making a change.

Many of the women priests feel very strongly that priesthood is, although not gender neutral, certainly capable of embracing both genders. They also strongly reject any labelling of women priests as not proper priests: 'The expression "woman priest" almost suggests a different kind of priesthood, and I want to resist that – but I don't want to deny any aspect of womanhood in fulfilling my priestly call.'

However, there are caveats to this optimism. The women also highlight the fact that for some people in the establishment, priesthood still carries masculinity with it: 'Priest is heavily loaded with maleness which makes it difficult for people to think of "women" priests – still thought of as a separate category. Women are not generally thought of primarily as leaders in the Church.' Also, many give warnings of the political struggle it will take for women to be allowed to be bishops.

Another cloud on the horizon is importantly, that they report that younger women entering the priesthood are not as political or ambitious for change. They have not experienced the long drawn out struggle to be ordained that has politicised the older women, and do not want to 'be told the old war stories'. So only time will tell the full story of whether transformation does take place.

Discussion

This book is largely based on four case studies of women in nontraditional occupations. However, while the assessment of their experiences and perceptions is necessarily selective, the treatment of women in these occupations appears to be representative of many other nontraditional professions when compared with other research (see for example Cockburn 1991).

The final question to be addressed is: are women changing these occupations or are they in the process of their engagement in this work being changed themselves? If the occupations are not changing, then women's career opportunities and chances of success are severely affected, creating a loss of their talent as expensively educated and trained staff.

Women participate in and assist in maintaining gender relations, therefore rationally we can assume that, by acting differently, they can alter these same relations. As capable agents they can choose to stop reproducing gendered systems, and thereby, despite structural and cultural constraints, change organisations. Chafetz (1990) argues that a different gender system has evolved out of the actions of women. Connell (1993, p. 149) notes how 'there is a long-term historical dynamic of practice and structural transformation ... Gender history is lumpy. There are moments of transition, when the conditions of prac-tice alter fast; there are periods of more or less steady shift in a given direction; and there are periods when a particular balance of forces is stabilised.' Women in non-traditional employment do contradict the norm, in that they have proved themselves capable of men's work. Thus, they threaten accepted beliefs about what it is to be masculine, and conservative notions about women's 'natural role'.

There is a continuing debate within feminism as to whether women should be seen as essentially different from men or essentially similar. Several analysts who favour the 'difference' approach argue that women's reproductive difference from men means they have a different life pattern, psychology and 'better' moral values (Spender, 1982; Gilligan, 1982; Griffin, 1984). Thus, women can be seen to have the potential to change non-traditional occupations. A different approach emphasises the effect of gender difference between the sexes that is socially learnt through a series of life experiences (Epstein, 1988). In this way, women could instead potentially be changed by non-traditional occupations.

However, Bacchi (1990, p. 259) argues that, damagingly, 'Debates amongst feminists along sameness/difference lines surface in contexts where there appear to be only two options, joining the system on its terms or staying out.' Young (1992) also suggests that women's attempts to overcome exclusion have taken two directions, assimila-tion or separation, neither of which have achieved the desired end. Cockburn (1991, p. 10) also eschews the sameness/difference debate, and argues that 'as women, we can be both the same as you [men] *and* different from you, at various times and in various ways. We can also be both the same and different from each other.' Fraser (1999, p. 7) also emphasises 'the need for women to be seen ... as both the same as and different from men workers ... implicit in my argument is a rejection of the binary opposition of sameness and difference'. This certainly seems to be evidenced in the study of women's experiences of non-traditional occupations in this book. Often women's approaches have to be pragmatic, being like men or more so when required, but also being different when it is advantageous. However, this must have a detrimental impact on any transformative aims they hold.

Maddock (1999, p. 200) argues that the 'conundrum for women is how to be credible in a male world; when to be credible they need to be accepted, they need to conform, and to be effective they need to be challenging and imaginative'. As the studies in this book show, 'getting it right' is hard for women in relatively uncharted, non-traditional occupations. They must not be too hard or too soft, or too masculine or too feminine. Also, they have the extra dimension on how this 'gender management' spills over into their family life. Organisational demands on the behaviour of these women as good managers, academics, engineers, are almost certainly not the same requirements that make a good wife or mother. Therefore, women need to discuss tactics and strategies together, but as the studies have shown their association is suspected and discouraged.

Men's resistance to women's success should not be underestimated. 'In a gender order where men are advantaged and women are disadvantaged, major structural reform is, on the face of it, against men's interests' (Connell, 1993, p. 285). The term 'backlash' was coined in the USA, where there was strong evidence of an anti-feminist movement. However, the male counterattack that Faludi (1992) describes at length has not been limited to the USA. According to Chafetz (1990) one type of opposition grouping that emerges to protect men's interests is 'vested interest groups'. These consist mostly of male organisational elites. Such groups fear that changes to the gender system will disrupt their social and economic status, 'thus denuding them of their most valuable resource: power' (p. 200). Certainly, there is evidence of both subtle and passive resistance from men in the studies in this book, and some more aggressive hostile behaviour.

Women's continuing and increasing labour force participation, and their maintenance of higher achievement over boys and men at every level of the education system, should increase their ability to enforce claims on male occupations. Walby (1997) argues that the effects of educational achievements for younger women and the decline in the significance of domestic tasks are providing better opportunities for some young women. In the light of this, and using Reskin and Roos'

(1990) conceptualisation of labour queues that have functioned as gender queues, with men ranked ahead of women for preferred occupations, we can ask whether this ranking is likely to change. 'Are employers likely to abandon sex as a ranking principle?' (Reskin and Roos, 1990, p. 315).

Employers already find themselves recruiting more women when they recruit the most highly qualified graduates, and thus should certainly increasingly experience and observe women successfully undertaking traditionally male professions. Reskin and Roos (1990) also suggest that women newcomers may try harder and be better qualified than their average male colleague. This is again evidenced in the studies reported in this book.

The first potential lever for change in enabling more women to enter non-traditional occupations – identified in Chapter 2 of this book – is the negative one of detrimental changes in conditions and rewards, that lead men to 'leave a sinking ship', leaving room for women. Interestingly, in all the four occupations in the present studies this has occurred. In academia, salaries have deteriorated relative to comparable professions, outside scrutiny and accountability to restricted economic budgets has increased, and there has been a subsequent increase in part-time and short-term contracts, disproportionately taken up by women. In the Civil Service working conditions have deteriorated since the changes made by Margaret Thatcher. Cockburn (1991, pp. 58–9) identifies these as:

> devolving control over spending to individual departments responsible for setting and meeting objectives within cost. Associated staff cuts – intensification of work ... falling standards of professionalism ... [being] increasingly expected to adopt modern business management methods ... [and] in recent years the drab corridors of the Service amid the filing cabinets, and the red tape have seen slow-motion patricide.

The Church of England is a notoriously low paying employer, and priests have also experienced greater strains and demands on their roles from increased and intensified social problems in society. There has been a subsequent shortage of male applicants for the priesthood, alongside the ordination of more women priests. In the USA in the 1980s the disproportionate feminisation of the clergy was blamed for the consequent loss of stature within the profession. White male divinity school enrolments plummeted, leaving a female majority in some schools (Katzenstein, 1998). Construction engineering also suffered a serious economic downturn in the 1990s, which led to many skilled workers and professionals being laid off. The subsequent upturn has left the industry with a skills and labour shortage, which has led it to look at recruiting more women. However, it has retained bad working conditions and a very 'macho' culture not attractive to many men, and hardly suitable for women's success (Bagilhole et al., 2000).

It would seem that as Reskin and Roos (1990) predict male occupations with deteriorating conditions continue to draw in some women. However, they argue that it might be a 'poisoned chalice' that women are drinking from by accepting worse conditions, status and pay than the previous male incumbents of their positions.

Ways forward?

How then is equality in the labour market to be achieved, if women's action by itself in this area is not sufficient? While men continue to see their interests being threatened by the arrival of women in male-dominated workplaces, voluntary transformation seems unlikely to occur. Here then is the central problem. The studies in this book show that the structure and culture of organisations, including their equal opportunities policies and women's experience of 'no change at home' inhibit their transformative action. As Connell (1993, p. 109) argues, men's authority is 'a core in the power structure of gender, contrasted with more diffuse or contested patterns of power in the periphery'. It is in this 'periphery' that we have witnessed the actions of women, and their strategic conduct. But the core in the power structure remains largely unchallenged. Some women may be drawing on their own agency in an attempt to transform the local or meso situations of particular workplaces, but they have a very hard and possibly impossible struggle.

Women's success will be determined by whether they are allowed competently to perform sex-atypical work in their own ways, and with this they will need some help. As Reskin and Roos (1990, p. 298) argue, women can pressure employers directly but without the 'threat of the government's big stick, their efforts are likely to be in vain'. Committed leadership in organisations actively working towards equal opportunities is essential, as are positive action programmes to overcome past disadvantage. A crucial catalyst to all this must be in the form of national government commitment demonstrated by the creation and implementation of effective, proactive legislation, and budgetary support. This means legislation that is monitored and its success evaluated, and that requires proactive, positive action from employers. More of the same equal opportunities policies based on equal treatment, or even family-friendly policies aimed exclusively at women, will not be sufficient to change and transform non-traditional occupations for women. As Maddock (1999, p. 225) argues:

> Equality feminism is not the answer. While single childless women may have the illusion of escaping the gendered landscape, those who are mothers will never be able to do this. Women may have the transforming skills, but most do not necessarily use them; some lose them over time and others become disillusioned; many resign from executive posts because they 'have had enough'.

This recognition has led several EU countries to introduce centralised, state-driven interventionist approaches to gender equality in non-traditional occupations, with quotas and targets becoming important parts of the strategies. Such measures are within the spirit of increasing acceptance in mainland Europe that affirmative action for women may be needed to tackle structural gender inequality (Ledwith and Manfredi, 2000). For example, in Sweden, since 1994 'every university must promote equality in all their activities not only in education and research but in appointing staff at all levels and in the administration'. New measures include availability of public funds 'to import', if necessary, women professors from other countries to posts in science and technology. Swedish higher education institutions are also required to meet, over a period of three years, recruitment targets set by the government. Failure leads to the freezing of some of their funding (Ledwith and Manfredi, 2000). Also, Norway and the Netherlands have adopted a policy of targets by introducing special acts promoting proportional representation of women in academia (Blokdijk-Hauwert, 1998).

From the evidence presented in the book, it must be concluded that the movement of women into areas of non-traditional employment, despite their potentially transformative capacities, is not of sufficient degree to signify any major shift in the gender order nor change in the systems in question. In contrast, many women seem to have to adopt the male model of these careers, and to restrict their 'domestic attachments' in their quest for success. It remains unlikely that either the men (or the women) who are winning under the existing rules within these occupations will become allies in changing their organisations' career systems. Especially if existing pervasive patriarchal assumptions remain consistent with organisational requirements.

Therefore, comprehensive changes are needed so that women can enter these occupations in greater numbers, and survive and thrive within them. We must stop looking for possible deficiencies or deficits in women themselves and see inequality as a problem for the organisations involved, placed fully and squarely on their shoulders. It is important to recognise the crucial part played by complex interdependent institutional factors in the process of excluding women from full participation and successful careers.

'Challenging Men' in the title of this book has been carefully chosen. Women, just by their very presence in male-dominated occupations, are challenging to men. They need to consider strategic ways forward to effect change, as individualistic solutions that women have adopted in the past have been unsuccessful. Hence, an exhortation to 'think about draining the swamp'. When people are under threat, discriminated against and disadvantaged, they are likely to behave unquestioningly, and try to change themselves to 'fit in'. In other words – 'when you are up to your ass in alligators you don't think of draining the swamp' (Bagilhole, 2001b, p. 1). However, this is a vital mistake.

Importantly, women in non-traditional occupations need the crucial assistance of positive action and targets from national legislation, and to work collectively and strategically to transform the organisational 'swamps', not themselves. Unless this is done, women will not successfully challenge and transform the organisations and the men within them.

Appendix: Details of Case Studies

Civil Service managers

The Civil Service provides a striking example of vertical job segregation, and an excellent framework and context for an in-depth investigation and illumination of the potential sources of women's under-achievement. Women still remain concentrated in very large numbers at the lower grades and few advance up its structure.

Funded by a full-time Nottingham University Postgraduate Studentship, a study of women managers in a major Civil Service department was undertaken. Initially contact was made with the London headquarters of the department, to discover the extent of help and cooperation they were able to offer to this study, which was to be based in the East Midlands. They expressed the view that the whole issue of women's underachievement in the Civil Service was one of deep concern, but also of a highly sensitive nature. Their suggestion was to pursue regional contacts and to interview willing staff in their free time. Therefore, the trade union that represented managers in the Civil Service was approached locally and they gave their full and extensive cooperation.

They distributed a brief preliminary questionnaire to their women members in the region. The returns were used to choose a sample of women managers who would be willing to be interviewed in their own time. Eventually, 50 women were chosen at random. Nearly two-thirds (64 per cent) were in the lowest managerial grade, and the rest were in middle management. Their length of service ranged widely from one to 35 years, but the majority (60 per cent) had between 10 and 19 years service and 10 per cent had worked in the Civil Service for over 20 years.

The aim was to identify the factors involved in their achievement, or lack of it. As a major part of this, it was very important to get their views and experiences of working in the Civil Service. Each interview took place in the women's free time, and usually lasted about one-and-a-half hours. A few of the interviews lasted much longer. These women felt the need to talk about their experiences as women in management, which they felt unable to do with their male colleagues. The first part of the interview was structured to obtain data on the personal details of the women's lives. The second part was semi-structured, raising points for discussion, to enable the women to express their views, opinions and personal experiences. Through the combination of these approaches, it was hoped to avoid a 'methodological inhibition' (Mills, 1959, p. 173) and to allow a more useful analysis of this complex issue. The desire was, as expressed by Acker (1980, p. 69), to 'study women as people rather than sex as a variable'.

In the semi-structured part of the interview data was obtained in three main areas, opinions on women working, experience of equal opportunities, and views on gender differences between men and women. This semi-structured form allowed the women to express their feelings, views and opinions. Data on the women's work experience had to be obtained in an exploratory way, which needed the women to suggest direction and structure to the interview. The aim was to capture the quality of these women's work lives as experienced by them. It is these work experiences which contribute to and sustain a sexual hierarchy of achievement in paid work. The subtle aspect of many work encounters, and the taken-for-granted quality of women's experiences of sexual differentiation, suggest that any attempt to use a precoded questionnaire would have been unhelpful.

The women were very enthusiastic when talking about themselves and their experiences, both inside and outside of work. Their families, homes and work lives were so intertwined that they were very involved in these areas and keen to share their experiences of life. I was invariably offered a barrage of comments after the actual interview had taken place. These I asked permission to transcribe and used them to enrich and contextualise the previous material. The qualitative data illuminated and brought to life the flavour of these women's working experiences.

Academics

Women constitute a minority of the full-time academic staff in UK universities and are concentrated in the lower grades. Statistical evidence points to the fact that an important reason for this is that discrimination exists within the academic profession. However, until recently there was little empirical information on the nature of this discrimination and the institutional processes that serve to maintain it. The study reported here was funded by a Loughborough University Faculty Research Grant. It sought to identify and illuminate these processes through the experiences and perceptions of women academics themselves. The purpose of the study was to explore women academics' perceptions and experiences of institutional processes, to discover what factors have influenced their own professional career, and what seemed to them to be the conditions relevant to the access of women to the academic profession.

A total of 43 women were interviewed from a university where women made up only 11 per cent of the full-time academic staff; a total of 58 women out of 510 staff. The sample was made up of all the women who were available and willing to be interviewed during the period of the research project. They came from across all the departments in the university where women were present, and across the range of academic posts. The university's departments were divided into four schools; engineering, pure and applied science, human and environmental studies, and education and humanities. In both the engineering and science schools women made up only 4 per cent of the full-time academics. In the human and environmental studies school they were 18 per cent, and in the education and humanities school 29 per cent of the total. The majority of the women interviewed were on the lecturer grade (77 per cent), 16 per cent were senior lecturers and 7 per cent professors.

A semi-structured interview schedule was used to allow the detailed investigation of the issues. This was developed to explore the organisational and professional issues which had been identified in previous studies of women's inequality in the academic profession. The women were asked open-ended questions about such things as their experiences in recruitment, probation, career development, appraisal, committee membership and their academic role. The interviews lasted from one to two hours and sometimes longer.

Sutherland (1985) was proved right in her assertion that, as research subjects, women academics are ideal. They proved to be enthusiastic and willing interviewees, and many were ready to talk analytically and frankly about their own experiences. Although the women interviewed came from departments that ranged across the arts and the sciences, and from many different disciplines, they expressed a commonality of experience around the issues of inequality and discrimination for women in academic life. As Acker (1984, p. 40) argued: 'women tend to be clustered in certain departments and relatively junior positions, which might well contribute to a sense of common consciousness among them, especially when this is seen as a consequence of common experiences of marginality within the institution'.

Construction industry engineering professionals

Construction has the lowest female representation in its workforce of all major industries and service sectors in the UK, and they are concentrated in clerical and secretarial positions, or other positions not directly involved in the construction process (EOC, 2001). Overall, only 1.45 per cent of qualified construction engineering professionals are women and they are not proportionately represented at middle and senior levels (Bagilhole et al., 2000).

In order to explore the influences on women's careers as professionals in the construction industry, a methodology was adapted from a successful study which analysed women's careers in the Norwegian engineering professions (Kvande and Rasmussen, 1993). This involved the investigation of the career influences and experiences of matched pairs of female and male informants. The informants were paired according to their career paths, experience, length of service to their organisation, and their educational and professional qualifications. The research was funded by an Economic and Social Council Research Grant.

Five of the 20 largest UK contracting organisations collaborated with the research project. They were all large multi-divisional organisations operating throughout the UK and mainland Europe. Good female engineering graduates were beginning to emerge from universities, and the companies were keen to utilise their talents. They were also concerned at the industry's lack of ability to retain women and hoped the study would give an insight into the ways their organisations had to change.

The companies provided a total of 82 informants (41 pairs). The majority worked in site-based roles, but a sample was also included from office-based positions including those which supported the main business functions. This allowed workplace sub-cultures to be explored within a variety of different settings within the organisational environment.

Using in-depth qualitative interviews, the informants were asked to discuss their career history and explain the nature and effect of the major determinants of their careers in their own terms. A cumulatively developing research instrument was adapted to focus on relevant aspects of each informant's career as they were interviewed. The interview transcripts were supplemented by a range of other qualitative data. These included work experience diaries that provided longitudinal accounts of the informants' day-to-day career experiences. These added rich insights which supported some of the general findings recounted by the informants during the career histories interviews.

The data reported in this book is from the 41 women interviewees.

Priests

A study of women 'pioneers' in the Church of England was undertaken by the author herself with no external funding. They are some of the first women priests to be ordained. Charlton (1997), in her study of American women clergy who had been ordained in the 1970s, offers a definition of pioneer, which is particularly appropriate for this group of women. 'A scout goes forward alone, without a map, faces danger, charts the territory, reports back. Pioneers, on the other hand, at least have a map, if rudimentary, and they have some company' (p. 605). These women priests are therefore pioneers. They are following on from women deacons, and do have female colleagues. However, in many ways they are 'going first [and] combining gender and work in a new way' (p. 599). This raises questions such as: as the combination of woman and priesthood is new, what does it mean to be some of those who go first? What does it mean to be doing things people have not 'seen' before? What are the lives and careers like of the women who embody the changes? What are the experiences of these 'pioneer' women priests?

While attending a conference, 31 of the most senior and experienced Church of England women priests from dioceses across the whole of England completed a questionnaire, with some closed, but mostly open questions. This allowed them to express their own views on various issues, which explored the relevance to them of the common themes experienced by women who enter male-dominated occupations.

As background, they were asked for their age, post-secondary qualifications, previous work experience, length of time as a priest, and experiences of lay ministry. Their marital and family status was established, and they were then asked to discuss their relationships and arrangements for housework and family responsibilities. They were asked for their perceptions of recruitment and promotion, whether women priests do different types of jobs to men, and whether they received the same rewards and working conditions. They were asked for their views about the prospects for women becoming bishops, and finally they were asked about any experiences of hostility or opposition from their male colleagues, superiors or the laity in their congregations.

These women made very enthusiastic informants. They were impressive because of the willingness and energy with which they engaged with these ideas, and their mettle, intellect and strength showed through, despite their reporting some very difficult and upsetting experiences they had endured at times.

References

Academy of Finland (1998) *Women in Academia,* Helsinki: Academy of Finland.

Acker, J. (1989) *Doing Comparable Work: Gender, Class and Pay Equity,* Philadelphia: Temple University Press.

Acker, J. (1990) 'Hierarchies, Jobs, Bodies: a Theory of Gendered Organizations', *Gender and Society,* 4(2), 56–62.

Acker, J. (1991) 'Hierarchies, Jobs, Bodies: a Theory of Gendered Organisations', in Judith Lorber and Susan A. Farrell (eds) *The Social Construction of Gender,* London: Sage.

Acker, J. (1992) 'Gendering Organisational Theory', in A.U. Mills and P. Tancred (eds) *Gendering Analysis,* London: Sage.

Acker, J. (1994) 'The Gender Regime of Swedish Banks', *Scandinavian Journal of Management,* 10(2), 117–30.

Acker, S. (1980) 'Women, the Other Academics', *British Journal of Sociology of Education,* 1(1), 68–80.

Acker, S. (1983) 'Women, the Other Academics', in R.L. Dudowitz (ed.) *Women in Academe,* Oxford: Pergamon Press.

Acker, S. (1984) 'Women in Higher Education: What is the Problem?', in S. Acker and D. Warren Piper (eds) *Is Higher Education Fair to Women?* Milton Keynes: Open University Press.

Acker, S. (1992) 'New Perspectives on an Old Problem: the Position of Women Academics in British Higher Education', *Higher Education,* 24, 57–75.

Acker, S. (1994) *Gendered Education: Sociological Reflections on Women, Teaching and Feminism,* Buckingham: Open University Press.

Alban-Metcalfe, B. (1987) 'Male and Female Managers: an Analysis of Biographical and Self-Concept Data', *Work and Stress,* 1, July–September, 207–19.

Alban-Metcalfe, B. and M. West (1991) 'Women Managers', in J.F. Cozens and M. West (eds) *Women at Work,* Milton Keynes: Open University Press.

Aldridge, A. (1987) 'In the Absence of the Minister: Structures of Subordination in the Role of Deaconess in the Church of England', *Sociology,* 21(3), 377–92.

Aldridge, A. (1989) 'Men, Women and Clergymen: Opinion and Authority in a Sacred Organization', *Sociological Review,* 37(1), 43–64.

Aldridge, A. (1991) 'Women's Experience of Diaconate', in *Deacons Now,* Advisory Council for the Church's Ministry, 15–18.

Aldridge, A. (1994a) 'Whose Service is Perfect Freedom: Women's Careers in the Church of England', in Julia Evetts (ed.) *Women and Career: Themes and Issues in Advanced Industrial Societies,* Harlow: Longman.

Aldridge, A. (1994b) 'Women Priests: from Exclusion to Accommodation', *British Journal of Sociology,* 45(3), 501–10.

Alimo-Metcalfe, B. (1995) 'Female and Male Constructs of Leadership and Empowerment', *Women in Management,* 10(2), 3–8.

Almquist, E. (1991) 'Labor-Market Gender Inequality in Minority Groups', in J. Lorber and S. Farrell (eds) *The Social Construction of Gender*, Newbury Park, CA: Sage.

Alvesson, M. and Y. Billing (1992) 'Gender and Organisation: Towards a Differentiated Understanding', *Organisation Studies*, 13(1), 73–103.

Anker, Richard (1998) *Gender and Jobs. Sex Segregation of Occupations in the World*, International Labour Office: Geneva.

Ansari, A. and J. Jackson (1999) *The Under-Representation of Black and Asian People in Construction*, London: Royal Holloway University/Construction Industry Training Board.

Arditti, R. (1979) 'Feminism and Science', in R. Arditti, P. Brennan and S. Cavrak (eds) *Science and Liberation*, Boston: South End Press.

Atkinson, P. (1983) 'The Reproduction of Professional Community', in R. Dingwall and P. Lewis (eds) *Sociology of the Professions: Doctors, Lawyers and Others*, London: Macmillan.

Atkinson, P. and S. Delamont (1990) 'Professions and Powerlessness: Female Marginality in the Learned Occupations', *Sociological Review*, 38(1), 90–110.

AUT (1992) *Sex Discrimination in Universities. Report of an Academic Pay Audit Carried Out By the Association of University Teachers' Research Department*, London: AUT.

Bacchi, C. (1990) *Same Difference: Feminism and Sexual Difference*, Sydney: Allen and Unwin.

Bagilhole, B. (1993a) 'Survivors in a Male Preserve: a Study of British Women Academics' Experiences and Perceptions of Discrimination in a UK University', *Higher Education*, 26, 431–47.

Bagilhole, B. (1993b) 'Managing to Be Fair: Implementing Equal Opportunities in a Local Authority', *Local Government Studies*, 19(2), 163–75.

Bagilhole, B. (1993c) 'How to Keep a Good Woman Down: an Investigation of the Role of Institutional Factors in the Process of Discrimination against Women Academics', *British Journal of Sociology of Education*, 14(3), 261–74.

Bagilhole, B. (1994) *Women, Work and Equal Opportunities*, Aldershot: Avebury.

Bagilhole, B. (1995) 'In the Margins: Problems for Women Academics in UK Universities', *Journal of Area Studies. Special Edition. Women in Eastern and Western Europe*, 6, Spring, 143–56.

Bagilhole, B. (1996) 'Travellers in a Strange World: Inequality and Discrimination against Women Academics and its Negative Effect on Higher Education', in K. Watson, S. Modgil and C. Modgil (eds) *Educational Dilemmas: Debate and Diversity*, London: Casell.

Bagilhole, B. (1997), *Equal Opportunities and Social Policy; Issues of Gender, 'Race' and Disability*, Harlow: Addison Wesley Longman.

Bagilhole, B. (2000a) 'Through the Upgrading of Skills to Empowerment: a Collaborative Project between East and West for the Career Promotion of Women in India', International Women's Conference, 'Women's Status, Vision and Reality, Bridging East and West', New Delhi, India, 27 February–3 March.

Bagilhole, B. (2000b) 'Too Little Too Late? An Assessment of National Initiatives for Women Academics in the British University System', *Higher Education in Europe, Special Issue: Gender and Higher Education*, XXV(2), 139–45.

Bagilhole, B. (2001a) 'Herding Cats: Managing Academics as an Issue for Equal Opportunities in Higher Education', Politics of Gender and Education 3rd International Conference, April, London.

Bagilhole, B. (2001b) 'Challenging Women in the Male Academy: Think about Draining the Swamp', Plenary paper Women in Higher Education (WHEN) Conference, 'In Bed with the Three-Headed Monster: Experiences of Research, Teaching and Administration for Women in Higher Education', Coventry University.

Bagilhole, B. (2002a) 'Challenging Equal Opportunities: Changing and Adapting Male Hegemony in Academia', *British Journal of Sociology of Education*, 23(1), 19–33.

Bagilhole, B. (2002b) 'Prospects for Change? Structural, Cultural and Action Dimensions of the Careers of Pioneer Women Priests in the Church of England', *Gender, Work and Organization* (forthcoming).

Bagilhole, B. and C. Dugmore (2001) *The Evaluation of Policies in Relation to the Division of Unpaid and Paid Work between Women and Men*, Tilburg, Netherlands: Work and Organization Research Centre, Tilburg University.

Bagilhole, B. and J. Goode (1998) 'The "Gender Dimension" of Both the "Narrow" and "Broad" Curriculum in UK Higher Education: Do Women Lose out in Both?', *Gender and Education*, 10(4), 459–69.

Bagilhole, B. and J. Goode (2001) 'The Contradiction of the Myth of Individual Merit, and the Reality of a Patriarchal Support System in Academic Careers: a Feminist Investigation', *European Journal of Women's Studies*, 8(2), 161–80.

Bagilhole, B. and E. Robinson (1997) *A Report on Policies and Practices on Equal Opportunities in Employment in Universities and Colleges of Higher Education*, London: Commission on University Career Opportunity, Committee of Vice-Chancellors and Principals of the Universities of the United Kingdom (CVCP).

Bagilhole, B. and M. Stephens (1999) 'Management Responses to Equal Opportunities for Ethnic Minority Women in a NHS Hospital Trust', *Journal of Social Policy*, 28(2), 235–48.

Bagilhole, B. and H. Woodward (1995) 'An Occupational Hazard Warning: Academic Life Can Seriously Damage Your Health. An Investigation of Sexual Harassment of Women Academics in a UK University', *British Journal of Sociology of Education*, 16(1), 37–51.

Bagilhole, B., A. Dainty and R. Neale (2000) 'Women in the UK Construction Industry: a Cultural Discord?', *Minorities in Science and Technology*, 6(1), 73–86.

Barkalow, C. and A. Raab (1990) *In the Men's House*, New York: Poseidon Press.

Bass, B.M. and B.J. Avolio (1993) *Shatter the Glass Ceiling*, Binghampton, USA: Center for Leadership Studies, Binghampton University.

Bates, Stephen (2000) 'Anglicans Take First Step towards Women Bishops', *Guardian*, 10 July, 10.

Becraft, C. (1989) 'Women Do Belong in the Military', *Navy Times*, 1, 47–51.

Benjamin, O. and O. Sullivan (1996) 'The Importance of Difference: Conceptualising Increased Flexibility in Gender Relations at Home', *Sociological Review*, 44(2), 225–51.

Bennett, J.F., M.J. Davidson and A.W. Gale (1999) 'Women in Construction: a Comparative Investigation into the Expectations and Experiences of Female and Male Construction Undergraduates and Employees', *Women in Management Review*, 14(7), 273–91.

Benschop, Yvonne, Lilian Halsema and Petra Schreurs (2001) 'The Division of Labour and Inequalities between the Sexes: an Ideological Dilemma', *Gender, Work and Organization,* 8(1), 1–18.

Benston, Margaret Lowe (1992) 'Women's Voices/Men's Voices: Technology as Language', in Gill Kirkup and Laurie Smith Keller (eds) *Inventing Women: Science, Technology and Gender,* Cambridge: Polity Press.

Bergqvist, C. and A.C. Jungar (2000) 'Adaptation of Diffusion of the Swedish Gender Model?', in L. Hantrais (ed.) *Gendered Policies in Europe: Reconciling Employment and Family Life,* Basingstoke: Macmillan Press – now Palgrave Macmillan.

Bett, M. (1999) *Independent Review of Higher Education Pay and Conditions: Report of a Committee Chaired by Sir Michael Bett,* London: The Stationery Office.

Bhavani, R. (1994) *Black Women in the Labour Market: a Research Review,* Manchester: Equal Opportunities Commission.

Bielby, William and James Baron (1986) 'Men and Women at Work: Sex Segregation and Statistical Discrimination', *American Journal of Sociology,* 91, 759–99.

Billing, Yvonne Due and Mats Alvesson (2000) 'Questioning the Notion of Feminine Leadership: a Critical Perspective on the Gender Labelling of Leadership', *Gender, Work and Organization,* 7(3), 144–57.

Blokdijk-Hauwert, T.M.M. (1998) 'Gender Equality in Higher Education in the Netherlands', paper presented at European conference of Gender Equality, University of Helsinki.

Bonney, N. and E. Reinach (1993) 'Housework Reconsidered: the Oakley Thesis Twenty Years Later', *Work, Employment and Society,* 7(4), 615–27.

Bourdieu, P. (1986) *Distinction: a Social Critique of the Judgement of Taste,* London: Routledge.

Bradley, H. (1989) *Men's Work, Women's Work: a Sociological History of the Sexual Division of Labour in Employment,* Cambridge: Polity Press.

Brannen, J., G. Meszaros, P. Moss and G. Poland (1994) *Employment and Family Life,* London: Employment Department.

Breugel, I. and H. Kean (1995) 'The Moment of Municipal Feminism: Gender and Class in 1980s Local Government', *Critical Social Policy,* 15, 147–69.

Brewer, J.D. (1991) 'Hercules, Hippolyte and the Amazons – or Policewomen in the RUC', *British Journal of Sociology,* 42(2), 231–47.

Brooks, A. (1997) *Academic Women,* Milton Keynes: Society for Research into Higher Education/Open University Press.

Brown, A.D. (1995) *Organizational Culture,* London: Pitman Publishing.

Brown, D. and N. Charles (1982) *Women and Shift Work: Some Evidence from Britain,* Dublin: European Foundation for the Improvement of Working and Living Conditions.

Brown, J. (1993) 'Sexual Harassment: Are Women their own Worst Enemies?', *Women Police,* Fall, 19–21.

Bruegel, I. (1994) 'Labour market Prospects for Women Ethnic Minorities', in R. Lindley (ed.) *Labour Market Structures and Prospects for Women,* Manchester: Equal Opportunities Commission.

Building (1995) 'QS Awarded £9000 Compensation for Sexual Discrimination by Contractor', 20 January, 13.

Building (1999) 'Minister Slams Industry Record on Minorities', 2 December, 14.

Burke, R.J. and C.A. McKeen (1996) 'Do Women at the Top Make a Difference? Proportions and the Experiences of Managerial and Professional Women', *Human Relations*, 49(8), 1093–1104.

Buswell, Carol and Sarah Jenkins (1994) 'Equal Opportunities Policies, Employment and Patriarchy', *Gender, Work and Organization*, 1(2), 83-93.

Butler, A. and M. Landells (1995) 'Taking Offence: Research as Resistance to Sexual Harassment in Academia', in L. Morley and V. Walsh (eds) *Feminist Academics: Creative Agents for Change*, London: Taylor and Francis.

Byanyima, W. (1994) 'The Role of Women Engineers in Developing Countries', Daphne Jackson Memorial Lecture, *RSA Journal*, CXLII(5454), 15–19.

Byrne, E.M. (1993) *Women and Science: the Snark Syndrome*, London: Falmer.

Cabinet Office (1988) *Equal Opportunities for Women in the Civil Service. Progress Report, 1984–87*, London: HMSO.

Cabinet Office (1990) *Equal Opportunities for Women in the Civil Service. Progress Report, 1990*, London: HMSO.

Cabinet Office (1991) *Equal Opportunities for Women in the Civil Service. Progress Report, 1990–91*, London: HMSO.

Cabinet Office (1992) *Equal Opportunities for Women in the Civil Service. Progress Report, 1991–92*, London: HMSO.

Cabinet Office (2001) *Equal Opportunities in the Civil Service. Data Summary 1999. Men and Women, Race, Disability, Age*, London: Cabinet Office, Government Statistical Service.

Caligiuri, C. and S. Cascio (1998) cited in Margaret Linehan and James. S. Walsh (2000) 'Work–Family Conflict and the Senior Female International Manager', *British Journal of Management, Special Issue*, 11, 49–58.

Carter, R. and G. Kirkup (1990) *Women in Engineering – a Good Place to be*, London: Macmillan Press – now Palgrave Macmillan.

Chafetz, J.S. (1990) *Gender Equity*, London: Sage.

Chafetz, J.S. and J. Hagan (1996) 'The Gender Division of Labor and Family Change in Industrial Societies: a Theoretical Accounting', *Journal of Contemporary Family Studies*, 27(2), 187–219.

Chapman, L. (1991) 'From Here to Fraternity: Interviews and Cold Porridge', *U C and R Newsletter*, 35,Winter, 10–15.

Charlton, J. (1997)'Clergywomen of the Pioneer Generation: a Longitudinal Study', *Journal for the Scientific Study of Religion*, 36(4), 599–613.

Cheng, C. (ed.) (1996) *Masculinities in Organizations*, Thousand Oaks, CA: Sage.

Chi-Chang, E.Y. (1992) 'Perceptions of External Barriers and the Career Success of Female Managers in Singapore', *Journal of Social Psychology*, 123(5), 661–74.

CIB (Construction Industry Board) (1996) *Tomorrow's Team: Women and Men in Construction: Report of the Construction Industry Board Working Group 8 (Equal Opportunities)*, London: Thomas Telford.

Civil Service Department (1971) *The Employment of Women in the Civil Service, CSD Management Studies 3*, London: HMSO

Clark, V., S. Garner Nelson, M. Higonnet and K.H. Katrak (1996) *Antifeminism in the Academy*, London: Routledge.

Cockburn, C. (1983) *Brothers: Male Dominance and Technological Change*, London: Pluto Press.

Cockburn, C. (1985) *Machinery of Dominance: Women, Men and Technical Know-How*, London: Pluto Press.

Cockburn, C. (1988) 'The Gendering of Jobs: Workplace Relations and the Reproduction of Sex Segregation', in S. Walby (ed.) *Gender Segregation at Work,* Milton Keynes: Open University Press.

Cockburn, C. (1989) 'Equal Opportunities: the Short and Long Agenda', *Industrial Relations Journal,* 20, 213–25.

Cockburn, C. (1991) *In the Way of Women,* London: Macmillan Press – now Palgrave Macmillan.

Cockburn, C. (1992) 'The Circuit of Technology: Gender Identity and Power', in R. Silverstone and E. Hirsch (eds) *Consuming Technologies,* London: Routledge.

Cockburn, C. (1995) 'Women and the European Social Dialogue: Strategies for Gender Democracy', V/5465/95-EN, Luxembourg: Equal Opportunities Unit, European Commission.

Coe, T. (1992) *The Key to the Men's Club. Institute of Management Report,* London: Institute of Management.

Collier, R. (1995) *Combating Sexual Harassment in the Workplace,* Buckingham: Open University Press.

Collins, N. (1983) *Professional Women and their Mentors,* Eagle Cliffs, NJ: Prentice Hall.

Collinson, M. and D.L. Collinson (1996) 'It's Only Dick: the Sexual Harassment of Women Managers in Insurance Sales', *Work, Employment and Society,* 10(1), 29–56.

Collinson, D.L. and J. Hearn (1994) 'Naming Men as Men: Implications for Work, Organization and Management', *Gender, Work and Organization,* 1(2), 2–22.

Collinson, D.L., D. Knights and M. Collinson (1990) *Managing to Discriminate,* London: Routledge.

Commission of the European Communities (1992) 'Commission Recommendation of 27 November 1991 on the Protection of the Dignity of Women and Men at Work', *Official Journal of the European Communities,* L49(39), 24 February, 1–8.

Connell, R.W. (1993) *Gender and Power,* Cambridge: Polity Press.

Couric, E. (1989) 'A NJL/West Survey, Women in the Law: Awaiting their Turn', *National Law Journal,* 11 December, 1–12.

Court, G. and J. Moralee (1995) *Balancing the Building Team: Gender Issues in the Building Professions,* Sussex: Construction Industry Board, University of Sussex.

Crompton, R. (1986) 'Women in the Service Class', in R. Crompton and M. Mann (eds) *Gender and Stratification,* Cambridge: Polity Press.

Crompton, R. (1994) 'Occupational Trends and Women's Employment Patterns', in R. Lindley (ed.) *Labour Market Structure and Prospects for Women,* Manchester: Equal Opportunities Commission.

Crompton, R. (1995) 'Women's Employment and the "Middle Class"', in T. Butler and M. Savage (eds) *Social Change and the Middle Classes,* London: UCL Press.

Crompton, R. (1999) 'Discussion and Conclusions', in Rosemary Crompton (ed.) *Restructuring Gender Relations and Employment,* Oxford: Oxford University Press.

Crompton, R. and F. Harris (1998) 'Explaining Women's Employment Patterns: "Orientation to Work" Revisited', *British Journal of Sociology,* 49(1), 118–36.

Crompton, R. and G. Jones (1984) *A White-Collar Proletariat? De-Skilling and Gender in Clerical Work,* Basingstoke: Macmillan.

Crompton, R. and N. Le Feuvre (1992) 'Gender and Bureaucracy: Women in Finance in Britain and France', in M. Savage and A. Witz (eds) *Gender and Bureaucracy,* Oxford: Blackwell.

Crompton, R. and K. Sanderson (1990) *Gendered Jobs and Social Change,* London: Unwin Hyman Ltd.

Cunningham, Rosie, Anita Lord and Lesa Delaney (1999) '"Next Steps" for Equality? The Impact of Organizational Change on Opportunities for Women in the Civil Service', *Gender, Work and Organization,* 6(2), 67–78.

Dainty, A., B. Bagilhole and R. Neale (1999) 'Women's Careers in Large Construction Companies: Expectations Unfulfilled?', *Career Development International,* 4(7), 353–7.

Dainty, A., B. Bagilhole and R. Neale (2000a) 'Women's Progression in the UK Construction Industry', *American Civil Engineering Journal (ASCE),* 126(3), 110–15.

Dainty, A., B. Bagilhole and R. Neale (2000b) 'A Grounded Theory of Women's Career Under-Achievement in Large Construction Companies', *Construction Management and Economics,* 18(1) 239–50.

Dainty, A., B. Bagilhole and R. Neale (2001) 'Men's and Women's Perspectives on Equality Measures for the UK Construction Industry', *Women in Management Review,* 16(6), 297–304.

David, M. and D. Woodward (1998) *Negotiating the Glass Ceiling: Careers of Senior Women in the Academic World,* London: Falmer Press.

Davidson, M.J. and R.J. Burke (2000) 'Women in Management: Current Research Issues Volume II', in Marilyn J. Davidson and Ronald J. Burke, (eds) *Women in Management: Current Research Issues Volume II,* London: Sage.

Davidson, M.J. and C. Cooper (1992) *Shattering the Glass Ceiling: the Woman Manager,* London: Paul Chapman.

Davies-Netley, S.A. (1998) 'Women above the Glass Ceiling: Perceptions on Corporate Mobility and Strategies for Success', *Gender and Society,* 12, 339–55.

Dececchi, T., M.E. Timperson, and B.B. Dececchi (1998) 'A Study of Barriers to Women's Engineering Education', *Journal of Gender Studies,* 7(1), 21–38.

Deem, R. (1996) 'Women and Educational Reform', in C. Hallett (ed.) *Women and Social Policy,* Hemel Hempstead: Prentice Hall/Harvester Wheatsheaf.

DeKeserdy, Walter and Martin D. Schwartz (1998) *Women Abuse on Campus: Results from the Canadian National Survey,* Thousand Oaks, CA: Sage.

Del Re, A. (2000) 'The Paradoxes of Italian Law and Practice', in L. Hantrais (ed.) *Gendered Policies in Europe: Reconciling Employment and Family Life,* Basingstoke: Macmillan Press – now Palgrave Macmillan.

Delamont, S. (1989) *Knowledgeable Women: Structuralism and the Reproduction of Elites,* London: Routledge.

Devine, F. (1992) 'Gender Segregation in the Engineering and Science Professions: a Case of Continuity and Change', *Work, Employment and Society,* 6(4), 557–75.

Devor, Holly (1989) *Gender Blending: Confronting the Limits of Duality,* Bloomington, Indiana: Indiana University Press.

Dex, S. and A. McCulloch (1995) *Flexible Employment in Britain: a Statistical Analysis,* Manchester: Equal Opportunities Commission.

DiTomaso, N., G.F. Farris and R. Cordero (1993) 'Diversity in the Technical Workforce: Rethinking the Management of Scientists and Engineers', *Journal of Engineering and Technical Management*, 10, 101–27.

Drake, Barbara (1984) *Women in Trade Unions*, London: Virago.

Druker, J. and G. White (1996) *Managing People in Construction*, London: Institute of Personnel and Development.

Dryburgh, H. (1999) 'Work Hard, Play Hard: Women and Professionalisation in Engineering – Adapting to the Culture', *Gender and Society*, 13(5), 664–82.

Duncker, Patricia (1999) *James Miranda Barry*, London: Serpent's Tail.

Dunnill, F. (1956) *The Civil Service: Some Human Aspects*, London: George Allen and Unwin.

Dzeich, B.W. and L. Weiner (1984) *The Lecherous Professor on Campus*, Boston: Beacon Press.

Eggins, H. (ed.) (1997) *Women as Leaders and Managers in Higher Education*, Milton Keynes: Society for Research into Higher Education/Open University Press.

Engineering Industry Training Board (1987) *Insight: Encouraging Girls to Become Professional Engineers*, Stockport, Cheshire: EITB.

England, P. and L. McCreary (1987) 'Gender Inequality in Paid Employment', in B.B. Hess and M.M. Ferree (eds) *Analysing Gender*, Newbury Park, CA: Sage.

EOC (Equal Opportunities Commission) (1997) *Management and the Professions. Briefings of Women and Men in Britain*, Manchester: Equal Opportunities Commission.

EOC (Equal Opportunities Commission) (2001) *Facts about Women and Men in Great Britain 2001*, Manchester: Equal Opportunities Commission.

EOR (1997) 'Cultural Change and Equal Opportunities: Learning from Opportunity 2000', *Equal Opportunities Review*, 75, September/October, 14–22.

Epstein, C.F. (1988) *Deceptive Distinctions: Sex, Gender and the Social Order*, New Haven: Yale University Press,.

Epstein, C.F. (1997) 'The Myths and Justifications of Sex Segregation in Higher Education: VMI and the Citadel', *Duke Journal of Gender Law and Policy*, 4, 185–210.

ESIB (1998) *Research and Results on Sexual Harassment and Violence at European Institutions of Higher Education*, The National Unions of Students in Europe, Kathrine Vangen and Rosi Posnik (eds), Vienna: ESIB.

ETAN (2000) *Science Policies in the European Union: Promoting Excellence through Mainstreaming Gender Equality*, Report from the ETAN Expert Working Group on Women and Science, European Commission, Luxembourg: Office for Official Publications of the European Communities.

European Commission (1997) *Key Data on Education in the European Union*, Brussels: European Union.

European Commission (1998) *European Social Policy. A Way Forward for the Union*, Brussels: Office for the Official Publications of the European Community.

Eurostat (2001) *The Social Situation in the European Union*, Luxembourg: Office for Official Publications of the European Communities.

Evans, J. (1997a) 'Men in Nursing: Exploring the Male Nurse Experience', *Nursing Inquiry*, 4, 142–5.

Evans, J. (1997b) 'Men in Nursing: Issues of Gender Segregation and Hidden Advantage', *Journal of Advanced Nursing*, 26, 226–31.

Evans, M. (1995) 'Ivory Towers: Life in the Mind', in L. Morley and W. Walsh (eds) *Feminist Academics: Creative Agents for Change*, London: Taylor and Francis.

Evetts, J. (1993) 'Women in Engineering', *Gender and Education*, 5(2), 116–24.

Evetts, J. (1994) 'Women in Engineering: Continuity and Change in Organisation', *Work, Employment and Society*, 8(1), 101–12.

Evetts, J. (1996) *Gender and Careers in Science and Engineering*, London: Taylor and Francis.

Evetts, J. (2000) 'Analysing Change in Women' Careers: Culture, Structure and Action Dimensions', *Gender, Work and Organization*, 7(1), 57–67.

Fagenson, E.A. (1993) 'Diversity in Management: Introduction and the Importance of Women in Management', in E.A. Fagenson (ed.) *Women in Management: Trends, Issues, and Challenges in Managerial Diversity*, London: Sage.

Fagenson E.A. and Jackson, J.J. (1993) 'Final Commentary', in E.A. Fagenson (ed.) *Women in Management: Trends, Issues, and Challenges in Managerial Diversity*, London: Sage.

Faludi, S. (1992) *Backlash: the Undeclared War against Women*, London: Chatto and Windus.

Ferguson, K.E. (1984) *The Feminist Case against Bureaucracy*, Philadelphia: Temple University Press.

Fielden, S.L., M.J. Davidson, A.W. Gale and C.L. Davey (2000) 'Women in Construction: the Untapped Resource', *Construction Management and Economics*, 18, 113–21.

Finch, J. (1983) *Married to the Job: Wives' Incorporation in Men's Work*, London: George Allen and Unwin.

Finch, P. (1994) 'News in Brief, Construction Women Hit Glass Ceiling', *Architects Journal*, November, 11.

Florman, S.C. (1984) 'Will Women Engineers Make a Difference?', *Technology Review*, 87(8), November/December, 51–2.

Fogarty, M., I. Allen and P. Walters (1981) *Women in Top Jobs 1968–1979*, London: Heinemann.

Fraser, K.M. (1999) *Same or Different: Gender Politics in the Workplace*, Aldershot: Ashgate.

Gale, A.W. (1991) 'The Image of the Construction Industry: How Can it be Changed?', in *Proceedings of 7th Annual ARCOM Conference*, University of Bath, September, 191-202.

Gale, A.W. (1994a) 'Women in Construction: an Investigation into Some Aspects of Image and Knowledge as Determinants of the Under Representation of Women in Construction Management in the British Construction Industry', PhD thesis, Bath University.

Gale, A.W. (1994b) 'Women in Non-Traditional Occupations: the Construction Industry', *Women in Management Review*, 9(2), 3–14.

Game, A. and R. Pringle (1984) *Gender at Work*, London: Pluto Press.

Garner, J.B. and S. McRandal (1995) 'Women in the Construction Industry: a Tale of Two Countries', in CIB W89, *Construction and Building Education and Research Beyond 2000*, Orlando, Florida: Construction Industry Board.

Gershuny, J., M. Godwin and S. Jones (1994) 'The Domestic Labour Revolution: a Process of Lagged Adaptation', in M. Anderson, F. Bechhofer and J. Gershuny (eds) *The Social and Political Economy of the Household,* Oxford: Oxford University Press.

Gilligan, C. (1982) *In a Different Voice: Psychological Theory and Women's Development,* Cambridge, MA: Harvard University Press.

Ginn, J. (1996) 'Feminist Fallacies: a Reply to Hakim on Women's Employment', *British Journal of Sociology,* 47(1), 167–74.

Glackin, M. (1999) 'Respect taskforce on brink of collapse', *Building,* 19 November, 11.

Glucksmann, M. (1990) *Women Assemble: Women Workers and the New Industries in Inter-War Britain,* London: Routledge.

Glucksmann, M. (1995) 'Why "Work"? Gender and the "Total Social Organisation of Labour"', *Gender, Work and Organization,* 2(2), 63–75.

Gonas, L. and A. Lehto (1999) 'Segregation of the Labour Market', in European Commission, *Women and Work: Equality between Women and Men,* Luxembourg: Office of the Official Publications for the European Communities.

Goode, J. and B. Bagilhole (1998a) 'Gendering the Management of Change in Higher Education: a Case Study', *Gender, Work and Organization,* 5(3), 148–64.

Goode, J. and Bagilhole, B. (1998b) 'The Social Construction of Gendered Equal Opportunities in UK Universities: a Case Study of Women Technicians', *Critical Social Policy,* 18(2), 175–92.

Gramsci, A. (1988) 'Some Theoretical and Practical Aspects of "Economism"', in D. Forgacs (ed.) *A Gramsci Reader. Selected Writings 1916–1936,* London: Lawrence and Wishart.

Grant, J. (1988) ' Women as Managers: What Can They Offer to Organizations?', *Organizational Dynamics,* 16(1), 56–63.

Greed, C. (1991) *Surveying Sisters: Women in a Traditional Male Profession,* London: Routledge.

Greed, C. (1997) *Cultural Change in Construction,* in *Proceedings of 13th Annual ARCOM Conference,* Kings College Cambridge, September, 11–21.

Greed, C. (2000) 'Women in the Construction Professions: Achieving Critical Mass', *Gender, Work and Organization,* 7(3), 181–96.

Gregson, N. and M. Lowe (1993) 'Renegotiating the Domestic Division of Labour? A Study of Dual Career Households in North East and South East England', *Sociological Review,* 41(3), 475–505.

Griffin, S. (1984) *The Roaring Inside Her,* London: The Women's Press.

Grosz, E. (1986) 'What is Feminist Theory?', in C. Pateman and E. Grosz (eds) *Feminist Challenges,* Sydney: Allen and Unwin.

Gruber, J.E. (1998) 'The Impact of Male Work Environments and Organizational Policies on Women's Experiences of Sexual Harassment', *Gender and Society,* 12, 301–20.

Gruber, J.E. and L. Bjorn (1982) 'Blue-Collar Blues: the Sexual Harassment of Women Autoworkers', *Work and Occupations,* 9, 271–98.

Guardian (1991) 'Sexual Harassment', 2 November, 12.

Guardian (1999a) 'Higher Education Statistics Reveal Gender Inequality', 12 June, 15.

Guardian (1999b) 'Archbishop Set to Resign over Women Bishops', 15 March, 8.

Gutek, B.A., A.G. Cohen and A. Tsui (1996) 'Reactions to Perceived Sex Discrimination', *Human Relations*, 49(6), 791–813.

Hacker, S.A. (1989) *Pleasure, Power and Technology*, London: Unwin Hyman.

Hadjifotiou, N. (1983) *Women and Harassment at Work*, London: Pluto.

Hagman, Ninni and Jeff Hearn (1999) 'Sexual Harassment and Higher Education', in Paul Fodelberg, Jeff Hearn, Lisa Husu and Teija Mankkinen (eds) *Hard Work in the Academy: Research and Interventions on Gender Inequalities in Higher Education*, Helsinki: Helsinki University Press.

Hakim, H. (1979) 'Occupational Segregation', Research Paper No.9, London: Department of Employment.

Hakim, C. (1991) 'Grateful Slaves and Self-Made Women: Fact and Fantasy in Women's Work Orientations', *European Journal of Sociology*, 7(2), 101–21.

Hakim, C. (1993) 'The Myth of Rising Female Employment', *Work, Employment and Society*, 7(1), 97–120.

Hakim, C. (1995) 'Five Feminist Myths about Women's Employment', *British Journal of Sociology*, 46(3), 429–55.

Halford, Susan, Mike Savage and Anne Witz (1997) *Gender, Careers and Organisations. Current Developments in Banking, Nursing and Local Government*, London: Macmillan Press – now Palgrave Macmillan.

Hammond, V. (1997) 'Cultural Change and Equal Opportunities: Learning from Opportunity 2000', *Equal Opportunities Review*, 75, September/October, 14–22.

Hampton, J. (2000) 'Where Are All the Female Managers?', *Construction Manager*, 6(4), 10–13.

Handy, C. (1993) *Understanding Organizations* , London: Penguin, 4th edition.

Hansard Society Commission (1990) *Women at the Top*, London: HMSO.

Hantrais, L. (1990) *Managing Professional and Family Life*, Aldershot: Dartmouth Publishing Co. Ltd.

Hartmann, H.I. (1976) 'Capitalism, Patriarchy, and Job Segregation by Sex', *Signs*, 1(3), 137–70.

Hartmann, H.I., R.E. Kraut and L.A. Tilly (eds) (1986) *Computer Chips and Paper Clips: Technology and Women's Employment*, Washington DC: National Academy Press.

Hartsock, Nancy (1990) 'Foucault on Power: a Theory for Women', in Linda J. Nicholson (ed.) *Feminism/Postmodernism*, New York: Routledge.

Hawkins, A.C. and D. Schultz (1990) 'Women: the Academic Proletarian in West Germany and the Netherlands', in S. Stiver Lie and V.E. O'Leary (eds) *Storming the Tower: Women in the Academic World*, London: Kogan Page.

Hearn, J. and W. Parkin (1987) *'Sex' at 'Work'*, Brighton: Harvester-Wheatsheaf.

Hearn, J., D.L. Sheppard, P. Tancred-Sheriff and G. Burrell (eds) (1989) *The Sexuality of Organization*, London: Sage.

Hemming, H. (1985) 'Women in a Man's World: Sexual Harassment', *Human Relations*, 38(1), 67–79.

Herbert, C. (1992) *Sexual Harassment in Schools: a Guide for Teachers*, London: David Fulton.

Higginbotham, Evelyn Brooks (1993) *Righteous Discontent: the Women's Movement in the Black Baptist Church, 1880–1920*, Cambridge, MA: Harvard University Press.

Heward, C. (1996) 'Women and Careers in Higher Education: What is the Problem?', in L. Morley and V. Walsh (eds) *Breaking Boundaries: Women and Careers in Higher Education*, London: Taylor and Francis.

Hirdman, Y. (1990) *The Gender System: Theoretical Reflections on the Social Subordination of Women, Report – Study of Power and Democracy in Sweden,* Uppsala: Maktutredningen.

Hochschild, A.R. (1983) *The Managed Heart: Commercialization of Human Feeling,* Berkeley: University of California Press.

Hochschild, A.R. (1989) cited in Margaret Linehan and James S. Walsh (2000) 'Work–Family Conflict and the Senior Female International Manager', *British Journal of Management, Special Issue,* 11, 49–58.

Holmer-Nadesan, M. (1996) 'Organizational Identity and Space of Action', *Organization Studies,* 17(1), 49–81.

Homans, H. (1987) 'Man-Made Myths: the Reality of Being a Woman Scientist in the NHS', in A. Spencer and D. Podmore (eds) *In a Man's World. Essays on Women in Male-Dominated Professions,* London: Tavistock Publications.

Hughes, B. (2000) 'Construction Needs Women', *Construction Manager,* 6(4), 9.

Hunt, J.W. (1992) *Managing People at Work: Manager's Guide to Behaviour in Organizations,* London: McGraw Hill, 3rd edition.

Institute of Management (1994) *The 1994 National Management Salary Survey,* London: Institute of Management.

Itzin, C. (1995) 'The Gender Culture', in C. Itzin and J. Newman (eds), *Gender, Culture and Organizational Change: Putting Theory into Practice,* London: Routledge.

Itzin, C. and J. Newman (1995) (eds) *Gender, Culture and Organizational Change: Putting Theory into Practice,* London: Routledge.

Jacobs, J.A. and S.T. Lim (1995) 'Trends in Occupational and Industrial Sex Segregation in 56 Countries, 1960–1980', in J.A. Jacobs (ed.) *Gender Inequality at Work,* Thousand Oaks, CA: Sage.

Jacobs, Jerry, A. (1989) *Revolving Doors: Sex Segregation and Women's Careers,* Stanford, CA: Stanford University Press.

Jacobs, Menno J.G., Gerard A.B. Frinking, Saskia Keuzenkamp and Tineke M. Willemsen (2000) *The Evaluation of Policies in Relation to the Division of Unpaid and Paid Work in the Netherlands,* Work and Organization Research Centre Report 00.06.001, Tilburg, The Netherlands: Tilburg University.

Jamieson, Kathleen Hall (1995) *Beyond the Double Bind: Women and Leadership,* New York: Oxford University Press.

Janeway, E. (1982) *Cross-Sections from a Decade of Change,* New York: William Morrow.

Jewson, N. and D. Mason (1986a) 'The Theory and Practice of Equal Opportunity Policies: Liberal and Radical Approaches', *Sociological Review,* 34 (3), 307–34.

Jewson, N. and D. Mason (1986b) 'Modes of Discrimination in the Recruitment Process: Formalisation, Fairness and Efficiency', *Sociology,* 20(1), 43–63.

Johnsrud, L.K. and C.D. Atwater (1991) *Barriers to Retention and Tenure at UH–Manoa: the Experiences of Faculty Cohorts 1982–1988,* Manoa: University of Hawaii.

Jones, Carol and Gordon Causer (1995) '"Men Don't Have Families": Equality and Motherhood in Technical Employment', *Gender, Work and Organization,* 2(2), 51–62.

Josefowitz, N. (1983) 'Paths to Power in High Technology Organizations', in J. Zimmerman (ed.) *The Technological Woman: Interfacing with Tomorrow,* New York: Praeger.

Jowell, R. and S. Witherspoon (1985) *British Social Attitudes*, London: Gower.

Kanter, Rosabeth Moss (1977) *Men and Women of the Corporation*, New York: Basic Books.

Katila, Saija and Susan Merilainen (1999) 'A Serious Researcher or Just Another Nice Girl?: Doing Gender in a Male-Dominated Scientific Community', *Gender, Work and Organization*, 6(3), 163–73.

Katzenstein, Mary Fainsod (1998) *Faithful and Fearless. Moving Feminist Protest inside the Church and the Military*, Princeton: Princeton University Press.

Kay, F.M. and J. Hagan (1995) 'The Persistent Glass Ceiling: Gendered Inequalities in the Earnings of Lawyers', *British Journal of Sociology*, 46(2), 279–310.

Keller, E. Fox (1982) 'Feminism and Science', *SIGNS*, 7(30), 589–602.

Kelsall, R.K. (1955) *Higher Civil Servants in Britain*, London: Routledge.

Kerman, L. (1995) 'The Good Witch: Advice to Women in Management', in L. Morley and V. Walsh (eds) *Feminist Academics: Creative Agents for Change*, London: Taylor and Francis.

Kessler-Harris, A. (1985) 'The Debate over Equality for Women in the Work Place. Recognizing Differences', in L. Larwood (ed.) *Women and Work. An Annual Review, Vol. 1*, London: Sage.

Kettle, J. (1996) 'Good Practices, Bad Attitudes: an Examination of the Factors Influencing Women's Academic Careers', in L. Morley and V. Walsh (eds) *Feminist Academics: Creative Agents for Change*, London: Taylor and Francis.

Khazanet, V.L. (1996) 'Women in Civil Engineering and Science: it's Time for Recognition and Promotion', *ASCE Journal of Professional Issues in Engineering Education and Practice*, 122(2), 65–8.

Kimmel, Michael (2000) 'Saving the Males: the Sociological Implications of the Virginia Military Institute and the Citadel', *Gender and Society*, 14(4), 494–516.

King, M. (1994) 'Women's Careers in Academic Science: Achievement and Recognition', in J. Evetts (ed.) *Women and Career: Themes and Issues in Advanced Industrial Societies*, London: Longman.

Kirkup, Gill and Laurie Smith Keller (eds) (1992) *Inventing Women: Science, Technology and Gender*, Cambridge: Polity Press.

Kossek, E.E. and S.A. Lobel (eds) (1996) *Managing Diversity*, Malden, MA: Blackwell.

Kozak, Marion (1976) *Women Munition Workers during the First World War, With Special Reference to Engineering*, unpublished PhD thesis, University of Hull.

Kvande, E. and B. Rasmussen (1993) 'Structures–Politics–Cultures. Understanding the Gendering of Organizations', in *Proceedings of the ISS Conference "100 ans de sociologie: Retrospective, prospective"*, Sorbonne, June, 1–36.

Kvande, E. and B. Rasmussen (1994) 'Men in Male-Dominated Organizations and their Encounter with Women Intruders' *Scandinavian Journal of Management*, 10(2), 163–74.

Lane, C. (1993) 'Gender and the Labour Market in Europe: Britain, Germany and France compared', *Sociological Review*, 41(2), 274–301.

Lanquetin, M.T., J. Laufer and M.T. Letablier (2000) 'From Equality to Reconciliation in France?', in L. Hantrais (ed.) *Gendered Policies in Europe: Reconciling Employment and Family Life*, Basingstoke: Macmillan Press – now Palgrave Macmillian.

Lantz, A. (1982) 'Women Engineers: Critical Mass, Social Support and Satisfaction', *Engineering Education*, April, 731–7.

Latham, M. (1994) *Constructing the Team*, London: HMSO.

Ledwith, S. and F. Colgan (eds) (1996) *Women in Organisations: Challenging Gender Politics*, London: Macmillan Press – now Palgrave Macmillan.

Ledwith, S. and S. Manfredi (2000) 'Balancing Gender in Higher Education: a Study of the Experience of Senior Women in a "New" UK University', *European Journal of Women's Studies*, 7(1), 7–33.

Ledwith, S. and J. Weaver (1995) *Harassment, Bullying and Intimidation. Report of Equal Opportunities Action Group*, Oxford: Oxford Brookes University.

Legge, K. (1987) 'Women in Personnel Management: Uphill Climb or Downhill Slide?', in A. Spencer and D. Podmore (eds) *In a Man's World. Essays on Women in Male-Dominated Professions*, London: Tavistock Publications.

Lehman, Edward (1987) *Women Clergy in England*, NY: Edwin Mellon Press.

Leventhal, G.S. and V.L. Garcia (1991) 'An Examination of Personal and Situational Factors which Affect Female Employees and their Managers', *Psychological Reports*, 68, 835–48.

Lewis, S. and J. Lewis (eds) (1996) *The Work–Family Challenge: Rethinking Employment*, London: Sage.

Lie, M. (1992) 'Technology Equals Masculinity?', Paper presented at the 4S/EASST Joint Conference, Göteborg, Sweden, 12–15 August.

Liff, Sonia and Ivy Cameron (1997) 'Changing Equality Cultures to Move Beyond "Women's Problems"', *Gender, Work and Organization*, 4(1), 35–46.

Liff, S. and J. Wajcman (1993) 'What Problem are EO Initiatives an Answer to?', Paper presented at the Labour Process Conference, Blackpool, March.

Liff, S. and J. Wajcman (1996) '"Sameness" and "Difference" Revisited: Which Way Forward for Equal Opportunity Initiatives?', *Journal of Management Studies*, 33(1), 79–94.

Liff, Sonia and Kate Ward (2001) 'Distorted Views through the Glass Ceiling: the Construction of Women's Understandings of Promotion and Senior Management Positions', *Gender, Work and Organization*, 8(1), 19–36.

Linehan, Margaret and James S. Walsh (2000) 'Work–Family Conflict and the Senior Female International Manager', *British Journal of Management, Special Issue*, 11, 49–58.

Lipmen-Blumen, J. (1976) 'Towards a Homosocial Theory of Sex Roles. An Explanation of the Sex-Segregation of Social Institutions', *Signs*, 3, 15–22.

Lipmen-Blumen, J. (1992) 'Connective Leadership: Female Leadership Styles in the 21st Century Workplace', *Sociological Perspectives*, 35(1), 183–203.

Lister, R. (1992) *Women's Economic Dependency and Social Security. Research Discussion Series no. 2*, Manchester: Equal Opportunities Commision.

Lorber, Judith (1994) *Paradoxes of Gender*, New Haven: Yale University Press.

Lukes, S. (1974) *Power: a Radical View*, London: Macmillan.

Lunneborg, P. (1990) *Women Changing Work*, New York: Bergin and Garvey Publishers.

MacDougall, G. (1997) 'Caring – a Masculine Perspective', *Journal of Advanced Nursing*, 25, 809–13.

MacLeod, Donald (2000) 'Female Trouble', *Guardian Higher Education*, Tuesday 4 April, 14–15.

Maddock, S. (1999) *Challenging Women: Gender, Culture and Organization,* London: Sage.

Maddock, S. and D. Parkin (1994) 'Gender Cultures: How They Affect Men and Women at Work', in M. Davidson and R. Burke (eds) *Women in Management: Current Research Issues,* London: Paul Chapman.

Management and Personnel Office (1982) *Equal Opportunities for Women in the Civil Service. A Report by the Joint Review Group on Employment Opportunities for Women in the Civil Service,* London: HMSO.

Mant, A. (1983) *Leaders We Deserve,* London: Martin Robertson.

Marshall, J. (1984) *Women Managers: Travellers in a Male World,* Chichester: John Wiley.

Marshall, J. (1993) 'Organizational Communication from a Feminist Perspective', in S. Detz (ed.) *Communication Yearbook,* Newbury Park, CA: Sage.

Marshall, J. (1994) 'Why Women Leave Senior Management Jobs: My Research Approach and Some Initial Findings', in M. Tantum (ed.) *Women in Management: the Second Wave,* London: Routledge.

Marshall, J. (1995) *Women Managers Moving On: Exploring Career and Life Chances,* London: Routledge.

Martin, J. and C. Roberts (1984) *Women and Employment: a Lifetime Perspective,* London: HMSO.

Martin, P.Y. (1996) 'Gendering and Evaluating Dynamics: Men, Masculinities, and Managements', in D.L. Collinson and J. Hearn (eds) *Men as Managers, Managers as Men,* London: Sage.

Martin, Susan Ehrlich (1980) *Breaking and Entering: Police Women on Patrol,* Berkeley: University of California Press.

Mavin, S. (1998) 'Is Organisational Gender Culture the Blockage to Women's Career Advancement?', Paper presented at Gender, Work and Organization Conference, Manchester, January.

McAuley, J. (1987) 'Women Academics: a Case Study in Inequality', in A. Spencer and D. Podmore (eds) *In a Man's World. Essays on Women in Male-Dominated Professions,* London: Tavistock Publications.

McIlwee, J.S. and J.G. Robinson (1992) *Women in Engineering: Gender, Power, and Workplace Culture,* Albany: State University of New York Press.

McNeil, M. (1987) 'It's a Man's World', in M. McNeil (ed.) *Gender and Expertise,* London: Free Association Books.

McRae, S. (1989) *Flexible Working Time and Family Life: a Review of the Changes,* London: Policy Studies Institute.

McRae, S. (1996) *Women at the Top: Progress after Five Years,* London: The Hansard Society.

McRae, S., F. Devine and J. Lakey (1991) *Women into Science and Engineering,* London: Policy Studies Institute.

Meadows, P. (1996) 'The Future of Work', in P. Meadows (ed.) *Work Out – or Work In? Contributions to the Debate on the Future of Work,* York: Joseph Rowntree Foundation.

Milkman, R. (1983) 'Female Factory Labour and Industrial Structure: Control and Conflict over "Women's Place" in Auto and Electrical Manufacturing', *Politics and Society,* 2(2), 159–203.

Milkman, R. (1987) *Gender at Work,* Urbana: University of Illinois Press.

Mills, A. (1998) 'Cockpits, Hangars, Boys and Galleys: Corporate Masculinities and the Development of British Airways', *Gender, Work and Organization*, 5(3), 172–88.

Mills, C.W. (1959) 'The American Business Elite: a Collective Portrait', in I.L. Horwitz (ed.) *Power, Politics and People*, New York: Ballantine.

Morgan, G. and D. Knights (1991) 'Gendering Jobs: Corporate Strategy, Managerial Control and the Dynamics of Job Segregation', *Work, Employment and Society*, 5(2), 181–200.

Morley, L. (1994) 'Glass Ceiling or Iron Cage: Women in UK Academia', *Gender, Work and Organization*, 1(4), 194–204.

Morley, L. (1996) 'Interrogating Patriarchy: the Challenges of Feminist Research', in L. Morley and V. Walsh (eds) *Breaking Boundaries: Women and Careers in Higher Education*, London: Taylor and Francis.

Mumby, D.K. and C. Stohl (1991) 'Power and Discourse in Organization Studies: Absence and the Dialectic of Control', *Discourse and Society*, 2(3), 313–32.

Neale, R.H. (1996) *Managing Construction Projects: an Overview*, Geneva: International Labour Office.

Nesbitt, Paula (1997) 'Clergy Feminization: Controlled Labor or Transformative Change?', *Journal for the Scientific Study of Religion*, 36(4), 585–98.

Newell, S. (1993) 'The Superwoman Syndrome: Gender Differences in Attitudes towards Equal Opportunities at Work and towards Domestic Responsibilities at Home', *Work, Employment and Society*, 7(2), 275–89.

Newton, P. (1987) 'Who Becomes an Engineer? Social Psychological Antecedents of a Non-Traditional Career Choice', in A. Spencer and D. Podmore (eds) *In a Man's World. Essays on Women in Male-Dominated Professions*, London: Tavistock Publications.

Nicolson, P. (1996) *Gender, Power and Organisation: a Psychological Perspective*, London: Routledge.

Northcraft, G.B. and B.A. Gutek (1993) 'Point-Counterpoint: Discrimination against Women in Management. Going, Going, Gone or Going but Never Gone?', in E.A. Fagenson (ed.) *Women in Management: Trends, Issues, and Challenges in Managerial Diversity*, London: Sage.

O'Leary, V.E. and J.M. Mitchell (1990) 'Women Connecting with Women: Networks and Mentors in the United States', in S.S. Lie and V.E. O'Leary (eds) *Storming the Tower: Women in the Academic World*, London: Kogan Page.

ONS/EOC (1998) *Social Focus on Women and Men*, London: Office for National Statistics/Equal Opportunities Commission.

Oppenheimer, V. (1968) 'The Sex Labeling of Jobs', *Industrial Relations*, 7(2), 219–34.

Packer, K. (1996) 'The Context-Dependent Nature of the Gendering of Technical Work: a Case Study of Work in a Scientific Laboratory', *Work, Employment and Society*, 10(1), 125–49.

Paludi, Michele (ed.) (1990) *Ivory Power: Sexual Harassment of University Students*, Albany, NY: State University of New York Press.

Paludi, Michele and Richard B. Brickman (eds) (1991) *Academic and Workplace Harassment: a Resource Manual*, Albany, NY: State University of New York Press.

Park, R.E (1985) *Final Report of the Social/Behavioural Science Evaluation of the SWINTER Land Trial, Research Report 85-1*, Willowdale, Ontario: Canadian Forces Applied Research Unit.

Park, R.E. (1986) *Overview of the Social/Behavioural Science Evaluation of the 1979–85 Canadian Forces Trial Employment of Service Women in Non-Traditional Environments and Roles, Research Report 86-2*, Willowdale, Ontario: Canadian Forces Applied Research Unit.

Pascall, Gillian, Susan Parker and Julia Evetts (2000) 'Women in Banking Careers – a Science of Muddling Through?', *Journal of Gender Studies*, 9(1), 63–73.

Phillips, A. (ed.) (1987) *Feminism and Equality*, Oxford: Blackwell.

Phillips, A. (1992) 'Universal Pretensions in Political Theory', in M. Barrett and A. Phillips (eds) (1992) *Destabilizing Theory: Contemporary Feminist Debates*, Cambridge: Polity Press.

Phillips, A. and B. Taylor (1986) 'Sex and Skill: Notes towards a Feminist Economics', *Feminist Review of Waged Work: a Reader*, London: Virago.

Phillips, L.M. and R.E. Park (1986) *Final Report of the Social/Behavioural Science Evaluation of the SWINTER Aircrew Trial, Research Report 85-3*, Willowdale, Ontario: Canadian Forces Applied Research Unit.

Platenga, J. (1999) 'Unpaid Work', in *European Commission. Women and Work: Equality between Women and Men*, Luxembourg: Office for Official Publications of the European Communities.

Platenga, J. and J. Rubery (1999) 'Introduction and Summary of Main Results', in *European Commission. Women and Work: Equality between Women and Men*, Luxembourg: Office for Official Publications of the European Communities.

Powell, C. (1983) 'Maid for the Job: Some Women in Building', *Building Technology and Management*, December, 6.

Powell, G.N. (1988) *Women and Men in Management*, London: Sage.

Powney, J. (1997) 'On Becoming a Manager in Education', in H. Eggins (ed.) *Women as Leaders and Managers in Higher Education*, Milton Keynes: Society for Research into Higher Education/Open University Press.

Pringle, R. (1989) *Secretaries Talk: Sexuality, Power and Work*, London: Verso.

Pritchard, C. (1996) 'Managing Universities is Men's Work?', in D. Collinson and J. Hearn (eds) *Men as Managers, Managers as Men*, London: Sage.

Purcell, K. (1989) 'Gender and the Experience of Employment', in D. Gallie (ed.) *Employment in Britain*, Oxford: Blackwell.

Putnam Tong, Rosemarie (1998) *Feminist Thought: a More Comprehensive Introduction*, Boulder, CO: Westview Press.

Ragins, B.R. and T.A. Scandura (1995) 'Antecedents and Work-Related Correlates of Reported Sexual Harassment: an Empirical Investigation of Competing Hypotheses', *Sex Roles*, 32, 429–55.

Rake, K. (ed.) (2000) *Women's Incomes over the Lifetime, a report to the Women's Unit, Cabinet Office*, Norwich: The Stationery Office.

Ramazanoglu, C. (1987) 'Sex and Violence in Academic Life, or You Can Keep a Good Women Down', in J. Hanmer and M. Maynard (eds) *Women, Violence and Social Control*, London: Macmillan.

Rasmussen, B. and T. Hapnes (1991) 'Excluding Women from the Technologies of the Future? A Case Study of the Culture of Computer Science', *Futures*, December, 1107–19.

Raynsford, N. (2000) *Keynote Address: Profiting From Innovation*, M4I Annual Conference 22 May, NEC, Birmingham, http://www.m4i.org.uk/conference/index.htm

Rees, T. (1992) *Women and the Labour Market*, London: Routledge.

Reimer, J.W. (1979) *Hard Hats*, London: Sage.

Rendel, M. (1980) 'How many Women Academics 1912–76?', in R. Deem (ed.) *Schooling for Women's Work*, London: Routledge.

Renzetti, Claire M. and Daniel J. Curran (1999) *Women, Men and Society*, Boston: Allyn and Bacon.

Reskin, B. (1988) 'Bringing the Men Back in: Sex Differentiation and the Devaluation of Women's Work', *Gender and Society*, 2, 58–81.

Reskin, B. and H. Hartmann (1986) *Women's Work, Men's Work; Sex Segregation on the Job*, Washington, DC : National Academy Press.

Reskin, B.F. and I. Padavic (1988) 'Supervisors as Gatekeepers: Male Supervisors' Response to Women Integration in Plant Jobs', *Social Problems*, 35(5), 536–50.

Reskin, B.F. and I. Padavic (1994) *Women and Men at Work*, Thousand Oaks, CA: Pine Forge Press.

Reskin, Barbara F. and Patricia A. Roos (eds) (1990) *Job Queues. Gender Queues: Explaining Women's Inroads into Male Occupations*, Philadelphia: Temple University Press.

Roberts, S. (1995) 'Women's Work: What's New, What Isn't', *New York Times*, 27 April, 6.

Rose, H. (1994) *Love, Power and Knowledge*, London: Polity.

Rosener, J. (1990) 'Ways Women Lead', *Harvard Business Review*, Nov/Dec, 119–25.

Rotella, E. (1981) *From Home to Office: U.S. Women at Work, 1870–1930*, Ann Arbor: UMI Research Press.

Rowbotham, Sheila (1974) *Hidden from History*, London: Pluto Press.

Rubery, J. (1999) 'Overview and Comparative Studies', in European Commission, *Women and Work: Equality between Women and Men*, Luxembourg: Office for Official Publications of the European Communities.

Rubery, J. and C. Fagan (1993) *Occupational Segregation of Women and Men in the European Community*, Luxembourg: Commission of the European Communities: Equal Opportunities Unit.

Rubery, J., M. Smith and C. Fagan (1996) *Trends and Prospects for Women's Employment in the 1990s*, Report for Equal Opportunities Unit, DGV, Luxembourg: European Commission.

Rubin, Jennifer (1997) 'Gender, Equality and the Culture of Organizational Assessment', *Gender, Work and Organization*, 4(1), 24–34.

Ruggie, M. (1998) 'Gender, Work and Social Progress', in J. Jenson (ed.) *Feminization of the Labour Force*, Oxford: Polity Press.

Savage, M. (1992) 'Women's Expertise, Men's Authority: Gendered Organisation and the Contemporary Middle Classes', in M. Savage and A. Witz (eds) *Gender and Bureaucracy*, Oxford: Blackwell.

Savage, M. and A. Witz (1992) (eds) *Gender and Bureaucracy*, Oxford: Blackwell.

Scase, R. and R. Goffee (1990)'Women in Management: Towards a Research Agenda', *International Journal of Human Resource Management*, 1(1), 107–25.

Scott, D.B. (1996) 'Shattering the Instrumental-Expressive Myth: the Power of Women's Networks in Corporate-Government Affairs', *Gender and Society*, 10, 232–47.

Scott, J.W. (1982) 'The Mechanization of Women's Work', *Scientific American*, 247, 169–87.

Sharma, S. (1990) 'Psychology of Women in Management: a Distinct Feminine Leadership', *Equal Opportunities International*, 9(2), 13–18.

Sheppard, D.L. (1989) 'Organizations, Power and Sexuality: the Image and Self-Image of Women Managers', in J. Hearn, D.L. Sheppard, P. Tancred-Sheriff and G. Burrell (eds) *The Sexuality of Organization*, London: Sage.

Sokoloff, N.J. (1992) *Black Women and White Women in the Professions: Occupational Segregation by Race and Gender, 1960-1980*, New York: Routledge Chapman and Hall.

Sommerville, J., P. Kennedy and L. Orr (1993) ' Women in the UK Construction Industry', *Construction Management and Economics*, 11, 285–91.

Spencer, A. and D. Podmore (1987a) 'Introduction', in A. Spencer and D. Podmore (eds) *In a Man's World. Essays on Women in Male-Dominated Professions*, London: Tavistock Publications.

Spencer, A. and D. Podmore (1987b) 'Women Lawyers – Marginal Members of a Male-Dominated Profession', in A. Spencer and D. Podmore (eds) *In a Man's World. Essays on Women in Male-Dominated Professions* London: Tavistock Publications.

Spender, D. (1982) *Women of Ideas (and What Men Have Done to Them)*, London: Routledge and Kegan Paul.

Staines, G., C. Travis and T. Jatrente (1974) 'The Queen Bee Syndrome', *Psychology Today*, 7(8), 55–60.

Stanko, E.A. (1988) 'Keeping Women In and Out of Line: Sexual Harassment and Occupational Segregation', in S. Walby (ed.) *Gender Segregation*, Milton Keynes: Open University.

Stanley, L. (1997) *Knowing Feminisms*, London: Sage.

Stiver Lie, S. and V.E. O'Leary (1990) (eds) *Storming the Tower: Women in the Academic World*, London: Kogan Page.

Sutherland, M. (1985) *Women Who Teach in Universities*, Stoke-on-Trent: Trentham Books.

Tallichet, S.E. (1995) 'Gendered Relations in the Mines and the Division of Labor Underground', *Gender and Society*, 9, 697–711.

Taylor, S. and M. Tyler (2000) 'Emotional Labour and Sexual Difference in the Airline Industry', *Gender, Work and Organization*, 14(1), 77–95.

Thomas, K. (1990) *Gender and Subject in Higher Education*, Milton Keynes: Open University Press.

Thomas, R. (1996) 'Gendered Cultures and Performance Appraisal: the Experience of Women Academics', *Gender, Work and Organization*, 3(3), 143–55.

Tuck, K. (1992) 'An Exercise in Asset Stripping', *AUT Bulletin*, January, 4.

Universities UK (2000) *Statistics on Academic Staff in UK Universities by Gender*, London: Universities UK.

US Department of Labor (1997)*The Glass Ceiling Initiatives: Are There Cracks in the Ceiling?*, Washington DC.

Villeneuve, M.J. (1994) 'Recruiting and Retaining Men in Nursing: a Review of the Literature', *Journal of Professional Nursing*, 10(4), 217–28.

Vinnicombe, Susan (2000) 'The Position of Women in Management in Europe', in Marilyn J. Davidson and Ronald J. Burke (eds) *Women in Management: Current Research Issues Volume II*, London: Sage.

Wajcman, J. (1996) 'Women and Men Managers. Careers and Equal Opportunities', in R. Crompton, D. Gallie and K. Purcell (eds) *Changing Forms of Employment. Organisations, Skills, and Gender*, London: Routledge.

Wajcman, J. (1998) *Managing Like a Man: Women and Men in Corporate Management,* Cambridge: Polity.

Walby, S. (1986) *Patriarchy at Work,* Cambridge: Polity.

Walby, S. (1990) *Theorising Patriarchy,* Oxford: Blackwell.

Walby, S. (1997) *Gender Transformations,* London: Routledge.

Walrond-Skinner, Sue (1998) *Double Blessing,* London: Cassell.

Walters, P. (1987) 'Servants of the Crown', in A. Spencer and D. Podmore (eds) *In a Man's World: Essays on Women in Male Dominated Professions,* London: Tavistock.

Walton, K.D. (1997) 'UK Women at the Very Top: an American Assessment', in H. Eggins (ed.) *Women as Leaders and Managers in Higher Education,* Milton Keynes: Society for Research into Higher Education/Open University Press.

Webb, Janette (1997) 'The Politics of Equal Opportunity', *Gender, Work and Organization,* 4(3), 159–69.

Webb, J. and S. Liff (1988) 'Play the White Man: the Social Construction of Fairness and Competition in Equal Opportunities Policies', *Sociological Review,* 36(3), 532–51.

Wells, Celia (2001) 'Working out Women in Law Schools', *Legal Studies,* 21(1), 116–36.

Westley, L.A. (1982) *A Territorial Issue: a Study of Women in the Construction Trades,* Washington DC: Wider Opportunities for Women.

Wheeler-Bennett, J. (1977) *Women at the Top,* London: Peter Owen.

Wheelwright, Julie, (1989) *Amazons and Military Maids: Women who Cross-Dressed in Pursuit of Life, Liberty and Happiness,* London: Pandora Press.

White, J. (1995) 'Leading in their Own Ways: Women Chief Executives in Local Government', in C. Itzin and J. Newman (eds) *Gender, Culture and Organizational Change,* London: Routledge.

Whitelegg, Liz (1992) 'Girls in Science Education: of Rice and Fruit Trees', in Gill Kirkup and Laurie Smith Keller (eds) *Inventing Women. Science, Technology and Gender,* Cambridge: Polity Press.

Whittock, Margaret (2000) *Feminising the Masculine? Women in Non-Traditional Employment,* Aldershot: Ashgate.

Wieringa, Saskia (1994) 'Women's Interests and Empowerment: Gender Planning Reconsidered', *Development and Change,* 25(4), 829–48.

Wilkinson, S.J. (1992) 'Looking to America: How to Improve the Role of Women in Civil Engineering', *The Woman Engineer,* 14(16), Spring, 12–13.

Williams, A. Paul (1999) 'Changing the Palace Guard: Analysing the Impact of Women's Entry into Medicine', *Gender, Work and Organization,* 6(2), 106–21.

Williams, C.L. (1989) *Gender Differences at Work: Women and Men in Nontraditional Occupations,* Berkeley: University of California Press.

Williams, C. L. (1992) 'The Glass Escalator: Hidden Advantages for Men in the "Female" Professions', *Social Problems,* 39, 253–67.

Williams, C.L. (1993) 'Introduction', in C.L. Williams (ed.) *Doing 'Women's Work',* London: Sage.

Willing, A. (1996) 'Giving the Girls a Go', *Chartered Building Professional,* August, 14–17.

Wilson, Fiona M. (1995) *Organizational Behaviour and Gender,* London: McGraw-Hill.

Witz, A. (1992) *Professions and Patriarchy,* London: Routledge.

Witz, A. and M. Savage (1992) 'The Gender of Organizations', in M. Savage and A. Witz (eds) *Gender and Bureaucracy*, Oxford: Blackwell.

Wright, R. (1996) 'The Occupational Masculinity of Computing', in C. Cheng (ed.) *Masculinities in Organizations*, Thousand Oaks, CA: Sage.

Wright, R. and J.A. Jacobs (1995) 'Male Flight from Computer Work: a New Look at Occupational Resegregation and Ghettoization', in J.A. Jacobs (ed.) *Gender Inequality at Work*, Thousand Oaks, CA: Sage.

Yates, J.K. (1992) 'Women and Minorities in Construction in the 1990s', *Cost Engineering*, 34(6), 9–12.

Young, I.M. (1992) 'Together in Difference: Transforming the Logic of Group Political Conflict', *Political Theory Newsletter*, 4, 11–26.

Yount, K. (1991) 'Ladies, Flirts and Tomboys: Strategies for Managing Sexual Harassment in an Underground Coal Mine', *Journal of Contemporary Ethnography*, 19(4), 396–422.

Zikmund, Barbara, Adair Lummis Brown and Patricia Mei Yin Chang (1998) *Clergywomen: an Uphill Calling*, Lexington: John Knox/Westminster Press.

Zimmer, L.E. (1988) 'Tokenism and Women in the Workplace: the Limits of Gender-Neutral Theory', *Social Problems*, 35, 64–77.

Zweigenhaft, Richard L. and G. William Damhoff (1998) *Diversity in the Power Elite. Have Women and Minorities Reached the Top?*, New Haven: Yale University Press.

Index

academia, 58–9, 63–7, 75

bureaucratic structures, 98

career development, 103–6, 136–7
appraisal, 105–6
Civil Service, 58–63, 75

engineering, 58–9, 67–70, 75
equal opportunities policies, 78–81,
133–48, 191
difference approach, 137–42
family-friendly policies, 79–81,
138–42, 162
hearts and minds approach, 142–7
level playing field approach, 134–7

femininity, 49–50, 52, 55–6, 68
feminisation of occupations, 13, 15,
21–2, 39, 58
feminism, 72, 77, 136, 176–7, 188–9
Christian, 72, 177

gender segregation of the labour
market, 2–3, 10–25, 26–43,
58–75, 96–9, 144, 166–71, 180–93
age and gender, 12
disability and gender, 12
dual labour market theory, 31–4, 38
Europe, 14–17
glass ceiling, 20–1, 36, 63, 99, 144
human capital theory, 29–31, 53,
119
internal labour markets, 34–8, 96–9,
166–71, 181–7: theories, 34–8
measurement of segregation, 13
potential levers for change, 38–43,
175–8, 181, 187–93: critical
mass theory, 39–41, 175;
negative levers, 38–9; role
models and mentoring, 41–2;
women's agency, 43, 175–8,
187–91

race and gender, 11
UK, 11, 14, 17–21
USA, 14, 21–4
gendering of occupations and jobs,
labelling of 'women's work' and
'men's work', 32–3, 44–57,
165–71, 181
'men's work', 48–52: leadership,
management and power,
48–50; technical skills, 51–2, 56
'women's work', 52–5, 165–75:
caring and emotional work,
53–5, 168–70; women's skills,
171–5
geographical mobility, 111–13

intersection of gender, race,
disability, class, age, sexuality
10–11, 32

male career model, 99–100, 116–17,
141–2, 149–53, 157–64, 175
male model of professions, 149–53,
157–64, 175
'queen bees', 161–4
management, 48–50, 86, 116, 152–3,
158–9, 171–3
masculinity, 36–7, 48–52, 56, 63, 123,
125–6, 150–3, 158
hegemonic, 36–7, 150–2
methodologies, 194

non-traditional occupations, 3–4,
58–9
definitions, 3–4

organisational culture, 36, 100,
114–32, 142–7, 149–53, 159–71,
175–8
chilly climate, 123–5
definition, 114–15
dress, 71, 153–4
gender regimes, 165–6

organisational culture (*continued*)
  homosociability, 36, 100, 115–16,
    118, 144
  informal socialisation, 149–53
  male-dominated networks, 118–23

part-time work, 63, 65, 141–2
patriarchy, 33, 37, 76, 96–8, 116, 150
priests, 58, 71–5

recruitment processes, 100–3, 115–16,
    136–7
  formal, 101–3
  informal, 100–1
relationship between paid and unpaid
    work, 27–31, 33, 38, 49, 53,
    76–95, 116–17, 160–1, 182–3
  assumptions about women's unpaid
    responsibilities, 77–9, 116–17

dual systems theories, 27, 33
  economising on domestic
    responsibilities, 86–9, 117
  men's domestic contribution,
    89–92, 117
  paid help, 92–3
  spillover theory, 76, 81
role models and mentors, 41–2,
    122–3

selection and promotion, 106–8, 115
sexual harassment, 37, 126–31

(un)equal pay, 63, 65–6, 71, 108–9

women masquerading as men, 1–2,
    153–64
women's networks, 119
working conditions, 109–11, 117